HONOUR THY FATHER

Eamonn McGrath

THE
BLACKSTAFF
PRESS

BELFAST

First published in 1970 by
Allen Figgis and Company Limited
This Blackstaff Press edition is a photolithographic facsimile
of the first edition printed by Cahill and Company Limited, Dublin

This edition published in 1990 by
The Blackstaff Press Limited
3 Galway Park, Dundonald, Belfast BT16 0AN, Northern Ireland
with the assistance of
The Arts Council of Northern Ireland
© Eamonn McGrath, 1970
Printed by The Guernsey Press Company Limited
British Library Cataloguing in Publication Data
McGrath, Eamonn
Honour thy father.
I. Title
823'.914 [F]
ISBN 0-85640-433-0

Every old man I see
In October-coloured weather
Seems to say to me:
'I was once your father.'

from 'Memory of my Father'
Patrick Kavanagh

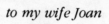

to my wife Joan

CHAPTER ONE

My father, who knew nothing of Moses Maimonides or Amalric of Bena and cared even less, caught his finely-veined nose delicately between finger and thumb and blew a ropy snot into the sawdust. With the toe of his boot he nudged the sawdust over it, patted it down, looked at it from every side like a cat burying its excreta. Then, with a scud of the shoulders and a deep snuffle, he abandoned it for ever and came back to his glass.

"Have another, Bill," the lame blacksmith said, running his hand in a halfhearted way down towards his pocket behind the singed apron that smelt of burnt hoof and horsedung.

"Will you whist," my father said. He went to the door that led to the bar and peeped through a diamond of glass the size of a playing card. He pressed the heel of his fist on the bell, then opened the door and shouted, "The same again, Wat, and a packet of biscuits for the child."

The blacksmith looked at me and stripped his black teeth to shoot a stream of tobacco-juice into the sawdust.

"He's the spit of you, Bill," he said. "You'll never be dead while he's in it."

"He don't take to the land," my father said and dismissed me from his mind.

I did not like the smell of the blacksmith and, young as I was, I knew he despised my father and would criticise him behind his back. I despised him too, but that was different. The blacksmith had his lame foot tied up in a black cloth. When he walked he hopped along by the wall holding the foot high as if he had just stepped into boiling water and was trying to ease the pain. I knew I should not be looking at the foot, but it fascinated me. I knew that underneath the cloth there was putrid flesh that stank. If contact with him had not disgusted me, I would have loved to have stamped on his foot and made him screech. I thought of driving over it with a steam-roller or stuffing it into a threshing drum.

"Books," my father said, "books are the ruin of him."

"There's only one good book," the blacksmith said, "you follow me now?"

"What book?" my father asked.

"The Lord's Book," the blacksmith said, "amn't I right?"

"Never read it myself," my father said, making it clear that he considered himself all the better for the omission.

"Books is sinful, right enough," the blacksmith said. "There's a power of sin in words."

"It's not natural," my father said.

The blacksmith tapped his head. "He's all right up here, I suppose?"

"God-dammit," my father said, "you'd no right to say a thing like that. Isn't he a son of mine anyway."

The blacksmith repaired the damage as quickly as he could.

"Sure, Bill, sure. I was only wonderin' if he had too much— you know—your family was ever noted for the good heads and I wondered—like—if there, maybe, was a little too much pressure on the skull. You follow me now?"

"I took him to the doctor," my father said. "He examined his water and said there was nothing wrong."

"The water's important," the blacksmith said. "I knew a man once that died for the want of making it. Did you ever think a thing like that could happen, now?"

"Wets his bed, too," my father said.

"Does he (the blacksmith looked serious)—you know. . . .?" He whispered to my father.

"Dammit, no! Not that!" my father said.

They both turned to look at me.

"Naw," the blacksmith said, after looking me over, "he wouldn't do a thing like that."

"I wouldn't put it past him," said my father.

Outside the street lamps were going on. A triangle of yellow light was flung over the wall into Wadding's yard, the tip of it striking like an arrowhead on the red door of the stable where our pony was waiting. The floor of the stable was concrete, cut into little squares like batches of buns on a baker's tray. The house smelled of horse-sweat and dung, which was pleasant, and of porter and urine, which wasn't. We relieved ourselves there. It was satisfying to watch the stream of urine rush off down the channels and expend itself in a long, snaking trickle just short of the door. It was my ambition to set up a record by sending a stream right under the door.

The pony would look at me in its mild, tolerant way. I would lean across its flank and close my eyes and think of boys in books, who had wonderful adventures with their fathers—clean, handsome, smiling men, who spoke properly and never drank porter or belched or got sick on the kitchen floor or shouted or threw things or put the whole house on edge and made everyone too miserable to speak, when all they wanted was to be nice to each other and live quietly and sleep and eat and do their work and be like other people to whom none of these terrible things happened.

Sooner or later, when he felt like it, we would drive home along the darkened road. The only sound the clip-clop of the pony on the sparking flint. All the mystery and terror of the night pressing in on us. The looming hedges alive with devils to pull my legs in the darkness where they hung out over the road. The dark hulk of my father under whose huge shadow I groped in anguish, like some doomed plant, straining towards the light.

Little squares of comfort would flower in the fields and I would grind my eyelids together, pretending I was asleep and would wake up presently behind one of those strange windows and be overwhelmed by a rush of love from a smiling man and woman, who would tuck me in and kiss me—and most of all one another—and tiptoe out hand in hand to have their supper before a warm fire, from which their voices trickled in to me full of stability and reassurance.

The rim of the upturned porter barrel on which I was sitting hurt my legs and I put my hands under them for cushions. My father and the blacksmith were talking of old times and of how a crowd of them had gone in a wagonette one Sunday afternoon to hear Parnell talk in Wexford. The porter touched old passions in them. Their faces were flushed, their voices raised. Some of the magnetism of the old leader still lingering in their voices caught my wandering imagination and I listened with eyes closed. It was the first time that I had felt any kinship with either of them that day. Something deep and ancestral stirred in me and I felt the pride and the pain of being Irish.

The blacksmith hummed a few bars of "The Blackbird of Sweet Avondale" and the melancholy of it affected us all. "They had no right to treat him like that," my father said. Then, seeing me with tears in my eyes, "wipe your eyes, boy. We'll be off soon."

It was a relief to cry. I cried for Parnell and what happened to him. I didn't know what it was, but I knew it was something awful and undeserved. I cried for all the Irishmen who had ever gone out and fought and given their lives. I cried for the ones who had starved and died in ditches, their mouths stained green from their last meal of grass and leaves. I cried most of all for myself, because I was a small boy, unloved and alone, because I hated the long days in the fields and the dry feel of clay on my fingers thinning turnips. I cried because that was my life and there was no changing it. Except dying. And that was the worst of all, because where could a boy hope to go, who did not love his father, except to ever-lasting damnation in the roaring flames of hell.

I dreamed of hell most nights. Hell was a fire like the huge open fire on the hearth in the kitchen. I would fall through the round holes in the grate and spin—down—down—into a burning pit. Then through another grate with devilish tongues searing my oozing flesh. Through a dark, roasting cavern with foul shadows reaching for me with razor talons. The marrow boiling in my bones and the shrivelled principle of life in me racing in retreat to make a last forlorn stand in some remote chamber of my heart. And always another grate to fall through more terrifying than the last.

When I awoke the bed would be wet and I would lie in the soggy mess, cold and terrified, but glad to be alive. Until I remembered the humiliation of having to confess in the morning that I had done it again. I would ask God to help me, then, and promise to be very good if it were gone by morning, leaving no trace. But it would be there when I got up, a shameful, yellow stain that stank. I would shake Holy Water on it and hope for a miracle. But, sooner or later, I could expect my mother's reproachful voice. "Last night again! A big boy like you! It's laziness, that's all. And your Sunday trousers too—your lovely blue serge Confirmation suit—ruined! What's wrong with you at all!"

In the daytime it happened whenever I got excited or afraid. I shook Holy Water on my trousers too. But I was a bold boy and God withheld his grace and his helping hand from me. Tying myself with twine was no good either. The cord bit into me and I could not stand the pain. Years before, I had been taken to a holy woman who rubbed a medal on me and that had failed too. For months I had been on the look-out for a bottle with a wide neck that I could strap on with some sort of harness and wear night and day. But I could never find one.

Mr. Wadding, the publican—everyone called him Wat—came in with a tray of drinks. He was a tall man with a brown shop-coat that was so much part of him that, when I saw him in his best clothes on Sunday, I always had difficulty in recognising him. He had an austere, melancholy face and a biggish nose, mottled like ripe cheese, which he fingered in a thoughtful way with finger and thumb when he spoke, feeling slowly over it like an explorer unsure of his ground and proceeding with commendable caution. He wore little round glasses with wire rims and sometimes pushed them up on his forehead when doing his accounts behind the partition in the grocery part of the shop. I thought he looked very like Mr. de Valera and, because of this, was greatly in awe of him. But he was a kindly man and would do his best to get my father out before he had taken too much. His view of life was summed up by the last line of an anecdote he liked to tell, when he felt in good humour. "And what d'you think he said to that?" he would enquire, looking from one to another of his audience. "There's always a something, he says, and when there's not, there's something else." And he would finger his nose and go off, chuckling gloomily to himself and repeating, "aye, when there's not, there's something else." With his intimates the anecdote itself had been dropped over the years and the tag-line was enough to set everyone laughing.

I always liked to hear Mr. Wadding and my father laughing over this, because it meant that my father was in good humour and had not yet reached the stage where his drinking became dangerous. He had a kind of plimsoll line and, once beyond it, the rest was inevitable. It was cheering to hear himself and Mr. Wadding laughing—even though the sycophantic blacksmith, who felt obliged to laugh more than was really necessary, upset the harmony of the thing.

Then, just as I was feeling that, perhaps, we would get home sober and without any flare-up when we did arrive, a strident voice, full of delays and inevitable debauchery, came ringing down the bar. Two hands shoved the leaves of the door apart and a head was thrust through. Confident, hat pushed well back, swivelling eyes bright as molten metal.

"Come in, Jem," my father said in the voice he reserved for his special friends. With a skip and a jump he bounced in, flexing his muscles, punching my father playfully in the arm, shadow-boxing at me, a bent cigarette drooping from his lips—a sort of middle-aged Pan with something of youth even still in his sallow, dissipated face.

"The hard Bill," he said. "What way are you?"

"Just pullin' and draggin'," my father said. "What'll you have?"

"Hold on a minute, now," Jem said and went to the door, shouting, "Wat!"

I sat there miserably, knowing how it would end, helpless to do anything about it. We were anchored for the night and the degree of drunkenness of both of them was the only thing in doubt. Mr. Wadding had come back and Jem was ordering drinks all round.

"What'll the boy have?" he asked my father.

"He's all right," my father said.

"Lemonade and biscuits for this young man?" Jem said to Mr. Wadding and looked enquiringly at me.

"I don't want anything. I'm not well," I said.

"What ails you?" my father asked.

"I want to go home," I said.

"We'll have a drink and then we'll go home, won't we, Bill?" Jem said jovially.

"One for the road," my father said, "that's all."

Jem made a feint at me and said, "Put up your fists, young fellow, till I see what you're made of."

I kept my hands by my side and, when he made a pass at me, I deliberately let him hit me. It gave me another reason for hating him—and it embarrassed him. He was full of apologies and insisted on ordering two packets of biscuits for me. I went out to the stable and was so preoccupied with worry over when we would get home and what would happen when we did, that I forgot to try for the record.

When I had finished, I stood outside the window, looking in at them. My father, short and massive, with long, ape-like arms, in his shapeless frieze overcoat, the brown stain like a high-water mark on his straggly, straw-coloured moustache. Whenever I wanted to think the worst of my father, I deliberately thought of that disgusting rag of moustache dipping into everything he drank and ate. Sometimes at the table he would, in his generous way—for he was generous, and affectionate too, in embarrassing, sentimental fits (as a child I had always been conscious of how his breath smelled, as he tried to kiss me, and avoided his embraces)—at table he would pass me some tit-bit from his plate and I would leave it lying there like some revolting bit of regurgitated food and try not to think of it. But my eyes would be drawn to it in a hypnotic way and my stomach would begin to turn over and, in the end, I would push my plate away from me and go out and be sick.

Jem Roche was prancing around in his usual fashion, like a footballer limbering up for a game, rubbing his hands together, taking little skips, slapping my father and the blacksmith and throwing his head back and roaring out great gusts of laughter. When he was sober and away from the pub—which was hardly ever—I admired and even liked him, because he had fought for Ireland and been wounded in a gun-battle with the Tans on his sixteenth birthday and been out with the Flying Column and on the run. He had been captured and imprisoned in Kilworth, from which he had escaped along with an uncle of mine—my mother's brother—and several other men, and had walked the long way back across the Munster hills and continued the fight. But I remembered him mostly—and resented him—for keeping my father in the pubs and for the disturbance he caused when they arrived at our house late at night after an evening's drinking. There would be shouting in the yard outside and drunken singing, and the voice of my mother pleading with him to go away. Maudlin philosophising in the kitchen till all hours, the smell of drink and cigarette smoke everywhere, and, in the morning, the half-filled glasses, porter rings on all the tables, drink splashed on the floor, bottles and corks underfoot, licks of vomit all over the fireplace and the stale smell of debauch on everything. My father waking in a foul mood and we all walking on tiptoe in dread of his wrath.

The blacksmith was eyeing them both speculatively and drinking his porter in the off-hand, unsparing manner of someone whose supply was assured—very different from his frugal nursing of the dregs when he was alone, waiting like a predatory spider for his next victim. I hated him for his meanness and his two-faced flattery. Even though I liked to be sent to his forge with a horse for shoeing and to press the shiny wooden handle of the black bellows—like a leather tar-barrel, I always thought—and loved the moment when the red-hot shoe was applied to the horse's hoof and a cloud of sour-smelling smoke curled up in curious arabesques to the roof, I hated him and his fat, white slug of a son, who spoke only in grunts—and smelled like a pig too with his sickly face like a bladder of lard and his big, watery, dead eyes.

They had forgotten all about me. There they were, cut adrift on a tide of euphoria, the world of reality and responsibility a fading stain behind them. I was too young to understand their need or forgive their weakness, though I knew the feeling well enough in myself. It came to me at moments of unbearable stress—while we were waiting at home for my father's return—when my wet bed was about to be discovered. I would rush upstairs to the old wooden trunk and drag out of it a wonderful book I had found, a huge volume with no covers. There were two columns of print on each page, containing all kinds of fascinating information about men who lived long ago—great heroes of Greece and Rome

—and the names of all the stars with wonderful maps showing their position in the heavens, and marvellous descriptions of strange lands and peoples, and some very difficult pages about a kind of men called Philosophers. It was there I had come across Moses Maimonides and Amalric of Bena and Aristotle. Because whatever they did seemed hardest of all, I had decided that I would be a philosopher some day.

Next to the philosophers I loved the writers. I knew their names and when they lived and what they had written and, though we had none of their books in our house, or any books except The Messenger, some Catholic Truth Society moral stories, and a few nondescript volumes that had been picked up at some auction somewhere for show and were gently mouldering in the mildewed grandeur of the parlour, I was able to form some idea of their contents from the references to their chief characters in the text. Tristram Shandy seemed so odd that I longed to know more about it and vowed it would be the first book I would buy when I grew up—if I ever did—and got money. The Life and Opinions of Tristram Shandy, Gentleman, by Laurence Sterne—which was a queer title in view of the fact that my book said Tristram wasn't born until halfway through the story and was barely christened before it ended.

When I went back in, there were two bottles of Orange Crush waiting for me—COUSINS & CO MINERAL WATERS WEXFORD on the diamond label and the strange words FOLLY SPRINGS underneath. There were two square, penny packets of Kerry Creams as well. I broke open one of the packets, split a biscuit across, bit the cream out of the middle and threw the rest into the darkness of the barrels behind me. I was sick of biscuits. I would probably regret my extravagance next day and for many days, because we didn't get many biscuits in our house and it wasn't often my father took one of us with him when he went out. So, it was either a feast or a famine with us.

My father, who never smoked cigarettes, was smoking a cigarette that Jem gave him. That was always a bad sign. There came a worse still, when he began to tell Jem of his father who had kept him at home from school when he was eleven and bought him a sheep to start him off in life. I knew all that was going to come after that. He would talk of his father's death and the number of priests at the Office and of how he had left home and bought a piece of land with the money he had saved, and sold that and bought a bigger bit. And then he would tell of the Landleague farm and how he had been boycotted and the land spiked and GRABBER GO HOME scrawled in whitewash on the walls—I was always ashamed of that bit. And so on to his present farm and the fine family he had, of whom I was by no means the worst, even though I was no good on the land and wanted to do nothing all day but read some old books that happened to be at home and had no business at all in a hardworking farmer's house. Then, they were off tracing relationships and I could relax again.

My trouble was that I could not be objective about my father. It would have been nice and simple if I could have hated him and left it at that. But there were times when I did not hate him at all. It was easy to hate him when he was telling all about himself and us to strangers. It made me feel as I felt when he brought me to the holy woman and made me take off my trousers for her—naked and ashamed.

But sometimes, when we were alone together driving in the pony and car to see some cattle he had several miles away on the Slob, I would ask him about these very same things and a kind of intimacy would grow up between us. I would look at his huge hands with their black and broken nails and a surge of pride and admiration would run through me at his strength and courage. He expanded in the fields and walked like a king among his cattle. The land made him kindlier, almost gentle, and I would feel sorry and bewildered that I was not a better son and could not share his enthusiasm for the soil.

The land seemed to be an extension of himself. He would pick up pieces of dried clay in the gaps and crumble them affectionately between his fingers, or he would pull a clump of grass and hold it up to the light to admire its texture, then smell it and rub it to his cheek before quietly putting it away from him, as if he were reluctantly parting from a lover. When I think of him now, lying under the green sod in that remote graveyard, I see him in his natural element and cannot imagine him as anything but happy to be reunited to the earth from which he came.

On the way home the mood would continue and I would ask him about Parnell and what he had said on that afternoon in Wexford long ago. Once, in a rare fit of confidence and remorse, he had told me that he was not a very good father to us and asked me to pray for him. Then we came to the village and as soon as we got inside the pub I had lost him again.

The biscuits and lemonade were coming faster and the talk was getting louder all the time. I stuffed some packets into my pocket to bring home. I would give all but one away and I would keep that in the cardboard box under my bed to console me when I woke, wet and apprehensive, in the middle of some fearful night. I liked eating in bed, but I was so timid of making any noise and being overheard below that it took me an age to eat a biscuit.

Once, when I was staying with my Aunt Nelly and my Uncle Ned—a big, serious-minded man, of whom I was in awe and whose bed I shared—I had spent an hour after going to bed, while the long summer evening stretched up the wall and darkness thickened in the corners of the room, trying to pluck up courage to take a bite from a green apple I had hidden behind a plate on the dresser earlier in the day. In the end, all I had the nerve to do was puncture it with my teeth and draw in the juice from the holes with my tongue. I had gone asleep that way and my uncle had found me when he came to bed with the apple between my lips, looking—as he laughingly described it to my Aunt next day— like a pig's head on its way to the table.

I had been as embarrassed about it as I was the day I unwound the steel measuring-tape in his tool-house and couldn't get it back into its case again. In the end I hid it and later, when I found that it had been re-wound correctly, I knew he had fixed it himself and said nothing. I was certain, then, that he thought me a sly, deceitful boy and, whenever I fancied he was looking at me in a thoughtful way, I would think of the tape and all the other things in his tool-house I had abused and misplaced and my guilt would burn in my face.

My young sister, Moll, was the only one to whom I confessed my faults. I didn't mind what Moll knew about me, because she was part of me. We had grown up together and were inseparable. We shared such childhood pleasures as slapping one another's naked bottoms in bed and bathing without clothes where the river formed a pool under overhanging sallies down in the bog between our land and Brett's. Once only in my life I had made her cry when, chasing her through the long grass, I had, for no reason that I knew, suddenly torn off her knickers and slapped her bottom very hard. I remember her surprised, pained face when she looked at me. I was as bewildered as she was and it was several days before we got back to slapping bottoms in a friendly way again.

CHAPTER TWO

ANOTHER friend of my father's had now arrived, a neighbour of ours whom I liked. Mick Rennick was his name and he lived alone on a fine farm near us. His usual salutation to my father—and to me—was to square up and ask for what he called a boxing match. It was odd—though it never struck me so at the time—that, though I liked Mr. Rennick to do this to me, I felt annoyed when Jem Roche did the same thing. I think it was because Mr. Rennick was a nice, easy-going man, who walked around his land with a sheep-dog trotting after him and his hands locked behind his back, as if he had nothing to do and all day to do it.

There was a hint of mystery about him too, which attracted me, because, although he had a wife, she didn't live with him. All I knew about her was that she lived somewhere "down the country" and he went to visit her on the bike on Sunday afternoons. Everyone said he was an indifferent farmer. If anyone's hay was wet or his corn unthreshable, it was sure to be Mick Rennick's. Still, he was one of those lucky, devil-may-care sort of men who prosper in spite of themselves. He had a friendly way that I liked of laying his hand on my arm to feel the muscle. It cheered me to see him come in. It meant more drinks, of course, and that couldn't be good.

He had a kind of public image that he had built up over the years, a deliberate distortion that gave him great pleasure and in which his friends humoured him. He pretended to be belligerent and always spoiling for a fight. But even I knew that it was all a joke and that no milder man lived in the parish than Mick Rennick.

"What dozen of yous," he said, coming in with one fist pounding in the palm of his hand, "will stand out till I flatten yous!" Jem Roche danced round him like a wasp round a placid old cart-horse.

"Women and children out before the slaughter begins," Mr. Rennick said, winking at me.

"Easy, now, Mick," my father laughed—that was another thing

I liked about Mr. Rennick; he put my father in good humour.

"Don't do anything you'd be sorry for."

"Come on," Jem Roche shouted, "I always wanted to take on the champ."

Mr. Rennick looked at him in disgust.

"Are you insured, boy?" he asked and we all laughed. Then Mr. Wadding came in to take his order and, when Mr. Rennick asked him how he was, he said he wasn't bad, but that there was always something and when there wasn't, there was something else and we laughed again and I felt better.

When he was halfway through his drink, Mr. Rennick produced a pack of cards from his pocket and they started to play Twenty-Five. I was pleased with this, because, though it meant we would be there until after closing time, the rate of drinking would be slower.

The place we were in was really part of a store where the bottling was done. There were barrels everyplace and they were using one as a table. A naked bulb on a long, cobwebbed cord hung directly over the barrel. Mr. Rennick had removed his hat and the light glistened on his bare crown. There were black sweat-marks in among the thin hair around the edge and I knew that it must have been years since he had washed his head. I had a habit of looking at men's heads to see if they were clean and always looked inside hats for tell-tale sweat-marks. Sometimes, if no one was looking, I would sniff at them compulsively, knowing that I would feel nauseated at the stale smell of human grease. I looked at men's heads in front of me at Mass, too, to see if they had nits. I never knew why I did these things and I wished I didn't. It was like scratching myself in certain places and smelling my finger. I would have given a lot to rid myself of such dirty habits.

Mr. Rennick was the only man I knew with a greasy head whom I liked. I hoped he would win at cards. He had a reputation for being mean—and enjoyed adding to his reputation. But I knew he wasn't mean, because he sometimes gave me a shilling. I had four of them in the box under my bed. I was saving them to buy Tristram Shandy when I grew up.

My father hated cards and only played to please Mr. Rennick. He accepted his losses as a sort of levy for Mr. Rennick's company.

His eyes were not very good. Play had barely begun when he pulled out of his waistcoat pocket a pair of wire-rimmed spectacles with lenses no bigger than a sixpence, which he had bought at Woolworth's for half a crown. He always insisted that they were the best glasses he ever had—which was no exaggeration as he never had another pair—and made an elaborate ritual of putting them on every Friday night to read *The Free People*. Sometimes he read pieces out in a halting, childish way. Occasionally, we children were sent out of the kitchen, when he began to read items that began with the heading SERIOUS OFFENCE. I always made it my business to look these up afterwards, though I could never make much of them. But I would wonder, when I woke in the middle of the night after the usual mishap, if my crime could be classed under that heading.

What puzzled me most about such items was the condemnatory way they spoke of something called "carnal knowledge". I didn't know what carnal knowledge was, but it seemed most odd that there could be anything wrong with any form of knowledge. To me the only crime connected with knowledge that I could even imagine was not having any of it. I never had the courage to ask anyone what it meant. There was the small consolation that, if carnal knowledge was denied to children, it seemed all right for grown-ups. Ned Rafter, our workman, was always allowed listen. I comforted myself with the thought that I would understand one day. But in the meantime not knowing was killing me.

When my father's glasses got steamed up, as they always did, I was called on to play his cards for him. Mr. Rennick, who, at cards, would have cut my father's throat for a penny, was very indulgent to me and sometimes gave me a trick when he could have beaten me. If he saw me hesitating over what to play next, he would nudge me and advise, "Heav', boy, heav'," and heave I would—with the Five, if I had it—and it was pleasant to see it hang the blacksmith's knave.

"No flies on this chap of yours," Mr. Rennick said to my father, putting out his hand, as if to snatch the pile of coppers in front of me. "That's three games in a row. You'll be putting him in the Church, maybe, and laying the foundation of a welcome for yourself above."

"There's the making of a bishop in him, at least," Jem Roche said.

"Whatever's in him," my father said, "there's no farmer in him. That's all I know."

"Farming," Mr. Rennick said, "is only for mugs, like us, or for gentlemen, like the Honourable Mr. Thimblehead beyond in Horetown."

"Honourable, begod!" Jem shouted, "and not a girl in the country safe with him."

They looked at each other over the rims of their glasses and then at me. There was a little trough of silence and then Mr. Rennick coughed and continued, "Why don't you send his lordship, here, to St. Patrick's, Bill? They do a great job on a fellow in there. Teach him all kinds of things."

"Teach him to swagger around with his hands in his pockets, looking down on us all!" my father said sarcastically. "Like that young pup of a Doran with a cigarette in the corner of his gob. Called me Bill to my face the other day. Morra, Bill, he says, without taking the fag out of his mouth. Bloody pup! And the mother telling how he passed in Latin and Greek—and he in no longer than it would take them to show him how to blow his nose, when he was home again. Couldn't learn him any more, I suppose!"

I would have liked to have gone to College. Our Principal Teacher, Mrs. Rochford's son, Pius—she was a religious woman and called all her sons after Popes (she had a Celestine, a Benedict and a Leo as well)—had gone to College as a day-boy to the Brothers and we were constantly being given reports on his progress. She would interrupt a class in Sums to announce, "Pius does all this by Algebra now, and in half the time. It's just amazing the things you can do by Algebra. Pius says you can solve any problem by X—(I wondered would it solve the problem of my father's drinking). Or she would say, "Pius tells me he can follow the Latin of the Mass quite easily now, and recite the Pater Noster (that's the Our Father) with the priest—in Latin, of course—every Sunday." During History class she would announce, "Pius informs me that the best scholars are now of the opinion that there were two Saint Patricks. Isn't that a strange thing, now!" Then she would beam on her second eldest. "Tell us, Celestine, who was the Pope who sent St. Patrick to Ireland?" Celestine would simper and pout and his mother would look at him dotingly with her mouth half open to fashion the answer with him, and he would reply, "Pope Celestine, Mammy!"

I hated all Mrs. Rochford's children. They were fat and sleek and pampered. Their lunch was brought over to them every day in a steaming basket. The smell always drove me frantic and set the saliva running in my mouth. In class after lunch, though I hated the sight of them, I would try to get beside one of them—between two if I could—because they smelt deliciously of dinner. I would try to get them whispering to me and inhale their food-laden breath. But, out in the playground I kept away from them and wished I weren't so timid and could pound and thump them, as everyone else did, to get their own back on their mother for so openly favouring them and treating the rest of us unfairly.

The other teacher, Miss Pelly, had a voice like a foghorn. She was always shouting at someone that she was sick, sore, tired, sorry, green, yellow, red, white and blue in the face, trying to get something into his thick head and that she'd prefer any day to go out and break stones on the Blue Hill. She helped the younger children make birds' nests out of Plasticine and fill them up with the oddest, most uneven, angular eggs anyone ever saw. Her other speciality was drawing a cat by joining a greater to a lesser spiral, putting a curl for the tail and tying a bow of whiskers across the mouth. She also taught Irish, which—considering neither she nor Mrs. Rochford had ever learned any—both did very well. But with more flamboyance and self-confidence than accuracy. The Inspector could never understand them nor they him. But—as they were at pains to tell us when he had gone—he had only Donegal Irish and that explained everything.

Every Friday morning Miss Pelly's old father would knock with his stick on the door and we would all shout, "Here's Mr. Pelly," and he would shuffle in on rheumatic legs with his Pension Book, which she would help him sign and then he was off in the ass-and-cart to draw it. The Canon came on Friday too. He would totter into the room on a pair of sticks, his white beard stippled with snuff. After the briefest of salutations to the teachers and solicitous enquiries on their part after his health—which was always precarious but never seemed to get any worse—he would look up at the round stain on the ceiling over Mrs. Rochford's table and ask, "How's the leak?"

The leak was always the same. On wet days she had to shift the table and we watched, hypnotised, while we stood around her doing Catechism, as the drops swelled on the ceiling, detached themselves and plonked into the coal-bucket. The Canon never once, Winter or Summer, forgot to inquire about the leak, but, beyond showing annoyance that it was still there, he never did anything about it.

We liked the curate, Fr. Donnelly, much better. He would gather us about the table to ask questions in Catechism. If he was pleased with our answers he would empty a pile of coppers from his pocket on the table and give them away to whoever could guess the date on them. We liked English pennies best and became very good at guessing their date from the head on them. It was the only bit of English history we ever learned—apart from a headline I once heard my father read from the Independent—KING GEORGE DIES AT MIDNIGHT. GALLANT BATTLE FOR LIFE FAILS. There was nothing about the Irish pennies to help us except their colour and that was often deceptive.

Dan Morgan stood beside me for Bible History, because he was convinced that I knew everything and would help him if he got stuck. We learned it all by heart and understood very little of it. But that didn't matter. If we could say it without stumbling, that was all that was expected of us. We chanted it out in a sing-song and, if once we lost the rhythm of the thing, we were finished. "Palestine where Our Lord lived," we would begin with a rush. One always had to rush. The words propped each other up and the whole thing would collapse like a pack of cards unless we were constantly shoring it up with a flow of new words. "Palestine where Our Lord lived is a small country on the south-eastern shores of the Medarranean (no one ever pronounced that properly —there wasn't the time). "It is less than half the size of Ireland, being about 160 miles in length and 80 miles in breadth. . . ." Or it might have been the other way round. We were always unsure of our figures.

Lizzie Collopy stood on the other side of me. Lizzie, who

came from the Mountain (which to the rest of us from the valley explained everything) always wore very short pinnies and never any knickers. I knew this for a fact because, whenever the wind blew, her skirt would fly up around her waist and I would see her white thighs and the sharp line like a knife-slash down the middle. All the other girls wore knickers. At least Nelly Moran did, because one day, coming from school, three of the bigger boys took it off her and threw it in the river, then ran off laughing.

Mrs. Rochford was forever making slighting remarks about our clothes or about the way our hair was cut. I dreaded going to school the day after my father had given me a haircut. Getting it was bad enough. He made us sit on a stool in the middle of the kitchen, put on his Woolworth glasses and, with a bold sweep of the horse-clippers, bared a strip from collar to crown. Then began the futile effort to match the rest of his performance to that first imaginative stroke. First his coat came off. Then his waistcoat. Then his glasses, which had steamed up. The scissors came into play to remedy some disastrous sweep of the clippers. We were pinched and pulled, our toes walked on, our ears nipped. God help anyone, though, who tried to cut *his* hair. He once chased Ned Rafter out the door and down the lane for nicking him. In the end he gave up in despair, leaving us like a badly-thatched rick. Having suffered all that we had to face the teacher.

When we came home my father would be waiting for us. "Well," he'd ask in a carefully careless way, "did she say anything?" When we told him, he roared about the kitchen like a wounded animal, banging his fist into the dresser in his rage. He threatened to come and have it out with her. My mother had a terrible time trying to placate him and persuade him to have sense. The next time it happened, we told him that nothing had been said, because we were terrified that he would come over and disgrace us like Maryanne Neale's father, who stormed down from the Mountain one day and made a boy, who had hit Maryanne with a stone over the eye, kneel down before the school and say three Hail Marys for her.

My father, whose kidneys were not good, was going oftener to the stable. I knew from the way he was chewing and spitting out the ends of Jem Roche's cigarettes that he had committed himself to another debauch. Once, I followed him out and, trembling in fear of his wrath, asked him to come home. He said he couldn't leave his friends. I began to cry and he threatened to clout me, if I disgraced him before his friends. Then he went back and I stayed outside a long time, snivelling and shivering, until Mr. Rennick came out and asked me what was wrong. I wished I could tell him all and have him pat my head and comfort me. But I couldn't say anything bad about my father to anyone else—it was unthinkable—so I said that I had a headache and the cool air was making it better. Perhaps he understood my problem very well, for he put his arm around my shoulder and brought me back in. Then he drew out his watch from his pocket, said how late it was and that decent people should be on the way home.

There was half-hearted talk of going and Jem went off to call a last round. But my father, who made a point of never being outdone in hospitality, called another as soon as Jem's was on the barrel and talk of going faded after that. Sometimes, I would catch my father's eye and plead with him, but he would frown at me and sink that awful moustache of his in his glass.

When closing time came, Mr. Wadding herded us nervously into his kitchen and there, on a comfortable seat that had once seen service in the back of a motor-car, I sat before the fire and felt heat creep into me. My trembling stopped. My head grew heavy. The voices of the men came to me from a distance. I blinked from time to time and faces swelled and receded, faces that shone out redly from the smoke, then broke up and floated away in fragments of greasy flesh beyond my line of vision. The tinkle of glasses faint as fairy bells, ringing in my inner ear. Floating away across a warm sea where the sun shone and golden apples blazed among the dark leaves. No sorrow there, nor care, no memory of grief, only the dark, healing draught of forgetfulness.

I woke to the shaking of my arm and my father's beery breath as he bent over me. They were all standing up and Jem Roche had a parcel clasped to his chest. It jingled as he swayed down the dimly-lit back passage to the yard. Mr. Wadding turned off the light in the yard before leading us across it and letting us out on the street. He had a word with my father about the pony which was still in the stable. Then the door clicked into place behind us and the bolt rasped across in a subdued groan.

Frost crystals glinted on the windscreen of Jem's car under the street light. He rubbed it with his cuff in big, ineffective sweeps, while Mr. Rennick pushed me into the back seat and got in beside me. I shivered and he spread an old coat over my knees. My father struck his feet against the running-board and fell across the front seat where he lay, breathing heavily, and showed no desire to drag himself erect. Outside, Jem was hawing on the windscreen. His breath froze as soon as it touched the glass. Then he was scraping at it with his finger-nails until it looked like a wire tray.

He disappeared from view and we heard him crank the starting handle. My father sat up suddenly.

"Did we bring the bottles?" he asked.

"They're here," Mr. Rennick said.

"Hey, Jem, where's Jem?" my father shouted. "Have you a corkscrew?"

"Dammit, give us a hand with this one," Jem said, coming round again. "She's cold."

My father got out and stood leaning unsteadily against the bonnet. Mr. Rennick got out too. They all went round to the front and I heard them arguing about which way it should be turned. It wouldn't start. They kicked the radiator and rocked the car.

"We'll push her," Jem said.

He got in again and my father and Mr. Rennick went round to the back. They heaved and groaned, while Jem shouted, "Push, dammit! Push!"

They heaved again and the car began to move. When it got up speed, Jem did something and the engine fired, then roared off and we shot down the street. I looked back and saw my father and Mr. Rennick standing in the middle of the street with their arms raised.

"Home, James, and don't spare the horses," Jem sang and kept going. He had forgotten about them. I coughed nervously and he looked back.

"Where's everybody?" he shouted.

I told him. He jabbed his foot on the brake, shooting me forward.

He reversed and shot back up the street again. He stopped the car and got out, holding the door open with exaggerated courtesy.

"Ladies first," he said.

"Making off with our porter," Mr. Rennick grumbled.

They got in, taking a long time to get their coats disentangled from the doors, opening them and banging them again, until dogs began to bark and upstairs-windows opened along the street. Then, we were away, the lights scything through the sleeping darkness.

At home my mother was sitting greyly at the fire and looked significantly at the clock when we came in. My father, blustery and unsure, said he was bringing his friends in for a minute to see his missus who was the best missus in the world. And, while she looked at him with cold, repugnant eyes, Jem told her she was blooming and, only that they were both married already, he'd be throwing his hat into the ring with the best of them and he didn't care who knew it.

My mother kept her counsel and said nothing, except that it was a late hour to keep a child out. I knew from her dead voice that she had gone through every possible rebuke before her anger had burnt out to a white ash and there was nothing left in her but a despair beyond words. The emptiness in her face brought tears to my eyes. I knew there was no hope for any of us in that loveless house.

Mr. Rennick said I was a good boy and they had taken good care of me and I would be a fine man one day. Life flickered for a moment in my mother's eyes. She patted my head in a fiercely possessive way and led me upstairs to bed. I wanted to throw my arms around her and tell her that I loved her and was sorry for all that had happened. But there was something about her—and always had been—that repelled intimacy. My hand in hers must have told her what I dared not, because she stroked my hair again and watched me undressing with tears in her eyes. When I was in bed, she put the Holy Water on my forehead and told me to say my prayers.

I listened to hear if she would go downstairs again. I heard the door of her room click. I lay there, listening, for a long time, but she did not come out again. As I said my prayers, I thought of her there in the darkness, waiting for my father to come up. I prayed that she and I and all of us might be forgiven our sins and die quietly in our sleep, before the hard light of morning called us to fresh pain.

The rest is a blur—like snatches of sound coming through a door blown back and forth in the wind. A clink of glasses from the kitchen. The scrape of a chair. Jem's voice in a wild laugh. My brother stirred in the bed opposite, asked if we were home and began to snore. A pulse in my temple throbbing away. A keening cry in the moors. Banshee? Vixen? Kitty The Hare on the lonesome roads of West Cork, the branches overhead clashing and moaning in the blackness, and a dreadful fate in store for someone with a name unfamiliar to our parts, like Murnane or Driscoll or Cowhig. Changelings and foul deeds of murder. Graphic illustrations in the OUR BOYS of brother's hand raised against brother.

My mother had brought home the magazine to me one week and I had devoured it, intoxicated with the smell of fresh ink, chewing and regurgitating the wonderful stories like a cow in the quiet of the night. The next week she brought it again—and every week after that. My grave, remote mother, who hardly ever smiled and sang only when she was alone—and then a low keen of sorrow. It seemed to me that anything of pleasure in my life had been given to me by her. Not a stir from her room. Not a sound.

On the Fifteenth of August she took us to the sea in the pony and car for our annual outing. The long, slow crawl over dusty roads. Half a day's work behind her and the other half waiting for her when she got home. Sand and waves and sunshine for one short hour. Lemonade and biscuits, sticks of candy from a Candy Car. A man breaking a rock on another man's bare chest. Crowds of men in blue serge suits sitting along the bank. Girls, arm-in-arm. Boys running and darting like fish through the throng. A circle of trampled grass and soft droppings around the pony when we went to yoke her. The long journey back in the cool of the evening. Cows lowing and calves bawling to be fed, when we got there. Our thoughts on next year and the possibility of having real buckets and spades when we went again. If only she would shout at him sometimes instead of that unassailable silence.

Later—much later—the sound of a motor woke me. Banging of doors, shouting of farewell. Grating of the lane gate—it needed oiling and always had, as long as I could remember. Uncertain footsteps across the yard, stopping under our window. A sudden jerk of violent retching and low moaning outside. I crept to the window and, dimly, in the light of the open door, saw the hunched bulk of my father close to the wall.

"They're here," my brother mumbled, turning in his sleep. I heard my father blow his nose. Then he staggered forward into the light—a black demon of terror, menacing our peace. He fumbled his way like a blind man around the doorway. The light disappeared and shutters of darkness dimmed my sight. It seemed an age before I heard him again, groping up the stairs on hands and knees. The door of their room slammed to behind him. I sat up in bed, listening—for I scarcely knew what—voices in anger, the sound of a blow. The silence surged in soft waves in the chambers of my straining ears. Nothing but the sigh of my expelled breath. No stir. No move in all that discordant house.

I got out and used the pot—in its way an oblique act of love. It would please my mother to find I had not forgotten. A dry bed would be like the fistfuls of wild flowers we sometimes picked for her to arrange in jampots along the dresser. She liked violets best. We picked them for her in the grass under the beech trees on blowy days in spring. She would press them to her nose. Her face would soften and she would tell us how she used pick them herself as a little girl long ago. It was strange to think of her as a little girl running and laughing and having her nose wiped and nits squeezed out of her hair.

No sound in all that dreadful darkness. I pulled the clothes about my head and willed myself to have one of the rare coloured dreams that came to me sometimes with a rush of brilliance. Drab places like our haggard would be transformed. Threshing day, perhaps. A red steam engine, blue drum (RANSOME SIMMS & JEFFRIES in white at the back where the grain came out), yellow pitcher. Ned Rafter and all the farmers' sons dressed in green and gold, handsome as princes out of a fairy tale. Afterwards, in my mind a warm, rainbow glow that needed only the shutting of my eyes to recreate the whole scene again. What was going on

behind that closed door? I tried to think of my own funeral in
colour, but all I saw was the black maw of a grave and my mother
crying on the edge.

It was daylight when I heard my father shouting. I heard my
mother's voice too in one short, sharp rasp and then the door
opened and she went downstairs. I heard him, then, shouting my
own name in a curiously plaintive tone, unusual for him. I rushed
out, shivering in my shirt. The door of his room was open and
even before I went in I got the smell.

He was standing by the bed, looking at himself in a stupid way
and rubbing his legs behind with his drawers, which he had
bundled up into a lump.

"We'll have to get the sheet off," he said. "Your mother
wouldn't help me"

I looked with nausea at his bony shanks with the white tufts of
hair on the shins. It was indecent to see my father like that. It was
like the time he took me into the Baths with him in Fethard and
took off all his clothes and got into the steaming sea-water and
wanted me to take off mine too and share it with him. I couldn't,
and neither persuasion nor anger could make me reveal myself to
him. I stood facing the door until he had finished—only looking
at him sideways, now and again, when he was looking the other
way, to verify that his shameful parts were the same as my own,
only more disgusting for being old. I tried to look away from him,
now, too, but my eyes kept coming back to him in fascinated
revulsion. The stench was sickening and I made no attempt to hide
my disgust.

"It came in a rush," he said in the placatory tone he used when-
ever there had been a row and he wanted to engage our sympathy
on his side. "I couldn't help it."

I said nothing, but caught the sheet by its utmost corners and
helped him take it off.

"You'd think by her that I done it on purpose."

He rolled the drawers in the sheet and handed them to me. I
left him sitting on the edge of the bed with his shirt-tails hanging
between his legs, his face grey as a dead fire and the purple veins
like decayed flesh on his cheekbones.

"He can wash them himself," my mother said.

But, when I had put on my clothes, I brought them out to the pump in the yard to wash them. I knew that, if someone didn't, there would be endless rows about them and everytime they were mentioned the whole shameful episode would be re-lived and we would all pay dearly for it.

With my stomach turning, I broke the ice on the pump-trough, beat out the wooden peg to let the water flow, held them as far away as I could from me with one hand and pumped with the other. I closed my eyes as I worked, in case I should lose my resolution. The water pained my hand and I could feel it stiffening to ice. When I thought they were fairly clean, I put in the peg and sloshed them around in the full trough with the stick we used for washing potatoes on cold mornings. Then I wrung them out and hung them on a gate beside a bag which had stiffened like a board overnight. Inside, I dipped my hands into a basin of hot water. The sting of the returning blood was worse than the bite of the frost.

"She washed them," I lied outside my father's door. But the first words of my mother, when he came down, groaning and holding his head, before we went to school, were that it was a shameful thing for a child to have to do. So, I had done no good at all, except give them further cause for quarrelling.

When we came home from school that evening, my mother had set up a bed for herself in the spare room. They slept apart from then on.

CHAPTER THREE

THE Saltee Islands were visible from our house. On fine days, I would stand on the ditch of the Long Garden and look out at them, green and becalmed on the blue horizon. A soft haze hung over them and a gentle breeze, moist with the ocean's breath, blew inland to extend its dominion over grass and young corn, stirring them into ripples and freshets, until I seemed to stand like an island myself in a green sea.

Sometimes, when things went wrong, I stood there and allowed myself to be swept away in the flood out among the islands and the wheeling sea-birds and the soothing lap of water against the ageless rocks. I had dreams of living there like a hermit in a beehive cell, wearing a habit tied with white cord, a rosary at my side with beads as big as seagulls' eggs and no one ever to disturb my peace—except, maybe, an angel from God to tell me how pleased He was with me and how I would become a saint and people in after times would come to see the imprint of my hand on the rock bed where I slept, and wash their sores and deformities in the water that collected in the hollow in the rocks that would be called St. John's Well after me.

I would live on locusts—Mrs. Rochford was always vague about what they were in the Bible History class—if there were any, and on honey, too, like my namesake, John The Baptist. And, maybe, an odd mackerel, too, because a man with an ass-and-cart came selling mackerel a few times a year and we loved them more than any other fish we ever got and, sometimes, when we had nothing else to do, we stood on the garden wall, watching the road and telling each other that God might be nice and send the mackerel man today.

Ned Rafter had a theory that the Saltees were slowly drifting westward and would maintain his belief, in spite of derision, outside the chapel gate on Sundays. Using the chapel pier and the chimney of Breen's house as guideline he—and his tormentors— would squint out to sea, then measure to the west and set up a stone to mark the exact line of the islands. It would be moved or lost by the time the next Sunday came round and then the argument—and the measurement—would start all over again. Sometimes, during the week, because I liked Ned, I would shift the stone to the east, if I remembered, but sometimes I made a mistake and shifted it the other way and upset all his calculations.

Accuracy was important to Ned. He often held up the work in the field—but never if my father was there—to demonstrate that the haycocks were not being made in perfectly straight lines or that some barbed wire fencing had been badly spaced. He had a fantastic memory and could remember easily when all the cows were due to calve, and that the half-Kerry with the crooked horn had calved last time in the River Field at half three in the afternoon of July 7th, which was a Tuesday and the very day that Jem Byrne, the pig-dealer, took bad of a weakness and was brought unconscious to hospital and put in the very next bed but one to a cousin of Peter Murphy's of Caroe on the mother's side, and towards evening it had come on to thunder and a man in Kerry had a narrow escape when the horse he was leading was struck by lightning and collapsed on top of him, breaking his left leg in two places, an item which he had read on the bottom right-hand column of page four of the following day's Independent, which had come wrapped round the bread at tea-time to the Near Meadow where he was putting the finishing touches to the last cock of fine-rakings.

He was very particular about his health, too, and would never drink anything but milk—preferably buttermilk and the sourer the better. In winter he wore hay in his boots and changed it every day, which annoyed my father, who considered it an unnecessary extravagance at his expense. Ned was considered near because he always walked home along the grass margins to spare the soles of his boots, though he once confided to me that he did it to save his head from the vibrations which, he had read somewhere, the hard surface of the road set up, doing irreparable damage to the delicate tissues of the brain.

When Ned was with us in the fields, my brother, Tom, and I hardly ever fought. If we did, he looped a paw around each of our necks and genially threatened to crack our skulls together like eggshells unless we gave over. But, if we happened to be alone, or with the other workman, Boggan, we were at it most of the time. There was something in our natures that couldn't agree. Tom had only to suggest that every pikeful of hay should be shaken to make a cock correctly for me to stop shaking and throw it together in shapeless lumps. If he saw me engrossed in the delicate work of heading it up evenly, he would fling a pikeful over the top and drown me. Neither of us would allow the other the privilege of putting the last cap—no bigger than a plate—on top. We kept putting on little bits to spite each other until the head looked sharp as a pencil and toppled off.

Boggan encouraged our rivalry and I hated him for it. Even when we were disposed to be peaceful he would find some cause for a quarrel. We might be thinning turnips and he would say, for no reason at all, "I bet John gets to the headland first."

Immediately we were off, throwing clay and turnips in all directions. It didn't matter who got there first. There were bound to be taunts and shouts and blows, with Boggan rubbing his thin hands and stripping his yellow teeth in a cackle of laughter.

We got our own back on him, sometimes, when he took a fit. He would be working away and then he would jerk in a spasm. His eyes would roll and down he would go, twisting and writhing, with his teeth clenched. We fell on him, then, and kicked him, or doused him in buckets of water until he stopped twitching and looked at us foolishly with his luminous, filmed eyes.

He slept on the loft over the cowhouse in an iron bed with a thin mattress from which the red fibre leaked. He was incontinent and wet the bed regularly. We took it in turns to go out and examine the floor and report whether he had done it again. Even I, who did it myself, was consoled to know that Boggan, a grown man of nineteen, was worse than I was. Later on, when he fell out with my father and left, we pelted him with stones until he went out of sight and when, years later, we heard that someone called Boggan had been arrested in the Midlands for killing an old man and burying his body under a ton of coal, we persuaded ourselves that it was our Boggan—even though my father and Mick Rennick said it wasn't—and agreed that it was no more than his due when he was convicted and hanged.

It was the second murder to come within our experience. Like the first it fascinated us because it involved (we were firm on that) someone we knew. But the first touched us even more closely. In fact, for the period of a grey Sunday afternoon in November of my eleventh year, shortly after the events of the last chapter, we were almost certain that we had a murderer in the family.

The murdered man had lived in an old Railway carriage at the bottom of a long lane leading to an outfarm that belonged to Nicky Breen, who was a first cousin of my father's. He had been found, his battered head stuck to the floor, by Nicky's son, Mike, a rough red-faced fellow with a cute look, whom we all hated because he was mean like his father and wanted to know everybody's business. A carriage lamp of Nicky Breen's had been found in the caravan with Nicky's fingerprints and spatters of the old man's blood on it and Nicky had been called to the barracks to explain how it came to be there.

We had learned all this from Ted Reville, the Cow Doctor, whom my father had sent for to cure a constipated pig. It was curious the way my father always sent for Ted when an animal was sick and never for the Vet. I think it was because he was a distant relation and my father, who had a very delicate sense of family, couldn't bear to hurt his feelings by sending for anyone else. Whatever it was, it cost him dearly. Ted would come on his bicycle, the bar laden with a triangular canvas bag, swinging like a cow's udder just short of the pedals. Inside were his tubes and syringes and a very professional-looking shop-coat. He would lean his bike against the wall, warn us solemnly to keep away from it, shake hands gravely with my father and mother, talk for an hour on family matters—never once inquiring for the sick animal—have his dinner, talk some more, smoke a cigarette, holding it between finger and thumb and sticking his tongue between his lips after every pull and spitting dryly twice—thugh—thugh. Then he would take off his flat hat, rub his bald head with a handkerchief, stretch himself out full-length on a form beside the fire with the handkerchief over his face and go to sleep.

When he woke, it was time for tea and after tea—perhaps—he would ask, as if he were Christ asking for the tomb of Lazarus, to be brought to the sick animal. He would prod it and poke it, feeling about with his fingers and pressing like a doctor testing for appendicitis.

"Ah," he would say, nodding his head, "when did its bowels move?"

Then he would ask for a candle and shove it up the pig's behind.

"If that doesn't work," he would tell my father, "send for me again."

But there was seldom need to. Ned Rafter would get out the spade and shovel the next day and my father would shrug and say philosophically, "Dammit, we should have sent for Ted earlier."

When Ted arrived on the Sunday afternoon in his blue serge suit and the shirt with the wing collar—his bike looking indecent without its swinging udder—and spat with his tongue through his teeth—thugh—thugh—very deliberately after every few words, we knew that something momentous had happened. My mother took his hat and my father gave him his own chair and we sat like mice on the long form under the window and waited with our breath held while he polished his dome and thugh—thughted.

"It's a—thugh—thugh—terrible business altogether," he began. "Terrible in a —thugh—thugh—Christian country."

"Do they know?" my father asked, looking very grave and biting the yellow end of his moustache. I knew he was thinking of the shame of having a cousin of his own hanged for knocking out the brains of a defenceless old man and stealing his life savings.

Ted looked at him with his myopic stare and thugh-thughted, looked at my mother with equal intensity and then over at us with our mouths open and our eyes distended.

"They know," he said in a dramatic whisper.

"Tell us," my father said. "Tell us, dammit. It wasn't . . . ?"

Ted held up one finger dramatically. "At this very minute— while I'm talking to you, now—they have him in Wexford barracks, taking down his confession."

"Who, man?" my father shouted.

"Now, sit down, Bill, and don't excite yourself. What I'm going to tell you will shock you as much as it shocked me."

"Why did he do it?" my father shouted in a frenzy, "a man like that with full and plenty?"

"A respectable man that everybody looked up to," Ted said.

"Who?" my mother asked, looking from one to the other, "who did it?"

"He struck him from behind with the carriage lamp," my father said, "just like you'd strike down a dog. What'll be the end of us at all!"

"It wasn't the lamp," Ted said. "They found an iron bar in the bog."

"Ted," my mother implored, "was it one of the Breens did it?"

Ted rubbed his crown and looked from my mother to my father and back again and then towards us and back again to my mother.

"The—thugh—thugh—children?" he inquired.

"Get out, get out, get out!" my father rose and scattered us with wild waves of his arms. "Out and play! Off that form! Out! Hurry! And shut the door!"

We fled before him, defeated and dejected, furious at not knowing for certain which of the Breens was going to be hanged.

"I hope it's Mike," I said, as we crouched under the kitchen window, straining to hear.

"Shh! Will you," Tom and my sister, Moll, said, "till we hear." But, though we huddled there for an hour, we never heard a word beyond the mumble of voices and the sound of my father pacing up and down the kitchen floor.

It was night before Ted went and we were let in again. The tension was gone and was replaced by something like irritation in my father's voice.

"Why did he have to come over like that with his whispering and thugh-thughting?" he said, "to frighten the lives out of us all?"

When he went out with the lantern to see the cattle, we coaxed it out of my mother.

The murderer was none of the Breens, but a well-to-do Protestant who had got himself into financial trouble (there was a woman somewhere in the story, too, who wasn't his wife, but we didn't hear of her until years after). We were all sorry that it hadn't been Mike, but all the neighbours said it was for the best and that, if the murderer had to be someone they knew, it was better that he was a Protestant rather than a Catholic, because, while they were all right—and Bill Watchorn, the butcher, kept a nice piece

of meat and raised his hat to the Canon—you couldn't trust them
and they'd all murder Catholics, if they got half a chance.

Later, when he had been convicted, a group of neighbours,
Catholic and Protestant, came round with a petition for reprieve
and asked my father to sign.

"He killed a poor, defenceless man—gave him a death you
wouldn't give to a dog," my father shouted. "Let him hang for it."

They read out the list of names for him, emphasising those of
our Catholic neighbours.

"I don't care who signed it," he said, "or who done it—
Protestant, Catholic or Jewman—hanging is too good for him."
And nothing they said could move him from that. They got
fifty thousand signatures from all over the county in spite of him,
but the man was hanged, all the same.

We still had our suspicions of the Breens and when, shortly
after, they built a new hayshed, we were certain it was done with
the old man's money. We looked at them in horror and fascination
on the few occasions when they came to see my father about
cattle. Once, we went so far as to print out the words THOU
SHALT NOT KILL on the lid of a shoe-box and tie it to the
tail-board of Mike's spring-car.

Sometimes, at night, I had dreams of his red face bending over
me, an iron bar in his raised hand to strike me down in case I
should reveal his guilty secret. To thwart his evil designs I wrote
MIKE BREEN KILLED JACK MIDDLETON FOR HIS
MONEY on a page of my exercise book, signed my name under-
neath, sealed it in an envelope, wrote TO BE OPENED AFTER
MY DEATH on it and put it away in the box under my bed.
When I thought of it again and looked to see if it was still there,
I found it open. What I had written was crossed out and the words
JOHN IS A BIG EEJIT were scrawled in its place in Tom's
handwriting.

The knowledge that he had ransacked my box and knew all
my secrets and would use the information he had gained to taunt
me and ridicule my pretensions filled me with dismay. God knows
what he had seen there. I hardly knew myself what it contained—
terrible things I had written on pieces of paper in moments of
stress, when my father was shouting and my mother in tears—

resolutions to run away—mad, irresponsible, evil things, like I DREAMED HE WAS DEAD AND WE WERE ALL LAUGH-ING—intimate things, like PLEASE GOD, STOP ME WET-TING THE BED AND I'LL BE A PRIEST—IF I'M LET. There was a copy-book, too, with these words in big letters on the cover:

THE LIFE AND OPINIONS OF JOHN FOLEY, GENTLE-MAN.

My name is John Foley. I am eleven years old. I live in Wexford on a farm. I do not like it. My father and my brother like it. I don't. They don't like me because I don't. I don't like my brother. He is always fighting. My brother is all for cows and corn and thinking he'll never be old enough to start ploughing. I don't want to plough, going up and down a field all day after old horses until your feet and arms drop off. And my father telling you how crooked the furrow is and you'd never be any good. Calves bawling to be fed and pigs and the rain and pulling turnips in the frost. I don't like it. I want to go some place else and do something else, I don't know what. But I'll never be let anyway, so it's all the same. . . .

I would have it all flung back at me, sooner or later. My brother was adept at finding out the tenderest and weakest spots in my defence and sinking the knife in. Somehow, he was always dis-covering me like a hermit crab between shells and exploiting my weakness. One of our more common habits which nearly always ended in blows, was to ridicule each other in crude rhymes. He usually bested me at this because he was quicker than I was. He would have it said and be folded up in laughter before I could think of something that rhymed.

"All the men . . .", he would shout by way of challenge, having already made up his own rhyme, and at these dread words (by a long-standing tradition, whose origin I have forgotten, our rhymes had to start that way) my mind would trip into panic and refuse to work.

"All the men," Tom would shout, "from here to Hook Head, Wouldn't stop John from wetting the bed."

Or, because I had sliced the top off one finger in a turnip-grinder and was very self-conscious about it, keeping it doubled in my palm most of the time:

"All the men, from here to Portlaw,
Couldn't put a finger on John's ugly paw."

The rhymes I made about his stupidity at school, his ignorance of Irish History, the fact that he couldn't spell, worried him not at all. He despised such things.

"I know NINETY EIGHT," he said, "and KELLY, THE BOY FROM KILLANNE and THE BOYS OF WEXFORD. The rest is not worth knowing. I know more about farming than you do. I know about manuring and rotating crops and what'll grow in a lay."

"It's a lea," I said, "you're pronouncing it wrong."

"Who wants to pronounce it like townies," he said, "with their fleas and leas!"

"I know all about crops, too," I said.

"I bet you won't tell me this, then," he said. "What kind of land is best for barley?"

And I couldn't.

"Where are your books, now!" he jeered.

"I bet you don't know what Timothy is," I said.

"Don't be codding," he said. "There's no such thing as Timothy. That's a fellow's name. A sissyish kind of name you'd find in books."

"It's the name of a grass," I said. "I saw it in the paper."

But he only laughed and jeered at me and called me Timothy afterwards, whenever he thought of it.

Our rivalry was fiercest of all in the games of handball we played. We had become good at the game, as there was a hand-ball alley beside the school and we served a long apprenticeship there during lunch-hour. But it was at home, playing against the gable of the house or against the front of the cowhouse that the games of blood were played. Tom, who was older and stronger than I, had the edge. Occasionally, I beat him by being cleverer and by refusing to concede an ace when another would have given up. Tom brought out a stubborn, competitive streak in me that ordinarily wasn't there.

He relied on strength and belted the ball so high and hard that it often flew back over my head and landed lifelessly on the dung-hill. The yard was full of hazards like that, which had to be taken into consideration in play. There was the door, against the bottom of which the ball fell dead. If it struck the lintel, it flew straight down, hit the bottom of the door and reeled out along the ground. The windows of the loft above were equally troublesome. But, with long experience, we learned to use them to make the ball behave in infuriating ways. We became so good at it that no one could beat us in our own yard.

Sometimes, my father sat on the wall and refereed. When he did, I always played better. I could concentrate on the game and be sure of getting fair play. I liked it, too, because it meant that the game would not end in blows. But the game was even tougher, when he was there. Something made us want to excel before him and win his praise. To me it was very important, because he seldom found praise for anything I did. Sometimes, at the end of a game, he would praise me and I was so pleased that I wished the world would end that very minute and leave me all eternity to glory in his approval.

But mostly, I earned only his wrath. There was the day he was turning in the pony—it wasn't really a pony, but a spirited young horse, trim, leggy, a flier, which he yoked under the Croydon. He was in a hurry to go to a funeral. He never missed funerals. For him it was a day of shaking hands, renewing old friendships and drinking as much whiskey as he could to show respect for the dead and regret at his untimely departure. His eye would moisten and his tongue would loosen to dilate on their long acquaintance and the many virtues of the deceased—chief of which usually was that he was "a dacent man", meaning that he could always be relied on to go on a drunken spree to the Curragh and match round for round with my father and the rest of the party. After the funeral, the mourning would continue at some convenient pub and he would arrive home in the despondent dawn, shouting that all the good men were dead and there was only himself left.

I was helping him turn in the pony. The field gate opened on to the lane and another gate led to the yard. The pony had a habit of galloping out of the field and turning down the lane towards the road instead of into the yard. I was sent down to close the road gate. It was a dull day and the trees near the road—sinister at the best of times—were full of menacing shadows. There was something stirring down there. A blackness, massive in bulk, threatening in shape, lurked under the scarfing branches. Huge, vague—like the presences I felt in the darkened room at night, stooping over me, their doomed breath on my neck, receding beyond the limit of my frightened vision when I turned to look, then, crowding back to tower above me, until I turned again in terror, my back against the wall, no weapon but my staring eyes to keep them at bay.

I could not face the unknown threat of the trees. Not even the prospect of my father's awful anger could make me. I turned back. What was I going to say? Confess I was afraid of shadows? In books there would be an understanding father who would take me by the hand, lead me down the lane and prick the irrational bubble of my fear. We would laugh together at it and I would walk into the darkest depths to show I was no longer afraid. A boy of eleven afraid! What would he say! What would my brother say!

I went back and told him the gate was shut. I had formed a plan that might save me. When we were turning the pony in, I would race across the field and cut him off at the place we called Half-Ways-The-Lane, where there was a stile. I would turn him back and no one need ever know of my cowardice. But he beat me to it. As I reached the stile, out of breath and in tears, he flashed past with a wild whinny and his tail flying. Out on the road and away. It was the last we saw of him for three days. The noise of his hoofs away beyond the Cross was like the drum-beat of doom, as I turned back to face my father.

He came towards me across the field at a lope. His arms—long as an ape's—swung to the knees. His short, broad fingers doubled into fists. He shouted at me. I ran for the house. He crashed across the stile and I could hear him pounding up the lane after me. I wondered would he kill me, this time, steamroll me, annihilate me. There would be one moment of pain and then a dazzling blackness as he felled me. The last thing I would see in life and the last thing I would feel would be the fist of my father. Struck in hate—that perverted form of love—it would be the most intimate contact we would ever have had. It would be the best thing for him—and for me, too, when he didn't want me.

But he wouldn't kill me. That was the trouble. He would beat

me and humiliate me. Then my mother would intervene and I
would be the cause of more trouble between them. He would hate
me more than ever and I would go in desperation, some day, like
poor, old Tom Pender, when his wife tried to commit him to the
asylum, and hang myself in the cowhouse.

My mother was at the table, having her eleven o'clock tea and
toast—which she had every day instead of breakfast—when I
ran in and flung myself under the table. She had her white cup
with the blue band raised half-way to her mouth and that was as
far as it ever got. There was a roar from my father as he passed
the window. The cup dropped from her hand and splintered on the
floor. She jumped up with one hand raised protectively, as my
father bellowed in and crashed to the door.

How shall I describe the indignities that followed—the shouts—
the threats! My father pounding the table. The words thick, and
tripping one another in an incoherent torrent. Shouting at me to
come out. My mother pleading with him to be calm. To be calm!
Telling him to be calm!

His anger was quickly diverted from me to my mother. As I
crouched there under the table, my knees trembling and every
bone softening to sludge, most of what had been wrong with their
marriage from the start was drawn down.

I can close my eyes, now, and see the brown leg of the table
with the grey gash where a splinter had been kicked loose, and
the woolly underside of the linoleum table-cloth, cutting off my
father's legs at the ankle. I can see his boots, tanned and ochred
with dried mud, the steel toecaps kicking angrily at the concrete
floor. Sometimes, they turned my way like questing terriers, the
studs glistening like teeth, and I shrank back out of their reach.
I never get the oily smell of linoleum now but I hear the voices
of my father and mother crying down my childhood.

I heard it all from the beginning. The marriage that had been
no marriage, because it had been arranged. My father, successful,
middle-aged, in search of an heir. My mother, eldest of an im-
poverished stock, sacrificed, as the eldest so often was in those
days, in the interest of the rest. Young enough to be his daughter.
I heard it all. The promises, the betrayals, the refusals to com-
promise, the withdrawals, the reservations, the withholding of self,

the things no longer spoken of, the indifference, the death of respect, of charity itself—until they stood, antagonistic figures in a bleak landscape, straining against the harsh bond that choked them.

I remember, in particular, talk of an unsuccessful honeymoon in a Dublin hotel, cut short because of some inadequacy on her part, which I could not understand, some brutality on his. I remember the voice of my mother, trembling with tears and a pain beyond endurance, shouting, "I tried! I tried!"

I remember my father, roaring her down in his great, broken, bull's voice, "You never wanted me from the start." A queer catch in his voice, as he added, "and, now, you've turned the children against me and I've nobody at all."

The talk came back to me again. I gripped the leg of the table, expecting to be pulled out at any minute.

"He's not like another," my father was angry, disappointed, aggrieved that a son of his could be so perverse.

"They can't all be the same," my mother said.

"That's right. Stand up for him. Encourage him in his lies."

"Do you always tell the truth?" she shot back coldly. "With your comings and goings, your excuses. Are they always true? The men you met that wouldn't be put off. As if you had no will of your own! The 'decent men' that are more important to you than your wife and family. Any lie is good enough for us, as long as you're hail-fellow-well-met with them. You're going out today and no one dare ask you when you'll be back, or what state you'll be in, or how many of your 'friends' will be with you to shout around the place in the middle of the night and frighten the children and leave the place like a pigsty. Truth! What do you know of truth or decency or anything else, except to get what you want and walk over people in getting it!"

To question his integrity was always to touch my father in a very tender place. He was off, at once, on a long, blustering tirade, roaring like a wounded lion, goaded beyond endurance at the ingratitude of us all, when he had slaved to build up a fine farm and keep us in full and plenty and would leave us well off at his death, which, he knew, we were all hoping for and none more than she, so that she might live riotously on his hard-earned

money and cast her eyes around for someone who would thaw
the frost out of her and enjoy an intimacy that had been denied
him, her lawful husband, whom she cared for no more than if he
were a piece of dirt at her feet.

Then he was off up the stairs to put on his Sunday suit, banging
doors and throwing things about and swearing dreadfully at the
top of his voice. I stayed under the table until he had gone off to
get a lift to the funeral from Mick Rennick. I was uneasy all day,
because I could not find out from my mother whether he had
decided not to beat me or had only postponed it until he got back.

The Croydon stood in the yard as a reminder of my guilt. Its
huge wheels with their thin spokes and the elegant, long, curved
shafts, its high-slung, graceful body on slender springs, made it
stand out like a thoroughbred among the lumbering farm-carts.
The Croydon—a sort of fancy gig—which my father had had
specially made, was his pride, He had wheeled it out himself that
morning and stood watching, while we washed the wheels and
polished the mountings.

He used it only on special occasions. Like funerals, or during
the Mission (which came every five years) when two roaring
Redemptorists thundered from the pulpit and children like us
nodded and dozed and were elbowed in the ribs, while the voices
bellowed on about the dangers of company-keeping or the awful
fate of those who neglected to say the Family Rosary.

Once, on a fine Sunday in Summer, it had been wheeled out
and we all went for a drive, sitting high above the green hedges,
back to back, floating along on feathered springs, with the dust
rising behind us and people in their Sunday best, coming from
the cottages along the way to look at us, sailing past. It was painted
black, with thin lines of yellow on the spokes and shafts. It had
yellow corduroy cushions with black buttons. We were all in love
with the beauty and grandeur of it, but most of all my father,
sitting upright in his Sunday serge, saying, "tch, tch, tch," through
closed teeth to encourage the horse, and flicking carelessly at low-
hanging leaves, as we passed under trees. His standing at the
funeral without it would be in doubt and it was all my fault.

All day, I helped around the house, building up credit with my
mother against my father's return. I swept the stairs. I cleaned out

the presses under the dresser that hadn't been cleaned out for years, exorcising the ghosts of old teapots and odd boots and corked bottles with dregs of turpentine or paint oil in the bottom, saucers with greenish-yellow residue that had once been a mixture of sulphur and linseed oil for ringwormed calves, empty polish boxes, washers, rusty nails, a bag of bluestone left over after some forgotten potato-spraying.

I cleaned the good knives and forks with bathbrick and the silver spoons that had been used only once when my grand-aunt—who had given them to my mother as a wedding present—came to tea. She never came again, because, being very highly related and having had an uncle a priest (in an age when having a priest in the family was something out of the ordinary, before every Tom, Dick and Lizzie Goggins that married the tinker could boast of one) she could not forgive my father for not having a lavatory in the house and for submitting her to the indignity of using the earth closet like the rest of us—or going behind a hedge like a common tramp.

Sometimes, I cried to myself over the spoons and wet the bathbrick, when I thought of how wicked I was to tell my father lies and let the pony escape. I knew he was right to be angry with me and that I should be beaten. It would have been better, if he had caught me before I had got to the house and thrashed me then. It would have finished at that and there would have been no row between them. Seeing me cry, my mother told me not to be afraid, that my brother, who had gone on his bicycle to look for the pony, would soon have him back and everything would be all right. That made me cry more, because I couldn't tell her what was really troubling me. I had no words to tell her that they could both beat me, and welcome, if only they loved and respected each other as a father and mother should.

To cheer me, she began to talk about sending me away to College, a subject they had spoken about—and disagreed on—once or twice before. The thought of leaving the farm pleased me, but I had very little idea why boys went away to school—except to become priests. I knew that I could never be fit for that and only boys, who kept their hands joined and looked at the altar all the time during Mass, and never told lies or committed sins or said dirty words, and whose fathers were well-off and wore collars and ties all the time, were fit to become priests.

Only once had I ever thought of becoming a priest and that was some years before, when a jolly Franciscan, on quest (as we called it), full of smiles and jokes and affability, had given me an apple, which he had collected at some other house (they took what was offered them—money, potatoes, duck-eggs, everything) and asked me if I'd like to go off with him and become a priest. I said I would, because I had fallen in love with his apples and his lovely red complexion, his brown habit and the beautiful smell of his soap-scented hands, which he laid on my head, and their short, clean nails and white skin—so different from the hands of my father, my brother and myself, with our black, broken nails and thick peasants' fingers, all red and grained with dirt. There would be no pulling of waterlogged turnips or washing of frosty potatoes in a monastery.

I was impressed too by the way he asked my mother to give the money, which she offered him, to his driver, as his vow of poverty forbade him handling the money he collected. It seemed very romantic to me, when my mother told me, afterwards, that the poor monks were often without a bite to eat in their monastery and were constrained to ring the church bell to let the people in the town know of their plight, and a few peals were enough to bring the generous townspeople running with food and fuel and whatever else might be needed.

He took me round with him to show him all the neighbours' houses and gave me more apples to cure my shyness. I had a wonderful day and was only embarrassed once, when he insisted on praising me to the Clearys, who had some kind of grudge against our family for something that had happened before I was born, and never spoke to us when we met, but passed by with deliberate aversion of the head, as if the sight of us was offensive.

The Franciscans had schools, my mother said, but they were too far away and too expensive. She wondered—half to herself— as she went about the kitchen, taking down the big keeler and getting the wheaten-meal and the buttermilk and the breadsoda ready for bread-making, whether it mightn't be possible for me to stay at her brother's house and cycle the five miles into College every day. She was always lamenting that her brothers, whom the master had declared good scholars, had never been given the chance. Two of them had spent a year or so at the Christian Brothers, but, when the Troubles started, they had become involved and their education had taken a grimmer turn. They had exchanged their books for rifles and taken to the hills. When it was all over, they were too restless to settle at anything and had drifted from one job to another, spending a while in the army and, finding it too tame in peacetime, trying their hand at insurance or construction work in England. In their time they had been Warble Fly Inspectors, Beet Agents, Seeds Salesmen, Cowmen, Stewards, Pig-Buyers, Threshing-engine Drivers, Potato Sprayers, Auxiliary Postmen. Everything for a while and nothing for long.

My uncle, Ned, although the youngest, had got the farm— mainly through default. It had never occurred to the others that they should come home and claim it. I didn't know whether I wanted to stay at my uncle Ned's and go to school from there or not. I felt guilty still about the steel tape and all the other things in his tool-house that I had tampered with or broken. The fact that he never said anything about them, but looked at me in that vague, yet penetrating way of his made it all the worse. Still, we liked him, especially when he came to visit us on his bicycle, once or twice a year. It would be on a Sunday afternoon and we'd all stand on the stile at Half-Ways-The-Lane, from which a straight stretch of road was visible, and wait for him. He always emptied his pockets for us and was thoughtful enough to bring each a separate present.

My mother looked younger, when he came. They would talk a lot and laugh and we'd hear about things that happened, when they were young and schoolchildren like ourselves. There would be tea and buns and apple-tart. My father, who liked uncle Ned, would take him out to see the cattle and the crops and we'd all hurry to get the milking done and the calves fed, until we could sit down again and listen to them talk.

In the cool of the evening, we would get his bicycle for him and fight for the privilege of wheeling it down the lane. My father would say goodbye to him at the gate and my mother and the rest of us would walk down to the road with him, while white moths flittered from the grass and heavy, black beetles lumbered, droning, across the hedges. My mother would ask him to come oftener. She would watch long after he had gone out of sight and, sometimes, stood there, brushing her eyes, until she remembered it was long past our bedtime and turned to shoo us home before her. For a few days she would be in a reminiscent mood and tell us about our grandparents who had died long before, about the old beggar-woman with the bandaged face, whom they called Mary No-Nose, about the chicken with the two heads and about the day she had gone with her father on the train to Tramore. I wished uncle Ned would come every week, because it was nice to see my mother like that. But it was a long journey—nearly twenty miles— and his visits were rare.

I knew my father had no regard for education, and, as he hadn't, I wasn't likely to be sent anywhere. He was in the habit of saying that all the Latin and what he called "that kind of stuff" a boy needed was the Serving of Mass. My brother and I served Mass and he was very proud of the fact. But he was forever lamenting that Dan Morgan served too. Dan was the son of a sharp little widow whose husband had been a labourer. She sometimes did the washing in our house. My father, who distrusted her and referred to her as "that little, wall-eyed woman", always had a quick check around to see that everything was still in its place, when she had gone. He believed that only farmers' sons and sons of people with money in the bank should be allowed serve Mass. His views on religion were much the same as his views on politics—only strong rate-payers and men of property should have the vote or the ear of God. Possession was virtue and to those who had, much would be given.

I was very conscious of his presence in the chapel behind me on Sundays. He watched our every move and, if we did anything wrong—moved when we shouldn't have, slouched or scratched our behinds—we would be sure to hear of it when we got home.

"I saw that pup of a Morgan picking his nose again, today. Don't ever let me see one of yous at a thing like that and all the people looking," he would shout.

"You didn't genuflect in the middle, when you came down with the Book," he said to me, "and the times you did genuflect your knee never hit the ground. Don't you know your knee should always hit the ground! Were you afraid of getting it dirty, or is it stiff in the joints you're getting?"

He was always on to us about running through the Confiteor, which we took at a gallop, because we were never sure of it and had to skate swiftly and lightly over it, as if it were very thin and dangerous ice. In all my time serving Mass I never relaxed on the altar until we had cleared the hurdle of the Confiteor.

Whenever I think of serving Mass now, I think of the morning I couldn't light the candles, because Dan Morgan—or whoever had put them out on the previous Sunday—had been in such haste that he had pulled the quencher down too far and flattened the wick in the soft grease, where it stuck, and, no matter how I turned the taper or stretched on tiptoe, I could not light it.

I was aware of a hush in the chapel and then the nightmare thing I had always dreaded happened. I heard the noise of the Sanctuary gate opening and the impatient footsteps and heavy breathing of my father coming up the steps behind me. As he reached up for the candle-stick in his heavy, black frieze coat— the yellowing wisps of moustache tailing away to the corners of his mouth—I thought of the eyes of everyone on us and hated him for drawing attention to himself and me in such an unnecessary way. He freed the wick and held out the candle for me. But my hand shook so much that I could not bring the flame and the wick together. The final indignity came when he roared in a whisper that rattled the organ loft (which contained nothing grander than a harmonium), "Dammit, boy, give it to me!" and took the taper from me and lit the candle himself.

All through the day my mother kept coming back to the same thing. There was only one salvation for me and that was going away to College. There was only one farm and Tom would get that. There would be nothing for me, if I stayed, but drudgery and conflict. At the best, I would get a job collecting insurance like Mikey Byrne, who cycled around with three fountain pens and as many pencils in his breast pocket and had the reputation of knowing more about insurance than any twenty men, a judgment that came into doubt later, when it was discovered that he had been collecting half a crown more from everyone than they ought to have been paying. But, by the time that came to light, he had gone on an extended vacation to England and was not available for questioning about his strange error.

In the evening, when Tom had returned without the pony, she brought it up again. My last recollection of her that day is the sight of her determined chin as she sprinkled Holy Water on us for bed and her saying that she was staying up until my father came home to tackle him about it.

But, like the pony, my father did not come back for three days. And when he did come, blustering and apologetic, one night with a party of friends—good fellows all, fresh from the races and bursting with fellowship, bibulous, garrulous, backslapping, laughing, bulging with bottles, their clothes creased from sleeping in cars, their collars dirty and awry—we were all roused from our beds to have biscuits and sweets forced upon us, while my mother stood in her night-dress at the head of the stairs, staring coldly down at my father looking up from the foot, with the tipsy laughter congealing on his disconcerted face and his self-esteem shattering like the bottles that dropped from his prodigal hands.

CHAPTER FOUR

THE College yard was like the deck of a ship. I stood at the railings, looking out over the rooftops and squalid gardens where weeds clawed for light, down into the bowl of the town where the river slid by ancient quays, and idle cranes hung like question-marks over the water. All around me was the sound of boys—running, shouting, wrestling, tumbling. Strange faces, strange accents. I stared out, not really seeing anything, not wanting to see, merely postponing the moment when I would have to merge and coalesce with the seething—terrifying—mass about me.

Somewhere a bell rang (I was about to be absorbed into a world of bells, but I didn't know that yet). I was slowly aware of the lessening of sound around me, as if one had stepped in from a storm and closed the door. Then a silence so absolute that I could hear the cling-ring of a bicycle bell in a street across the river. The familiar sound touched some unbearable chord of loneliness in me and I began to cry again. I leaned across the railings with my head on my hands and let the tears flow, making no attempt to wipe them away. Down my face they ran, salty at the corner of my mouth, dribbled from my chin to my hands and down into the barren gardens twenty feet below.

A hand was laid across my shoulder and a voice—a not unkindly voice, but one with authority in it—said, "What are you doing out here? Why aren't you in at your tea?"

The pressure of his arm turned me round and I looked down, ashamed to be caught crying. Through the tears I saw the leather cincture hanging, the black hemline of the habit, the rounded toes of the neat, black shoes. I sniffed and rubbed my eyes which were swollen and sore with crying. He put his hand under my chin and pressed it firmly upwards.

"What is your name?"

I told him.

"Come," he said and smiled so that a wrinkle spread from one

47

corner of his mouth, "it isn't the end of the world, now, is it?"

His face was dark, his hair very black. He had a black hood, such as I had seen in pictures of monks, on his shoulders. The pressure of his hand on my arm steadied my shivering. I felt thirsty and very hungry. I had cried all day since morning and —for the moment—there were no more tears in me. Just a nothingness, as if my eyeballs were pressed up to a blank wall.

"You'll feel better about it tomorrow," he said, "everybody does. Hate starting myself."

He squeezed my arm to show how he shared my feeling.

"We'll have you enjoying yourself before you know where you are. Hurling, football, handball, table-tennis. You have football boots, of course?"

Of course. They had been on the list and—like the silver napkin-ring, which I was never to use—my mother had bought them, though I had never played football and never even seen a pair before. It didn't seem to me a great attraction, now, either.

"We'll have you on all the teams in no time," he said. "But, come on, now. A footballer must eat. Let's see if we can't find you something nice."

He led me by the arm through a ball-alley and a boxroom, piled to the ceiling with trunks and cases, through a short, windowless corridor lit by a single bulb, through a heavy door into a huge room with tables of boys lining the walls and down the centre. He led me to a vacant seat at a table with boys of my own size. They all stopped for a moment to look at us, their cheeks bulging with bread.

"Make way for a hungry man," the priest said. "And you, Murphy," he said to a biggish boy with a lick of red hair in his eyes, "see that he is properly looked after—and take him to his dormitory, when tea is over. He'll tell you his name and you'll find the lists on the doors. First Junior, I expect."

When he had gone I told Murphy my name. He poured a cup of tea for me out of an enamel teapot, big as a bucket, which he brought from the kitchen.

"Jam tonight, because it's our first night," he said. "I wish you'd 'a sat some place else. I had bagsed the stuff on that plate."

I looked at the plate. There was a spoonful of jam on the side of it and two prints of butter about the size and thickness of pennies. I pushed the plate over to him.

"Aw, Murph," someone said, "that's lousy. He's only a new fellow. Give him his butter."

"He can have his lousy butter," Murphy said. "I wasn't going to take it. I only said I had it bagsed, if nobody came."

He pushed it back to me. He cut me a piece of bread to show he had no ill-will. I began to eat.

"Hey!" Murphy said, "you want to look out for McGaw."

I looked at him, wondering what he meant.

"Leave him alone, Murph," a boy said, "he's only new. He doesn't know McGaw."

He turned to me. "You don't know McGaw, do you?"

"I don't know anybody," I said.

"There, Murph, what did I tell you! He doesn't know McGaw. He doesn't know anybody."

"He knows us," Murphy said.

"He knows Black Jack," the boy beside me said.

I looked at him in a puzzled way and they all laughed.

"Father Turley," Murphy said. "He brought you in. We call him Black Jack. But you'd better not let him hear you. He doesn't like it."

I was shocked at their irreverence and blushed at the suggestion that I might ever refer to a priest by a nickname. I had been brought up to believe that people went to hell for less.

"He's the Dean," another boy said.

"Looks after us all," Murphy said.

"Sleeps in a room off the Top Dor," another boy said.

"Sees we go to bed."

"Sees we get up."

"Sees we wash our ears."

"And blow our noses."

"Speak for yourself, snotty!"

"He's a real father to us," Murphy said in a facetious voice, "ain't he, boys?"

This was a great joke. They all spluttered and coughed pieces of bread across the table.

"Our Father, who art in the Top Dor," another boy said, when they had laughed their fill. They were off again, until a big boy from another table shouted, "Shut up, scum!" and they all made derisive sounds like sheep bleating and subsided.

Up at a little table at the top of the room Father Turley rang a bell and we stood up and said Grace After Meals. Then Murphy took me upstairs to the dormitories and we searched for my name on the lists pinned to the doors. It seemed strange to see my name there, staring out at me from the middle of a string of names I had never heard before—Guerin, Mockler, Field, Cunnane, Barnes, Tubridy, Young, Costello, Fitzsimon. It looked hemmed in and besieged and leaped gratefully out at me, when I ran my eye down the list, like my face appealing for recognition from a shop window, as I passed along the street. It was odd to think that I was known and expected in this strange place where I knew nobody. I wondered whose hand had written it and if he knew anything about me. Anything bad was what I meant.

Down the length of the dormitory were two rows of beds, facing outwards from the walls. In the narrow space between the two rows was a third row, placed head to foot down the centre of the room. There was a passage of about a foot on either side of them—and absolutely no privacy. Out there one would be in full view of the whole dormitory. I saw that all the best beds, around the walls, were already taken. We made the rounds of them, noticing the suitcases or bundles of clothes laid on each. The counterpanes had been stripped off and were hanging in neat folds from the bottom bars of the beds. There were only two beds out in the middle with the counterpanes still on. I chose one and Murphy helped me to strip the counterpane off.

"You must fold it twice down the middle," he said, "then join the two ends and fold again across the bottom bar. You'll hear about it from Sister Benedict, if you don't."

I was shy of opening my case when he was there, but he sat on the bed, as if he meant to stay there for the rest of the night and, in the end, I had to. I took out the shiny, new keys on their string from my pocket and opened the case. With my body between the case and Murphy, I lifted one corner of the lid and felt around inside for the sheets, pyjamas and towel.

I wasn't too happy about him seeing my new pyjamas, either,

because I was afraid he would guess from their newness that I had never worn a pair before and had been used to going to bed every night at home in my shirt. I laid out a new toothbrush and a tube of toothpaste as well. I didn't mind whether he knew that I had never washed my teeth with a brush and paste before—only with a rag and salt—because washing teeth at all seemed to me to be one of those daft adult things that boys could see no reason for. I had tasted a bit of the toothpaste the night before and liked it. It was just like peppermint and, even if I didn't use it to wash my teeth, I felt I could always eat it.

Murphy showed me a room off the dormitory with rows of open lockers from floor to ceiling. He said I was to keep my soap and brushes and things there. I found an empty locker and put in my new toothbrush, a bar of yellow soap called Coal Tar, which smelled beautifully and was so different from the common Sunlight we always used at home. It was the last I saw of them. Toothpaste and soap were gone, when I went to look for them in the morning. I was too frightened to ask if anyone had seen them or to report that they were missing. I did notice after a week that Murphy had a yellow bar of soap, and blushed to the roots of my hair, when he caught me looking at him in the washroom, in case he thought I might suspect him of stealing mine.

Boys were continually coming in to the dormitory and wandering around. Sometimes, they sat together on beds and talked. They looked at me with mild curiosity and returned to their conversation or wandered out again. They all seemed to know one another and their casual greetings and easy familiarity increased my despondency and sense of isolation. Murphy had gone off and I didn't know what to do for the rest of the evening. I was afraid to ask anybody, because it would draw too much attention to myself. I slipped out, when I thought no one was looking, and wandered around brown, dimly-lit corridors, until I found a lavatory. I went in and sat down and, behind the privacy of the closed door, I cried hopelessly again.

When I had cried myself dry, I found a washroom and cooled my smarting eyes with water. Then, because I was thirsty, I had a long drink from the cold tap. The water was lukewarm and tasted of scented soap. I had never taken water from a tap before and thought miserably of the well at home and the ice-cool water which we loved to scoop up in our hands on hot days, dashing and slopping it into our mouths and over our faces. In the mirror my eyes and face looked swollen, my expression empty and hopeless as a gutted building.

Back in the dormitory some boys were preparing for bed. I sat on the edge of mine, watching them covertly to find out how they went about it. When they got as far as shirt and trousers, I watched very carefully to see what they would do next. I was appalled at the thought that I would have to take off my trousers out there in front of everybody. I wondered how it could be done decently and hoped to find out by watching the others.

The first boy to strip himself eased his arms out of the braces, then opened the fly and, with one swift movement, slid the trousers down over his haunches and at the same time sat down on the bed and pushed the front of his shirt between his legs. Then he lifted his feet out of the trousers and slipped them into the legs of the pyjamas. With the same swift movement, this time in reverse, he stood up and pulled up the pyjamas at the same time. Then he casually hauled off the shirt and donned the pyjama jacket.

I watched while two more boys did the same, before I had the courage to try myself. I got as far as slipping the braces off and there I stuck. I had a furtive look round to see if I was being watched and it seemed to me that all eyes were on me. I decided to take off my socks first. When I had them off, I held them up to the light, as if I were looking for holes, and, behind the screen that they offered, I had another look round. From what I saw I was more than ever convinced that the time was not yet propitious. I made great show of turning back the bedclothes and digging the pillow. I sat down on the bed and had a hurried bite round the nails of both hands. Then I saw the door of the Locker-room standing ajar. With the feeling that I was escaping from a great indignity, I took up my pyjamas and sidled towards it, doing my best to give the impression that I had no intention or desire of going inside, but was at the mercy of some inevitable drift that was floating me there like flotsam on the tide.

Once inside, I closed the door behind me. I had my fly open

and was about to drop my trousers to the floor and step out of it, when a movement at the window made me jump. I saw in the gloom —I hadn't put on the light—two boys leaning out the window and I caught the red glow of cigarettes in their hands. I buttoned up my trousers again.

"Get out of here for feck's sake and close the door!" one of the boys hissed.

I backed out into the dormitory again and made for the door. In the privacy of the lavatories I changed and examined myself critically in the glass of the Washroom for several minutes. What I saw was not very reassuring. The pyjamas were too big for me. The legs touched the floor and I had to pull them up to keep them from tripping me. The arms came down to my fingertips. I rolled them up to the elbows like shirtsleeves, but they looked even more ridiculous that way. It was quite a while before I could force myself back to the dormitory. On the way, I had to stop and slacken the cord which I had tied too tightly. It was biting into my waist, but, when I eased it, the pyjamas slid perilously low and I had to tighten it again. It still wasn't right and I despaired of ever getting the trick of it.

When I went in, the dormitory was fuller. I had a distinct impression that the noise and chatter stopped for an instant as I appeared. There was a titter here and there. I felt that they knew I had never worn pyjamas before and were laughing at the uncouth figure I made. I put away my clothes in the Locker-room. The smokers had gone but the tang of tobacco still lingered. As I came back to my bed, my eye, sliding about for some neutral, inoffensive ground, met those of a pair of boys sitting on the bed beside mine. Before it swerved away again in embarrassment, I saw them nudge each other and laugh. They had the same look in their eyes as a group of boys I had seen once, urging dogs on to a squealing rabbit, which they had dug from its burrow and bludgeoned with a spade.

I kicked my shoes under the bed, threw back the bedclothes and jumped in. As I did so, there was a great guffaw, which struck my ears at the same time as I became aware that there was something strange wrong with my bed. I could not get my feet down into it. The more I strained and pushed the more it resisted me and the more the boys laughed. The more they laughed the more desperately I threshed and flailed about.

I was still kicking, when a sudden silence fell on the place and an authoritative voice, a voice I recognised, said, "What's going on in here?"

No one made any reply. Footsteps came very deliberately down the dormitory and stopped at my bed. I looked up diffidently into the eyes of Father Turley.

"Is anything the matter?" he asked.

"My bed," I said and began to snivel. "I can't get into it."

There was a titter which quickly died, when Father Turley swung round.

"They made a French bed for you, did they?"

"I don't know, Father," I sniffed.

While I hung my head, Father Turley asked, "Who is responsible for this?"

There was no answer.

"Roche," he said, addressing one of the boys I had caught laughing at me, "do you know anything about this?"

"No, Father."

"Hurley," he said to a boy down near the door, "do you know?"

"I've just come in, Father," Hurley said.

"Very well!" Father Turley said. "Nobody knows anything— as usual. Now, I want two boys—you, Roche, and you, Finnegan —to make this boy's bed. Correctly! And, if I hear of any more victimisation of new boys like this, I shall punish the whole dormitory."

He stood there, supervising the making of the bed, while I sat miserably on another bed, my pyjamas clutched to me, not knowing what way to look. I needed no one to tell me that by bringing Father Turley down on them like that I had incurred the enmity of the whole dormitory and would pay for it in a thousand ways later.

When the bed was ready, I crept in and hid my head under the blankets. Father Turley went off and the hubbub started again. I stretched my ears to hear if anything was being said about me. I heard nothing. But, presently, someone walked up to my bed and pulled down the blanket that was covering my head. I looked up in fear and saw a biggish boy looking down at me. His face, I was relieved to see, was not unfriendly.

"You," he said, "what's your name?"

I told him.

"Listen," he went on, "you're never to tell on another fellow." He raised his voice. "Do you hear that, all you new lousers, you're never to tell on another fellow."

"No," I said.

"When Black Jack asked you what was wrong with your bed, you should have said there was nothing wrong."

"I didn't know," I said timidly.

"Well, you know, now!"

"Yes," I said.

"Pull the louser out, Collins," someone shouted.

"Shut up!" the big boy said, then added charitably, "th' old eejit didn't know any better. And he'll never do it again. Will you?"

"No," I said.

"Pull him out, all the same—just for the gas," the same voice shouted and several others joined in, crying, "out with the louser."

"Shut up!" Collins roared. "Who's running this dor, anyway!"

A series of boos came from all sides and derisive calls of, "You, Mr. Prefect, Sir—I don't think!" and, "Big Chief Collins—him very important man!"

Collins made a rush and clouted the nearest booer. There were cries of, "Aw, Collins, don't come the heavy!" But the clouting had its effect and there was no more booing. They seemed to have forgotten me and I withdrew under the clothes again.

Shortly after, Collins, who seemed to be in charge, shouted, "Lights out in five minutes!" and, grumbling and protesting, they began to prepare for bed. Then Father Turley came in again, said, "Goodnight, boys!" and turned off the light.

Silence for a few minutes after he had gone. Then someone whispered, "Is he gone, lads?" and a voice from the other end replied, "No, I'm not. Do you want a goodnight kiss?"

Laughter around the dormitory, sounds of kissing, and Collins shouting, "Cut it out, fellows!"

But the whispering continued for a long time.

I remembered that I had not said my prayers. I was about to get out of bed to go on my knees, but the fear of drawing attention to myself again kept me where I was. As soon as I began to pray, I thought of home. I wondered if they would be kneeling down at this very minute to say the Rosary. I could hear my father saying, "Give us my old beads and we'll say the Rosary, in the name of God."

My brother would have to get it for him, now that I wasn't there. They'd all kneel down—my mother at the chair near the fire, my father on the other side, Moll at her own little stool. Tom would have the New Form all to himself at last and be glad I wasn't there any more to fight with him about it and make my father cross, so that he'd put the two of us kneeling up straight as ram-rods, against opposite walls, without any support for our wilting spines.

How we galloped through the decades, waiting impatiently at the end of each Hail Mary for my father and mother to catch up. How, when the Rosary was finished, we prayed, at my father's insistence, for a string of dead—mostly his relations (the demands of my mother's family on his prayers never troubled him)— that seemed to go back to Adam's time. I wiped my eyes in the sheet, and the only prayer I could say was, "Please, God, let me wake up in the morning in my old bed at home!"

It seemed a lifetime since I had awakened there to the sunlight creeping up the yellow wall and the sound of my mother stirring about in the kitchen. It didn't seem possible that it was barely fifteen hours since I had stood at the bedroom window in my shirt, looking out over the September fields, heavy with dew, to the wheat-field where the stacks, crinolined and waisted like ladies from a bygone age, curtseyed and nodded to one another through the mist. Down in the land behind the house I could hear Boggan turning in the cows, his thin, petulant voice carrying clearly in the morning air. Up the lane, his gleaming boots swishing through the wet grass, the tissues of his brain delicately cushioned, came Ned Rafter. The sight of him, so careless and unconcerned, making sucking sounds with his teeth, as he passed under me, struck like a hammer at my heart and I was conscious, for the first time, of the change that was about to be made in my life.

The known and familiar seemed suddenly very precious. I envied Ned his predictable, orderly existence. Whatever happened to me, he would still go about his work, as he had always done—always would do—milking the cows, getting his instructions for the day, drinking his buttermilk, drawing his pay on Saturday. All day and every day seeing those trees and that particular bit of sky and the green islands infinitesimally drifting westward. Looking out at the world from a known vantage point, secure in his anchorage, sure of his place. Not like me—about to be set adrift, without steer or compass, knowing I must, but dreading the voyage, without words to put my fears into shape. Nothing but a sense of upheaval, a tearing apart, and the dumb acceptance that it was inevitable and—though I could never feel it—for my ultimate good.

A big, new case with expanding hinges was packed and ready in the corner of the room. The new suit—the first with long trousers—which my mother had bought out of her own egg-money—was hanging behind the door. A nice suit. Creases sharp as razor blades in the trousers. A decent suit by country standards—navy blue and a close weave. Very suitable for a farmer's son. Not the kind of thing you'd find on a cottager, as my father was grudgingly compelled to admit, or on "one of them hair-oil townies you'd see stopping to rack his hair in a shop window". A white shirt and a red tie. Which gave Tom the opportunity to call me John Bull and to jeer:

> "Green, white and yella—
> The brave Irish fella.
> Red, white and blue—
> The dirty English crew."

Down in the kitchen they were finishing their breakfast. My father was impatient, asking Ned Rafter sarcastically if his teeth were bad, for Ned was a deliberate eater and had read somewhere that each mouthful should be chewed at least thirty times. They were to begin drawing in the harvest and my father fumed, as Ned chewed on at his regular pace and remarked mildly that the dew was so heavy that there wasn't a chance of the corn being dry enough for another hour. "'Twill all be lost," my father shouted, "if the weather changes. And, here, when we want every hand we can, they (looking crossly in the direction of my mother) must send the child off to College to have his head filled with notions."

My mother, who had been through it all many times before with him, said nothing, but went about her business, giving Moll instructions about the dinner (Mrs. Morgan was coming to help her) and how much milk was to be left back from the evening's milking—in case she was late for it—and which calves were on skim milk only and how the chickens should be fed and which boxes they went into.

I could not eat anything. I drank some tea from my mug. Half way through, it struck me that I might never drink from it again and I went outside so that nobody would see my face. I wandered around, looking into houses, storing up their smells, letting the young calves suck my fingers, dipping my hand into rain-barrels, jolting the wheels of carts and rattling chains— collecting pieces of my life to take away with me and sustain me in the ordeal before me. It was all too much and I slunk inside again and upstairs, where I sat on my bed, looking at the case, hating it and all it stood for, until my mother in her Sunday clothes came to look for me.

"If your father sees you like that," she said, "he won't let you go at all."

The pony was ready at the gate when we went down. Tom tied the case to the seat on one side, and my mother and myself sat at the other. He untied the reins and handed them to her. "We'll have everything done when you come home," he said.

Moll, to whom I could not bring myself to speak since the evening before, was standing in the doorway rubbing her eyes. My father was nowhere to be seen.

The first load of corn came lurching into the yard and Ned Rafter, sitting on top, waved his hand. I waved timidly back and began to cry without any hope of ever stopping again. "There's a good boy," my mother said. "Everything will be all right."

Moll ran out and put something into my hand. Then she ran in and did not appear again. The thing in my hand was hard and round. I knew, without looking at it, that it was the strange, red and white stone we had picked up together on the strand the day we swore never to marry, because married people always quarrelled, but to live together in our own little house and never fight or disagree.

Tom stood there, not saying anything, and I could think of nothing to say to him. I wanted to shake hands with him. But the shock of discovering that I had loved him all the time, without ever knowing it till now, made me unable to make any gesture of farewell.

We were just moving off, when my father appeared from the fields in his shirt-sleeves, carrying a pike. I knew, now, that I loved him, too, and always would, no matter what he did or said. I hoped he had come to say goodbye to me.

"Not gone yet!" he said gruffly. Then he dug his hand into his pocket and pulled out a ten-shilling note.

"Here, boy," he said, "you might want that."

Then he turned away and in a different voice said, "God be with you—and be a good boy."

He went off to the haggard, without looking back, a stoop to his shoulders and the pike dragging after him.

I did not look back until we were at the top of the hill leading to the village. The house lay down underneath us among the sheltering beeches. Splinters of light leaped from the galvanized roof of the hayshed. Underneath, someone was piking sheaves from a load of corn. Later in the day, the roof would get very hot— too hot to touch. I thought of the day I had climbed the bench of hay with Moll, and we had taken off our clothes and lain, naked, in the soft, sweet hay under that burning roof, and of the time we had laid out a galvanized sheet in the sun, then collected all the eggs we could find and fried them on the hot zinc. The experiment had failed and was hardly worth the beating we got for it.

My mother gave me her own handkerchief to dry my eyes. "You won't be very long away," she said, "and it will be Christmas when you come home. I'll send you the OUR BOYS every week."

I was still in mourning for Christmas and had not yet reconciled myself to the death of Santa Claus. I refused to believe that he would come no more, and often, still, went into the parlour where we had hung our stockings in the hope that he would brighten some drab day in the middle of the year by coming to me, because I believed in him so faithfully, and prove them all wrong. So her mention of Christmas, instead of cheering me, was only another reminder that all the certainties of my life were being swept away.

She took a bar of chocolate out of her handbag and gave it to me. The knowledge that she had saved it for me, had deliberately put it away in anticipation of this day and moment, affected me very deeply. The gesture with which she held it out to me was, somehow, the culmination of all she had ever done for me. I have never eaten a bar of chocolate over which I cried more, or which I enjoyed less. But, of all the bars I have ever eaten, it is the only one I remember.

Going through the village, I was glad to see that the place was almost deserted and there was no one in the street whom we knew. I caught a glimpse of Mr. Wadding through his window, with his glasses on his forehead, peering at his ledger on the slanting shelf before him. He looked up as we passed, and I would have liked to have waved, but, while I was making up my mind whether I should or not, he looked down again and my chance was gone.

For the sake of appearance, on our way through the village, we had begun to talk of trivialities, but our conversation had no roots and wilted quickly as soon as we had passed the last house in Church Road and were in the country again. Sometimes, to distract me, my mother would suggest that I should walk some of the steeper hills to take the weight off the pony and give my legs a stretch at the same time. The exercise did me good. I would walk behind, holding on to the car, stealing looks at her as she sat erect, scarcely touching the back-rest, with the reins caught firmly in both hands, as if she didn't trust the pony—she didn't— and expected him to bolt if she relaxed her vigilance for a single instant. At the top of the hill I would get in again and the pony would smarten into a trot. The motion was not disagreeable. It set up a repetitive rhythm in the brain that precluded consecutive thought and inhibited brooding.

We reached my uncle's, which was as far as my mother intended to take me, in time for dinner. For me it was a sorry meal, but, mercifully, nobody pretended to take any notice of me. While they exchanged family news, I moped at the end of the table. My aunt Nelly cut me a thick slice of cake she had made and insisted on wrapping up the rest for me to take with me. When nobody was looking, she wiped my eyes in her apron, gave me half a crown and said she would come and see me at the week-end. She never did come, considering it wiser, perhaps, to leave me alone, until I had settled down.

When the time I dreaded came, at last, my uncle and aunt said goodbye to my mother at the door and I went with her down the lane. I led the pony for her, knotting and unknotting my hand in his mane in my distress. Earlier, when I was yoking him, I had thrown my arm in abandon round his neck and shouted foolish endearments in his ear. When we came to the road, we stopped. I looked at my mother, hoping, somehow, that she could say something or do something that would reconcile me to everything. She looked back at me, full of compassion and concern. I came nearer and she put her hand on my head. I broke down completely. She continued to pat my head in mute consolation.

"You'll make yourself sick," she said at length.

When there was still no sign of me stopping she said, "Maybe I'd better take you home."

Her words cut through me like a healing knife. They did not lessen my agony, but they spoke to a part of me that had been building towards this day for as long as I could remember. By putting the alternative into words, she had brought me back to it. As soon as she said it, I knew that, whatever hardships might come of it, the choice had been made long ago and there was no going back.

"I don't want to go home," I said.

"Good boy!" she said and there was a note of triumph in her voice.

"Don't cry any more, now."

"I can't help it," I said.

"Will you be all right?"

"I will," I said.

She put out her hand and I took it.

"Write after a few days when you get settled," she said.

I clung to her hand for a long time. Then she gently disengaged herself and, as she moved off, said, "Go to bed early tonight and have a good sleep."

I could hardly see her through the tears, as she drove off. At the turn of the road she waved. I felt a terrible urge to run after her and call her back. Then she was gone and I stood there a long time, waving at nothing, before I could compose myself sufficiently to go back to the house.

Afterwards, all emotion was drained out of me. When my uncle Ned brought out his own pony and car, I said goodbye to my aunt Nelly, thanked her for the cake, which she had remembered and run in for just as we were about to start, and waved to her, dry-eyed and calm, until we got to the road. We left the pony in a yard in town. The man in charge, who knew my uncle, sent a boy ahead of us to take my case up to the College on a handcart. My uncle bought me sweets in a shop with a red-haired woman behind the counter, and we followed the hand-cart up the steep, narrow streets like mourners after a funeral.

At the College gates he said goodbye to me and slipped a shilling to the boy, who looked at it, spat on it carelessly and put it in his pocket. Then he picked up the handles of his cart and went whistling down the street. I watched my uncle follow him. He waved once and I waved back. But, even before he had gone out of sight, I had forgotten him. I was thinking of my mother and wondering how far she was on the road. I thought of how my tears must have distressed her and hated myself for causing her pain. I thought of her, driving along between the high hedges in the quiet of the evening, the pony snorting and shaking off the flies. There would be work to be done when she got home, the separator to be cleaned, bread to be made. My father gone, perhaps, and no knowing when or how he would return.

I cried again, then, and for the rest of the evening, whenever I thought—as I did most of the time—of her and them. Now, in bed, I thought of them again. As the dormitory quietened down and breathing spread like a whisper around the room, it was easy to close my eyes and pretend I was at home again. I kicked off the lower part of my pyjamas, which I found strange and irritating, and, with the clothes pulled over my head, tried to re-create for myself the sounds of home—the shuffle of animals in a stall, the grating of the lane gate on its hinge, the low susurration of conversation from the kitchen, the sad whistle of curlews over the wet moors.

But the bed felt different, the sheets smelled new, the pillow was not my own. I ended the day, as I had begun it, crying.

CHAPTER FIVE

I AWOKE to the clang of a handbell. It rang and sang and jangled along the corridors, a tingling tangle of sound. Boys were leaping out of bed all over the place. I was out myself and half-way to the Locker-room for my clothes, when the cut of a hand on my bare bottom and a snicker around the dormitory reminded me of the pyjama trousers that I had discarded. Overcome with shame, I rushed for the door, a hand before and aft for decency, the skin of my face feeling stretched and burning. It was a bad start to the day.

I hung about the Locker-room in shirt and trousers and fumbled with my shoes in a corner for a long time, before I dared to come out again. In the Washroom I had to wait, while a row of boys finished their washing. When the boy I was standing behind had finished, he turned away from the basin and, finding me in his way, gave me a cuff on the side of the head and said, "Scram!"

When I got back to the basin again, another boy had taken his place. When he had finished, someone standing behind me caught me by the two ears and lifted, until I was standing on tiptoe. Then he turned me round and slipped in behind me. He was a big boy and I was relieved when he didn't hit me and said nothing as I stood behind him and watched him take out a razor from its case and begin to shave himself. He hadn't any hairs that I could see. It mystified me, then, when he turned to the boy at the next basin and said through a mouthful of lather, "You're lucky, boy, you don't have to shave. Mine gets thicker all the time. I'll soon have to shave every day. Either that or grow a beard."

"Black Jack wouldn't stand for that," the other boy said. "It's against the rules."

"Who cares!" the big boy said scornfully.

I thought he must be a very depraved boy to speak like that about a priest. I wondered if he was a Catholic at all.

When he had finished and had dried his razor with great care, he stepped aside. I was just about to begin washing, when another big boy with a whistle in his hand rushed in and shouted, "Everybody out! Time for prayers."

I folded my towel again and went back to the dormitory. It was deserted. I put on the rest of my clothes as quickly as I could and went off to find where prayers were being said. After wandering round for a while and seeing nobody and hearing nothing but the gush of water in some distant cistern, I bumped into a boy on a corner and asked him to direct me.

"They're finished now," he said. "Everybody's gone to Mass."

"Where?" I asked.

"Down that way," he said. "Out the front door and the chapel is straight across."

I thanked him and was setting off, when he called me back and, lifting his fist, laid it on my chest just under my chin.

"Listen!" he said "Don't ever mention you saw me here or I'll lay you out."

"No," I said, frightened. "No, I won't. Honest to God, I won't."

"Scram!" he said. "You'll be late."

I went, but, search as I would, I could not find the front door or the chapel.

I wandered upstairs and downstairs, along corridors and into rooms, strange dormitories, classrooms with desks such as I had never seen before—desks with lids that lifted up, with a compartment inside full of books—a room with STAFF written on the door, which I didn't dare open, a room with pigeon-holes along the walls, stuffed with football boots and togs, hurleys stacked in racks, a smell of liniment and embrocation about the place.

Once, near the Boxroom, where I recognised my own case, I pushed through a door into total blackness. There was a damp, mildewed smell and in the light slicing in from the corridor I began to make out lumps of coal. Then I got the pungent smell of tobacco smoke and a voice hissed, "Feck off! D'you hear!"

I jumped with fright and backed out, banging the door in my haste. I found a lavatory and sat there, until I heard doors slapping and racing feet and I guessed that Mass was over. Two boys came whistling into the lavatory and stood at the urinal. "I'll get you a place at Dawlach's table," one of them was saying. "Smith and Bonzo and Bardolph and Big Buttons and all the fellows are there."

"That'd be super," the other boy said. "But is there any room?"

"Of course, there's room. We'll funt out Half-a-Bikky—we don't want a creep like that—and you can have his place."

"That'd be super," the other boy said again and they went out.

I followed them out at a distance. Another bell was ringing and boys were running madly towards the sound. I ran myself and was soon caught in a milling mass outside the door of a room I recognised as the Refectory. When the bell stopped, the door was opened from inside and there was Father Turley, surveying the mob.

"The stampede of the Gadarene Swine!" he said.

Under his stern glance the shoving and shouting stopped and we went in in some semblance of order. I was jostled and pushed from one table to another by boys who came along and claimed the place I was standing at. In the end I found myself at the bottom of a long table with boys of my own size. Father Turley said Grace. There was a scraping of forms, a ringing of spoons on porridge plates and breakfast began.

The porridge was a cold slab of sticky stodge with a blue collar of milk around the edge. When it was eaten, two boys from each table collected the plates and brought them to the kitchen. They came back with brown, chipped-enamel teapots that had a handgrip near the spout, and poured tea from a height into the cups, making a great splash and a head of foam. Milk had already been added, but there seemed to be no sugar and there was none on the table. A boy at the head of the table was slicing a loaf of bread. There was a scramble for the crust and boys were bagsing—as they called it—the crusts on the next loaf, that hadn't arrived yet, and even the one after that. One boy shouted, "I bags the crusts of the first fresh loaf," and there were ironic cries of "What a hope!" and "You'll be lucky!"

Here and there, scattered through our table and the one next to us, were boys like myself, who looked on rather than took part. They were the ones who had their tea poured last, who sat and were too diffident to ask someone to pass the bread. Like me, they stared at everything and blushed when they were caught staring. Sometimes, they exchanged a timid smile with one another—a thing I had not dared do yet. In the main, they looked frightened and defeated, though I could not imagine any of them feeling as frightened and defeated as myself. They had, at least, begun the process of assimilating. They had managed to remain anonymous in the dormitory. They had, presumably, been in time for prayers and Mass. They had made a better start than I had.

An uncouth-looking boy who sat beside me—he was obviously not a new boy—and had been sufficiently kind to cut and pass me a slice of bread, when he saw me sitting there in embarrassment, with my eyes on the loaf further down the table, turned to me and said, "Listen, if you want to go in a hurry after breakfast, your best bet is the top Jacks. Not the one on top of the first flight. That's no good. They all go for that. But the one on the next flight."

I looked at him without comprehending.

"Whatever you do," he said, "don't go near the one here on the ground floor. At other times—all right. But not in the morning. The Seniors use it then. They'll kick you into a pulp, if they find you there in the morning."

"Yes," I said, hesitantly.

"You get me?"

"No," I confessed, hoping he wouldn't be offended at my stupidity.

"The Jacks," he said. "Lavatories, if you like. Only don't call them that here or they'll laugh at you. You'll want to run for them like mad after breakfast, mind! Everybody does. You should see Big Tom Traynor. He's always first. Everybody stands out of his way or he'd trample them. First inside the door at the head of the stairs, that's his. Nobody else would dare use it until he's finished."

I looked at him in wonder. Such things were more simply ordered at home. If the earth closet was occupied, we went behind the ditch and relieved ourselves there.

"You want to mind, too," he went on, "or some fellows will try to make you run and bags a place in the queue for them. And just when your turn comes and you're bursting to go, in they'll stroll and take your place and you'll have to wait until they've finished—that's if you are able to wait," he concluded darkly.

"Whatever you do," he said after a few minutes, when I thought he must definitely have exhausted the subject, "don't go into the one next to the room with STAFF on the door. That's for the masters. Or the one marked PRIVATE off the Top Dor. That's Father Turley's. Real posh they are inside. Matting on the floor. Nice seat. Big roll of real Toilet Paper. I did it once myself in Father Turley's—one day I was sick and they were all out on a walk. Man, it was like in a hotel. Did you ever hear the Queen of England has one with a padded seat?"

"No," I said.

"You'd think Kings and Queens would be so grand they'd pay someone to do it for them," he said, "but they all have to do it, don't they? Even a bishop. The Pope, too, if it comes to that!"

After breakfast, as he had warned me, there was a stampede for the Jacks. Boys queued on all the stairs and everywhere was the sound of cisterns re-filling. Luckily—or I might have waited till Doomsday—I received no call.

A bell was ringing again and boys were running. I had no idea why it was ringing or where they were running. But it was a new fact of life that I was beginning to absorb. A bell rang and one ran. I ran now. The trouble was that they were going in different directions. I ran downstairs after a group of boys, but, just as I caught up with them, they rushed into a room, the last one in slamming the door in my face. I was wondering whether I should open the door and go in after them, when another group came running along a corridor shouting, "Hurry!" and shot up the stairs. I panted after them, but when I got to the top they had disappeared. Immediately, I was swept down a corridor by another crowd. Again I was left standing outside a closed door and could not find the courage to go in.

I went down the stairs again and knocked timidly on the first door. There was no reply, and when I listened there was no sound. I stood in irresolution for a long time with my hand on the knob. I walked away, then came back and stood on tip-toe, listening. There was no sound and no longer any boys to be seen or heard.

I wandered around—down corridors and into corners. There

was a door open near the Refectory and I peeped through. A fat girl in blue and grey stripes was polishing the floor. She saw me and came over.

"Is it a knife you want?" she said. "They all want a knife."

"No," I said.

She looked at me curiously.

"Well, what *do* you want? Forty times a day they come, asking for knives. Sister said we weren't to lend out any more knives. They'd scald you. Just when you'd be down on your knees, scrubbing, they'd come, looking for knives. They'd come, all right, but they'd never bring it back, when they've cut their cakes —or whatever they do be doing with them."

I waited for her to stop. I wanted to ask her where everybody was and if she knew where I should be. But, before I could ask, she was off again.

"You wouldn't be the little Sullivan fellow from out the country with an uncle Jack above on Dawson's Hill, would you?"

I shook my head.

"That's a pity," she said, "because I'd 'a known your uncle Jack real well, if you were. You're a new chap, God love you. I'd know yous from the lost look o' yous."

She looked at me sympathetically.

"You'd like to see your Mammy, now, wouldn't you?"

I blinked my eyes and said nothing, because I was afraid that if I opened my mouth I would begin to bawl.

"Look," she said, "I'll give you a knife. But don't, on your life, tell anybody I gave it to you. Sister would kill me. But, anytime you want a knife, ask for Kitty—that's me—and I'll give it to you. But you must bring it back when you're done, d'you hear?"

I was about to ask her where everybody was, when there was a rustle behind me and the whisper of beads.

"What are you doing here?" a thin, testy voice said.

"Jesus!" Kitty hissed and began to polish vigorously. I jumped. A broad, stumpy nun with lips like a tight incision was standing beside me.

"Why aren't you in your classroom? Don't you know boys are forbidden to talk to the girls?"

"He's only new," Kitty sprang to my defence, "he don't know nothin' about nothin'."

"That will be enough, Kitty," the nun said. "Now, tell me your name."

I told her.

"You should be in your classroom," she said. "Did nobody tell you that?"

I had never spoken to a nun before and didn't know how to address her properly.

"No, Ma'am," I said at length.

She pulled the stitches a little tighter before she said, "Run along, now, and don't let me find you hanging around the kitchens again."

I was slinking off down the corridor when she called after me. "Little boy!"

There must have been something about my dejected air that softened her, because, when I turned and came back, she looked less formidable and spoke more kindly.

"Would you like a piece of cake?"

I was so surprised that I could say nothing.

"Come back after class and we'll see what we can do for you. Now, off to your class and tell the teacher I kept you."

I nodded in bewilderment and backed away, until I got to a safe distance, then turned and fled. I was hardly to know that, when I came back later, she would fail to remember me and threaten to report me to Father Turley if she ever caught me near the kitchens again.

It was Father Turley who came to my rescue in the end. I was standing at a green baize notice-board at the end of a corridor, reading yellowing sheets with curled edges, relics of bygone football games, with draws for tournaments and lists of boys' names, when he came along and, with his arm around my shoulder, steered me back into the mainstream of school life again.

He took me with him downstairs, through the Boxroom— my case was still there—across a yard which was also a handball alley, into a small building on the other side. He opened a door with the figure "I" on it and brought me in. It was a classroom with boys of my own size, sitting with their backs to us at long benches.

Standing at the blackboard, facing the class, was a very tall man with long, black hair sleeked back.

"Another for you, Mr. Ronan," Father Turley said.

The tall man smiled at Father Turley, looked me over fleetingly and said, "That makes twenty-five barbarians so far."

This was, obviously, some sort of joke, because Mr. Ronan rubbed his long fingers together, as he said it, and laughed, and Father Turley smiled before replying, "I'm sure Mr. Cuffe and yourself will make good Grecians out of them before they leave."

A place was found for me in the last desk.

"We'll put you here for the present," Father Turley said. Then he laid his hand on my head and made me blush beetroot by saying, "If the size of this is any indication, we'll have you up in front in no time."

Everyone looked around curiously to see the size of my head, and it seemed to me that their looks made it swell even bigger in embarrassment. Later, his words were to be remembered and I was to get the first of my many unflattering nicknames—MOON-FACE.

After consultation with Mr. Ronan, Father Turley opened a press and began to give out copies and books. At first, he gave seven copies to everyone. Then, while he continued to add books to the pile of copies beside us, Mr. Ronan told us to write our names and the name of a subject on each copy. To help us he wrote, in very neat capitals, the names of the seven subjects we would be studying on the board.

IRISH
ENGLISH
LATIN
GREEK
HISTORY
GEOGRAPHY
MATHEMATICS

The sight of the copies and the smell and smooth feel of the new books pleased me. We wrote our names on the books as well. I took great care with mine, as I didn't want to spoil such beautiful

books with blots or careless handwriting. When he had finished
distributing books, Father Turley gave us a talk on keeping our
copies and books neat and tidy. Then he showed us how to make
out a time-table and made us copy one he gave to Mr. Ronan to
write for us on the blackboard. The time-table listed the classes
in the seven subjects for the week.

When Father Turley left, Mr. Ronan told us we were about to
begin Greek. He showed us Greece on the map and told us of the
clever, inventive race of people who lived there long ago. He said
their language was a key that could open for us the door to their
culture and civilisation. That Greece had been a great centre of
learning and experiment, when the rest of the world was sunk in
ignorance. That they had been great mathematicians and astrono-
mers, poets, dramatists, sculptors and philosophers, when such
arts and sciences were unknown to the rest of mankind. That they
were great soldiers, too, and great athletes and had introduced
the Olympian Games. He said that, as Irish boys, the descendants
of a race noted for their scholarship and sharp intellect, we had a
great deal in common with the nimble-minded Greeks. He showed
us that we already knew some Greek words, words that had been
borrowed from Greek by our own language, words like "eaglais"
(church) from the Greek "ekklesia".

He wrote the Greek alphabet for us on the board and called a
number of boys out to write English words in the strange, new
lettering. The familiar words in the odd script made us laugh. Then
he told us to write our names, as closely as we could, with the
Greek symbols. When he asked who had finished, the excitement
of doing something new and interesting made me forget my shy-
ness and I put up my hand. Mr. Ronan came down and looked at
my copy.

"Very good!" he said. "John Foley, isn't it?"

"Yes, sir," I said and blushed with pride.

Mr. Ronan went up to the board and wrote down my name as
I had written it.

"Now," he said to the class, "I want you to look at this. John
Foley has noticed something. Who can tell me what it is?"

Nobody answered.

"Well," Mr. Ronan said, "I'll tell you. He has noticed that

there is no letter 'J' in Greek, so he has, very sensibly, substituted 'I' for it. He spells his name IOV, JOHN. How many Johns are there in the class?"

Five boys put up their hands.

"How many spelled their names like John Foley?"

Two hands went up.

"Good!" Mr. Ronan said and rubbed his fingers together. "We are making progress."

While he went around examining the copies of the other boys, I looked with fascination at my own name on the blackboard and studied the alphabet, so that I would be ready for the next task and win Mr. Ronan's approval again. I felt that I had already learned a great deal and was anxious to learn more. I was not at all pleased when a bell rang and class finished, and, when a boy casually cleaned the board and rubbed out my name, I felt as indignant as a scholar would, if he had erased the inscription on some ancient monument.

Mr. Ronan was followed by a big, square priest with the aggressive head and manner of a Mussolini. He strode up and down with his hands behind his back, as if he were addressing his troops, and called us "men".

"Now, men," he began sternly, almost before the door had closed, "you will see from your time-tables that I have you on five days a week for English and five days for Latin. Let me tell you what I shall expect of you. I shall tell you once and tell you no more.

"I have ways," he continued, looking us over with a frown and drawing a cane from an opening at the side of his habit and waving it solemnly—as if he were performing a religious ceremony—before replacing it. "I have ways of dealing with men who do not live up to my expectations. And here let me assure you that my expectations are high. I do not ask every man to do his best. I ASSUME that he is already doing his best. What I shall require of him is to do that little bit more. Do I make myself clear?"

He looked around, as if daring us to say no.

"Yes, Father," we said dutifully.

"It is the amount that you can do, plus—PLUS, I said—that something extra which seems beyond your grasp—only seems, mind—because by the grace of God and your own hard work, I hope to bring it within reach—it is this that will satisfy me. And nothing less. Do you understand now, men?"

"Yes, Father," we said again.

"Now," he continued, "my methods are simple. I can state them in a word. MEMORISE! Memorise, memorise, memorise! And when you're tired of memorising, go and memorise some more. If you can say it, you know it. That will be my constant standard of judgment. The Gospel says, 'by their fruits you shall know them'. Let me say now, once and for all, that, in this class, by their words I shall know them. The man who pleases me best will be the man of many words. Provided they are the right words. Remember that, men. Relevancy is all.

"Now," he said briskly, opening a book with a red cover, "we will begin by memorising portion of a poem. Open your poetry books at page six. There you will see a poem. Can anyone tell me what a poem is?"

He looked expectantly around the class, but there was no answer.

"Come on, men," he encouraged, "answer the question."

A boy in the front desk mumbled something that I couldn't hear.

"Speak up, man."

"It rhymes, Sir."

"Anything else?"

The boy had exhausted his invention and could say no more. The priest looked authoritatively at several other boys, but could elicit no answer from them.

"Let me tell you then," he said at length. "I shall tell you once and tell you no more. A POEM IS A GROUP OF WORDS ARRANGED IN A CERTAIN ORDER. When you learn it, you must repeat them in that order. That is the important thing. There are other things, of course, but we must take the most important first. Tell me, now, again, what is a poem?"

"A poem is a group of words arranged in a certain order," the first boy he looked at said.

"Good! Don't ever forget that. Later, we shall find other things in it like Personification and Similes and Metaphors. But, for the moment, I shall be satisfied if every man remembers that a poem is basically (he waited with mouth held open, encouraging us to join him)—A GROUP OF WORDS ARRANGED IN A CERTAIN ORDER.

"Now, then," he continued, smoothing down the page of his book, until it lay flat, "let us read the poem. But, first, let me remind you of another definition of a poem. A POEM IS A NUT WHICH MUST BE CRACKED IN ORDER TO REACH THE KERNEL—A TIN WHICH MUST BE OPENED TO GET THE BULLY-BEEF. Now, the nutcracker, men—or, if you like, the tin-opener—is in here."

He tapped his head solemnly.

"Do you follow me?"

"Yes, Father," we said.

"Very good! Let us proceed. THE SOLITARY REAPER."

I looked at him with great respect as he read the poem, chewing through it avidly, sucking the juice out of it with his determined lips. It seemed to me that he was a very clever man and it would take me all my time to understand him and maintain the high level of scholarship that he expected of us.

It was only later that I discovered how really important he was, no less a person than the Rector himself, who normally did not teach at all, but liked—it was said—to take First Year, so that he might have an opportunity to weigh them up and root out any incipient threat to good conduct before it had time to get entrenched. There were those who did not scruple to suggest that his gifts were purely administrative and that he had never trained as a teacher. His methods were different from those of the other teachers, certainly. Before he left us, after that first class, he summed up the whole educational process, as he saw it, in three words which he wrote on the blackboard.

"Here it is, men," he said, wetting his finger and rubbing it on the point of the chalk, "write them down and never forget them."

Then he turned and, drawing up the sleeve of his habit to reveal a striped shirt-cuff, wrote with a flourish these words:

SCRUTINISE
MEMORISE
REVISE

When I looked up from my copy, after writing them down, he was gone and a man with a round, smiling face had taken his place.

"How are all the lads?" he said in an ingratiating tone.

One boy with more courage than the rest said, "Well, Sir."

The teacher looked at the blackboard, then laughed and said in a hearty, currying way that made me feel uneasy, "Aha! Look at the jawbreakers. Scrutinise, memorise, revise, eh? Would I be right in saying Father Creame was here?"

He looked around expectantly until the boy who had spoken already said, "We had a priest, Sir."

"Big man?" the teacher asked. "Like this?" He squared his shoulders, jutted his head forward, unmistakably assuming some of the characteristics of the man who had just left.

"That's him, Sir," several boys, encouraged by his familiar and irreverent manner, said.

"Skim Milk—Skim for short—that's what the boys call him," the teacher said and laughed. "Good, isn't it? Creame—Skim Milk!"

There was a nervous titter.

"He's the Big Boss around here," the teacher said. "You'd want to watch your Ps and Qs with him. No smoking. No letters from girls—though, I suppose, you're a bit young for that. Father Creame's the one who hires and fires. Just let him catch you and—phut!—you're out."

He took a small notebook from his inside pocket and a pen from the pocket of his waistcoat.

"The first thing," he said, "is to get your names. Maybe, I'd better give you my own first."

He brushed back a stray lock of hair from his forehead, which, I noticed, was a mannerism of his, and took up a piece of chalk. Then he shot up his hand and sang out like a child in High Infants, "Please, Sir, Sean O Tuama is ainm dom."

He laughed, a wild, comedian's laugh, showing most of his tongue and wrote SEAN O TUAMA—OLLAMH LE GAEILGE on the board.

"Notice the 'Ollamh' bit," he said. "I like that. I always make the wife—God help her—call me Professor. I refuse to speak to her unless she does. Your breakfast is ready, Professor. Shall I pour your tea, Professor? I'm lucky she doesn't pour it over my head. But, then, I treat her very nice. Ours is a refined—refained, a beg your pardon—a refained house. The Queen, I call her— after her namesake, you know, Elizabeth, the Virgin Queen. Though the wife's hardly that. But I shouldn't be talking of things like that to nice, respectable boys like you. Though, 'pon my oath, there's too much of that hush-hush business in this country.

"Now, where was I? (This was a phrase of his with which we were to get very familiar). Names? Yes. As I was saying, Twomey is the name, a good, old West Cork name, from Skibbereen way— Wesht where the shnipe an' de shtones do be awful plenty—like" (he put on an exaggerated accent).

"Are there any boys here from Cork?"

Several boys put up their hands.

"Aha!" Professor Twomey said (I had begun to think he was a very strange man for a professor) and began to chant in a peculiar sing-song that was barely intelligible:

"AROO FROM CARK?"

"I AM. AROO?"

"DO OO ATE SHPUDS?"

"I DO. DO OO?"

"HOW DO OO ATE 'EM?"

"SHKIN AN' AAALL. . . ."

The boys who had put up their hands seemed to have heard this before and they all laughed. Then he asked them what part of Cork they came from and a long conversation ensued in which names of places I had never heard of before predominated. The rest of us fidgeted, and I remember feeling that I wasn't going to like Professor Twomey very much—or he me—if coming from Cork made such a difference.

His Irish, when, eventually, he got round to it, was fluent and musical, very different from the stuff I was accustomed to hearing from Mrs. Rochford and Miss Pelly. I didn't understand very much of what he said, but I listened in fascination to the way he gurgled his Rs like a dog, growling low in the throat, and the slender belling of Ls, and, most of all, a ringing NG sound, tingling and lingering like a note struck on a tuning fork. I had never heard Irish spoken like that before, but, I knew from a stirring deep within me, some submerged race memory on the borders of my consciousness, that it was the language of my ancestors, spoken as it should be spoken. To sit and listen was to open a door that had been long since closed and find inside something forgotten, yet oddly familiar, as warm and reassuring as a memory of the breast and the comforting hand of a mother. For some reason that I could not explain, the same feeling of loss as I had experienced when my father and the blacksmith talked of Parnell came over me, and I had to blow my nose very hard to keep from crying.

When he dropped into English again, I had no more difficulty.

Before he went, he told us of a pantommie he had produced in the town, of the quarrels and jealousies over parts and how he had dealt ruthlessly and efficiently with them; of the business-man, who refused to let his young wife go on in the part of Principal Boy (I wondered if he had made a mistake here—for how could a woman be a boy?), when he saw the scanty costume she would have to wear, of some pompous personage who was offended by one of the topical jokes which referred to him in a slighting way. He assured us that the jokes were most witty, because he had written them himself and her majesty—the Queen, that is—had laughed, until she burst her stays, and all the people in the shops were telling their customers about them for weeks afterwards.

The songs, too, were very well executed, but he thought it rather a pity that there was no one on the female side to match the clarity and distinction with which he had delivered his own songs. The men had sung well when he was on the stage to lead them, but, on their own, tended to falter and lack fire. There was, he said, one fellow who fancied himself, because he had taken lessons in Dublin and, consequently, thought it beneath him to take direction from anybody. Everyone had been pleased when he had gone flat as stale porter in the middle of his solo and been booed by the audience, who were only waiting for him to make a mistake, because he was one of those insufferable fellows who thought he knew it all.

At the end of the class, Professor Twomey and the teacher who had come to take his place remained talking just inside the door. Father Turley came back again with some more books which he distributed, and joined in their conversation. Some boys talked in whispers. I looked through my books, not reading them, but savouring their newness, opening them, running my nose down the centre, sniffing the fresh ink, feeling the smoothness of the illustrations in the Greek Reader, wondering what the strange set of lines and three-sided figures in a book, called "Céimseata Scoile" by Hall & Knight, were supposed to be.

A boy beside me was eating sweets, slipping them out of his pocket in an underhand way, stripping the paper off under the desk and edging them into his mouth, when he thought nobody was looking. Although he caught me looking at him more than once, he made no attempt to offer me one. He had nice clothes and I could see from his pale hands and face that he was a town boy, used to wearing good clothes every day of the week, unlike me, who wore my good suit to Mass of a Sunday and put it away in brown paper, when I came home, until the following Sunday again. I was sure he would have come from a house with carpets on all the floors, and have had rashers and eggs for his breakfast every day. His father would wear a collar and tie—not like the rough, striped flannel, fastened at the neck by a stud, worn by my father—and he would shave every day and be something like a big shopkeeper or a bank manager or a school-teacher and pronounce his words properly—and look down on people like my father who didn't. I wished I were sitting near someone of my own kind, who wouldn't be so likely to despise me.

Just as the bell rang again, Father Turley made some announcement, which I didn't catch, and everybody raced out. I followed the crowd back across the yard into the Refectory. Dinner was a square of meat, the size and toughness of the heel of a shoe, soapy potatoes that stuck to the knife and an inquisitorial dessert, full of prying eyes, the like of which I had never seen before. During the meal the noise was deafening, except when Father Turley rang the bell and called everyone to order. But it built up again and there were several bells, before Grace came round, and we bolted out like crazed cattle, running blind into the light. The tendency to push and run, when there was no apparent reason for hurry, seemed to have something to do with being in a crowd. It was an instinctive reaction. I felt it in myself and pushed and ran as strongly as anybody.

CHAPTER SIX

OUTSIDE in the yard, boys lounged in the thinning September sunshine. Rows of backs against a wall. Tiered, down a flight of steps. Lining the railings, overlooking the decayed gardens. The crisp crack of a half-solid from the alleys. The soft bounce of a sponge ball.

I stood in the shadow of our classroom and watched. I had not yet found my place. Perhaps, I never would. Would always remain a watcher. Two boys I recognised from my own class went by. Their heads together. Not seeing me. The watcher. Alone.

When a whistle blew, I went into the classroom and sat down at my desk, left hand under my head, waiting. The hard edges of my books were, somehow, reassuring. Red, yellow, green, dark-blue, the Joseph's coat of knowledge. Another whistle outside. Feet on concrete. Distant shouts. But nobody came. No tide of alien flesh to engulf and hide me.

Feet outside. A big boy, with a whistle in his hand, stuck his head in. Even before he spoke, I knew I had isolated myself again. Had blundered. Had broken some unspoken law of the herd. It scarcely mattered that I had done it through ignorance. I had done it.

"What are you doing here?" he shouted.

"I thought—" I began, jumping up, and stopped, hardly knowing what I had thought.

"Half Day," he said. "Didn't you know that! Hurry on and get your togs and boots. We're off to the park. You're holding the whole school up."

He caught me by the arm and flung me out in front of him. I rushed across the yard and into the Boxroom, looking around for my case. I could not see it immediately and, with the prefect standing over me, began to claw desperately at row after row of cases, tumbling them on the floor, pulling them on top of myself, as if by tugging at them all in turn I must come to my own in the end.

"Stop!" he shouted. "Listen, you bloody little fool, don't you know your own case? Use your bloody eyes. Go right along the line and *look* for it. *Look* for it. D'you hear!"

I went along the line and, mercifully, found it quickly. I hauled it down and pulled out my new football boots and togs. I was fumbling with the lock, when he pushed me aside, drove his foot down on the lid, locked it, flung the key at me and tossed the case into a corner, where it teetered on one end and subsided against the wall.

Outside, Father Turley was lining the boys up, two by two. As I passed along the line to the front, where the small boys were, I was kicked several times in the backside and hit smartly, once, with a hurley.

"Get a move on," the big boys roared.

When I got to where Father Turley was, they were all arranged in pairs and there was no one to walk with me. Father Turley re-arranged the line to make room for me by moving a boy backwards right along the line. Everyone protested to him about this, because, it seemed, boys had regular partners, and he had broken them all up to accommodate me. When the re-arranging was complete, he dropped back to the end of the line and a whistle sounded. Two by two, we marched out through a small door in a high wall and paraded up the hilly streets of the higher part of the town.

Almost as soon as we had begun to move, the line re-adjusted itself. The boy who had been pushed back to make room for me elbowed me out of his way. His place behind was immediately filled and there was nothing for me to do, except tag along on my own between two pairs of boys. I felt very conspicuous and my face was burning. Every time I tried to edge in beside a pair, they shuffled me off or dropped behind, leaving me on my own again. Nobody wanted to have anything to do with me.

The streets were the widest I had ever seen. When we passed through an ancient gateway, where the ruins of the old town walls were still to be seen, they opened out as wide as a football pitch. The low, mean-looking houses on either side made them look wider still. It seemed very dreary to me, without much traffic, or people walking about. Half-way up, a pyramid of granite with a cross on top, isolated as a tidal reef, divided the street in two.

Water splashed from a drinking fountain beside it, as a barefoot child, one hand on the knob, his head bent, tried to get a drink. We passed a pub with a thatched roof and square-paned windows. The name CLUSKEY—WINES & SPIRITS was painted in yellow on a lavender shingle over the door. As we passed, a countryman with a shirt fastened by a stud—just like my father—but with no moustache—came out, rubbing his mouth with the back of his hand and spat into the gutter.

At the top of the town there was a view of the country—trees and stacks of corn in a field. We turned down a narrow road to the right and came between high walls to the playing-fields. There were a couple of pitches with red and white goal-posts, a pavilion, whose zinc roof gleamed in the sunlight—and Father Creame, walking up and down through the long grass at the side, reading his breviary.

Boys spilled into the field, whooping and calling, punting footballs to each other, racing and tumbling for possession. Someone struck a hurling ball high in the air over the goal-posts.

I sat on a wooden seat inside the gate and looked at my football boots. I had never seen a pair before and the cleats on the soles fascinated me. I was wondering whether I should put them on, when an older boy came over to me.

"Let's see the boots," he said. He took them out of my hand, without waiting for an answer, and examined them.

"Nice and light," he said. "What size are they?"

"Eights," I said.

"I think they'd fit me," he said.

I said nothing, but looked at him in mute protest.

"Mind if I try them on?" he asked.

"I want them meself," I said, feeling desperate.

"I only want to try them on," he said. "No harm in trying them, is there?"

He sat down beside me and pulled off his shoes. When he had my boots on, he stood up and walked around, flexing his instep and kicking at wisps of grass.

"Grand fit," he said.

A ball came towards us and he ran to meet it, taking it on the roll with my new boots and lofting it in the air.

"Hey, Bonzo! Come on!" someone shouted to him and he ran to join a group of boys around the goal, with an airy wave of his hand to me and a shout, "Won't be a minute. Just a few kicks to try them out. That's all."

I followed him up to the goal-posts to be near my boots. But they had picked teams and he was moving off down to the other side of the field. I walked down the sideline, but it seemed to me that, whenever I got near him, he sheered off somewhere else and deliberately kept out of my way.

I was passing near Father Creame, when he shut his breviary with a snap and strode over to me.

"Why aren't you playing games, man?"

I jumped and began to stammer something about my boots.

"Every man must play games, I repeat MUST," he roared, without waiting to hear what I had to say.

"What is your name?"

I told him.

"Master Foley," he said, "I must warn you that I shall punish most severely any man who does not take part in games. Games are compulsory, I repeat COMPULSORY. Get out there, now, and play. Play hard, Master Foley, and work hard. That's our motto here. See that you never forget it."

"Yes, Father."

"Off with you, then. See those boys over there? They've got a football. Run, man. Put your back into it. Remember, I'll be watching."

Feeling that his eyes were making gimlet holes in my back, I put down my head and ran diagonally across the field. I blundered through a group of boys, felt the ball strike my instep and followed the looping line it made towards the sideline. The voice of Father Creame came like a far bellowing over the thunder of feet and the angry cries behind me.

"That's it, Master Foley. Now, kick it again, man."

With a desperate lurch, I kicked again and, just before I went down under a jerking mass of boots and bones, I saw the ball loft high to fall on the pavilion roof and bounce into the field beyond.

I was almost suffocated with the weight of boys on me. Toecaps raked my ribs. My legs were bruised. My face was pressed into the ground. I smelled grass and clay and human sweat. I heaved over on my side, got my head out between a pair of legs and breathed again. Boys were picking themselves up and shaking themselves off. They were shouting at me.

"You're not in our game."

"Clear off, scum!"

"Make him get our ball first. Breaking up our game like that!"

"We'll duck him when we get back," a boy proposed.

"That's what we'll do. We'll duck him," they all shouted.

A boy with red hair stooped down and dragged me to my feet.

"D'you hear that, you little runt? We're going to duck you when we get back."

"That'll larn him," another boy said and they all laughed.

"Now," the red boy said, "get us our ball, and feck off."

"Hurry, or we'll duck you twice," someone else said.

I got up and ran to fetch their ball. Something—a sod or a lump of hard cow-dung (I didn't look back to see)—struck me on the head.

"Hurrah!" they shouted. "Good shot!"

Other things, hard and soft, fell around me, as I fled out behind the pavilion and flung their ball back.

"Don't forget your ducking," someone shouted and they laughed.

"Come on, for God's sake, and kick the ball," a voice said.

The ball was kicked up and they raced away after it. I peeped out over the hedge to see if Father Creame was still watching. He was stalking briskly away, with his breviary closed and, as I watched, he went through the gate and on to the road. He would hardly be back.

My rejection by the boys made me feel very lonely and I moped around the ditch of the second field, rubbing my eyes furtively. I drifted gradually to a corner of the field where the laughter and cheers of a group of boys attracted me. The laughter stopped when I stood near the edge of the circle, and eyes inspected me.

"Aha!" said a fat boy in long trousers, at last, "here's the very man."

He laughed and they all laughed with him. I blushed in confusion and was about to move away, when he said, "Don't go. We've a game to show you."

"That's right," a boy beside him, with black, curly hair and hot, shining eyes, said, "we've a game to show you."

I knew from his tone that I wasn't going to like their game, whatever it was.

"I'm no good at games," I said in a voice barely above a whisper. This amused them very much.

"He says he's no good at games!" they roared, nudging each other. "No good at games. Did you hear that! No good at games, he says!"

"This one's easy," the black boy, whom they called Curly, said.

"As easy as losing your—" a voice began and was shouted down by a wave of, "Shh! Don't spoil the game," from every side.

"Will we show you?" the fat boy asked.

"Go on. Show him, Fatser," the others said.

"Will I?" Fatser looked at me.

"I—I—I don't know," I said, stalling. But, from the way they were looking at me, it was clear that I was going to be shown, whether I liked it or not.

"It's to try how many it takes to lift you," Fatser explained.

"You'll have to sit down."

I sat down. A boy sat in front of me, between my legs, and held my two ankles. Another boy sat behind me and looped his arms through mine.

"Now, lift!" Fatser said.

They made as if to lift, but nothing happened.

"Another hand," they shouted. "Now, Curly!" and they laughed again.

Curly got up and I knew by the way he came over that it was not to lift me. His eyes were very bright and he was breathing in an excited way, as he bent over me.

"Come on, Curly!" they shouted. "Show him the trick."

Curly reached up and undid my braces. I struggled, but the others had a tight grip of my feet and arms. When the braces were loosened, he caught my trousers by the legs and pulled them down. The boy at my feet disengaged his hands and swept them off. He jumped up and threw them in the air.

"Hurrah!" everyone shouted. "It worked! The trick worked!"

As I struggled free Curly lifted my shirt and smacked me hard on the bare bottom. At the same time, Fatser lifted it in front and everyone cheered. Overcome with shame, I broke loose and ran to reclaim my trousers. But they passed it from one to the other, throwing it over my head and shouting. In the end, tiring of the sport, they tossed my trousers to me where I stood at some distance from them, with my shirt-tails between my legs. I put them on, while they shouted for Curly to come and help me. I was terrified lest he should come and take them again, but he made no move.

"What do you think of him?" Fatser asked him.

"Not bad," Curly said, "not bad at all. We might be able to train him yet."

"He might do for a night," Fatser said.

"None o' that," Curly said. "I saw him first."

"Aw, Curly," several boys said, "you always see them first."

I wondered if they could be talking about me. As soon as I had my trousers fastened, I slunk away and, when I thought I was out of sight, I ran. But the mocking voice of Curly followed me.

"Be seeing you, sweetheart!" he shouted. And again there was laughing.

I spent the rest of the evening looking over the ditch near the pavilion, watching—for the return of Father Creame, for the boys who had threatened to duck me, for Fatser and Curly, for anyone who could be a threat to my peace. I was becoming, though I didn't know it, what many boys in College are forced to become, a dodger. A dodger of games. A dodger of prefects and priests and supervising nuns. A dodger of other boys—of the bullies and cowards and cheats, the exploiters, the thieves, the terrorists. In time, I would become a liar with the cunning of an animal—a hunted, maligned, intimidated creature for whom survival was the only virtue.

When the whistle went for our return and boys began to form in line at the gate, I came out from hiding and slipped in among some boys from my own class. The well-dressed boy who had sat beside me in class, eating sweets, recognised me and smiled. He had no partner and I had no partner, so, when the prefect came along, forming us in pairs, we stood together in loose and mute alliance.

The boy who had taken my football boots ran up, as we moved off, and flung them at me. He dropped back in the line behind us without a word of thanks. The sight of my new boots, muddied and scored and smelling of his dirty feet, made my eyes prick again. The lovely, black leather had white streaks along it where sharp nails from other boots had scraped it. One of the laces was broken and, when I looked at the soles, I saw that a cleat was missing from the heel of the left boot.

I was washing them under the tap in the yard, after getting back, when the boy who had taken them—Jack Kehoe, he said his name was—came over and offered to buy them for 7/6. I knew my mother had paid 21/- for them—and, besides, I didn't want to sell them, and certainly not to him. He threatened to beat me and to get all his friends to help him, and swore he would make life miserable for me, as long as I was there, if I didn't let him have them. He was prepared to give me ten shillings for them, as a token of goodwill, though they were hardly worth that now, being second-hand and scored.

There was nothing that I could do except let him have them. He gave me no money for them either, but said he would get Father Turley to add ten shillings to his bill at Christmas and to deduct the same amount from mine. Every time I saw him in them afterwards, I hoped he would break his neck, but he never did. Instead, he went on to win glory for himself and for the College on the hurling field and somewhere in the Recreation-Hall there is probably, to this day, that picture of him, holding the Inter-College Junior Cup and smirking—in my boots.

There was a free evening after tea. Many boys were writing letters in the Study Hall, where we had been given a desk and to which—on the instructions of Father Turley—we had taken our books after tea.

I decided to write home. I didn't really want to write, because home was something I was afraid to think about until I was safe in bed with the lights out. But the Study Hall seemed the safest place for me. I was worried that the boys who had threatened to duck me would remember their threat and pounce on me, if I showed my face in the yard. I didn't know what exactly ducking was—I was to learn the following day, but not at their hands. I only knew it was something to be avoided.

I sat at my desk in the Study Hall and, as soon as I had written the address and "Dear Mammy", the tears started, as I knew they must. They dropped on to the page, making dark, uneven blotches on the white paper. When they fell on the writing, the ink thickened and swelled into grotesque distortions. I thought of tearing out the page and starting again. Then it struck me that I should leave them there, so that my mother would see how miserable I was and come and take me home. But I knew that, whatever happened, that would be no solution. So I tore out the page and started again.

I now recognised that it was the emotional words like "Mammy" and the names of Moll and Tom, when I asked for them, that were likely to be my undoing. I kept my handkerchief in readiness, whenever I had to write them, and, in this way, made fair progress. But, every few minutes, the sight of the familiar names would be too much and I would have to stop and indulge my weakness. It was strange—but not hypocritical—to ask about my father. After that blinding revelation in the yard, when I was leaving, I knew that we were bound indissolubly together and, though I could hardly feel proud of him, or he of me, the claim of the blood would be always paramount.

I asked about Ned Rafter (I cried for a long time over Ned). I even asked about Boggan and wondered why I had ever disliked him. I asked about the animals, whether the Red Cow had calved yet (more tears, as I thought of her, licking gently over the wet hair of her calf) and if the chicken, whose leg Moll and I had put in splints, had recovered. I asked about Mr. Wadding and Mr. Rennick. About the only one I knew, for whom I did not ask, was the blacksmith. I thought of him, but felt it would be Pharisaical of me to ask.

I said I was getting on very well and could write my name in Greek and had got a whole lot of new books, and intended working very hard. I said I missed them all very much (tears again), but that I was getting on all right and had walked down from the park with a boy in a very nice suit, from Dublin, who told me he had never seen a cow, but had travelled all over Dublin on buses—

double-decker buses, he said, with people upstairs, as in a house, a thing I had never heard of before. I said that I liked him very much. His name was Kieran Maher and he was my best friend.

When the letter was written, a boy showed me the letter-box, outside the Senior Dormitory, in which letters had to be placed unsealed, so that they could be censored later by Father Turley. The idea of censorship was something new to me. I thought with misgiving of the intimate things I had written about and blushed at the thought of a priest reading them. But that was the rule, and the boy said I would have to obey it.

I climbed the stairs to the Senior Dormitory, dropped some more tears into the open envelope and pushed it into the wooden box. There was a typewritten note beside the opening, which verified what the boy had told me.

ALL LETTERS MUST BE PLACED
IN THIS BOX UNSEALED

It was, like the bed in the middle of the dormitory, a symbol of College life.

CHAPTER SEVEN

My first Christmas holidays.

"Tell me, John, boy," my father said, "you must have learned a lot in that College in three months. There's one thing I always wanted to know. Did they ever tell you what is meant by 'The Lamb of God'?"

"Isn't it Jesus Christ?" I said.

"I know, boy. I know. But *why* did He say 'I am the Lamb of God'? What was His meaning, d'you know? Why did He call Himself a lamb? I always wanted to know. But I could never get anybody to tell me."

"I don't know," I said hesitantly. "I never thought about it."

I was ashamed to confess my ignorance. I felt my father would be critical of it and wonder if good money hadn't been wasted in sending me to College.

"I was sitting next to old Canon Codd, once, in a wakeroom and had a mind to ask him," he said, "but he kept on talking about his hens—he always kept hens in the vestry—and I didn't like to interrupt him. Then the man of the house, Tom Furlong (Mick's father over in Aghabee—the wife was waking) came over to take him down to the parlour for a drop of punch and I never got another chance."

My mother looked up from her knitting.

"I always knew what that meant," she said.

My father looked at her crossly and without any great faith.

"Aye, you did?" There was an edge of sarcasm on his voice.

"In them days," she said, "people used offer sacrifice of a lamb in the Temple, and Our Lord meant that He was to be offered like a lamb as a sacrifice to God."

"Is that a fact?" he said in a disputatious tone.

"I learned that in school and I never forgot it," my mother said proudly.

"Some of us didn't get a chance of going to school." My father was testy. Then to me:

"Find out for me when you go back, boy."

"Why don't you believe me when I tell you?" my mother said sharply. "If it was Jem Roche now, or someone like that, you'd believe it all right."

It had been so friendly and peaceful, but that was the end of agreement. We were sitting around the fire, toasting our shins—blazing logs on the open hearth—spit of resin, ooze of juice—Moll on the stool by the fan, lazily twisting the wheel, Tom whittling a stick with a pen-knife, my father, his boots off, his feet in the ashes, his pipe making a water-logged snore, the oil-lamp, mellow, yellow, throwing soft shadows. Quiet, peaceful, idyllic on my first evening home for the Christmas holidays.

I had walked out to my uncle Ned's, and spent the night there, sleeping with him in the same bed where I had gone asleep a lifetime ago with the apple in my mouth. After tea, uncle Ned had gone off to a neighbour's house. When the lamp was lit, aunt Nelly had got down the cards and we played Twenty-Five and ate Christmas cake and drank lemonade and laughed—aunt Nelly was a jolly sort—and talked and played more cards. She gave me *The Holly Bough* with its red, Christmassy cover and warm, cosy Christmas stories to read, while she made tea. I sat back in the heat of the fire and thought of the Christmas Number of the OUR BOYS waiting for me at home, and my mother coming for me on the following day, and the long, intimate journey home together, and all the holidays before me.

We picked a hambone for supper and laughed over our greasy fingers. After a few more games of cards, we began to yawn and, the clock showing a quarter to twelve, we lit our candles and went upstairs.

I liked the smell of tobacco from my uncle's room and the low pitch of the roof after the high, bare dormitory in College. I examined all his tiepins and cufflinks on the dressing table and his string of ties in the wardrobe and had a peek through the books and magazines that were strewn about on top of it. In bed I gathered the blankets about me and settled down to read a story from *The Holly Bough*. But my mind was so full of pleasant things that I couldn't concentrate and read the first paragraph over and over again, with long, dreamy intervals in between, in which

I listened to the quiet noises of the night—the sigh of wind about the eaves, the hollow ticking of a clock in the kitchen beneath me.

I awoke, in a warm fuzz, to darkness and my uncle nudging in beside me. Then off again, to dream of snow and bells ringing and light streaming from warm houses with open, welcoming doors.

Morning, then, and the joy of my mother's arrival. Her hand on my head when we met—the only gesture of affection that her reserve would allow her, but it was enough. The pony nuzzling into my hand as I fed him hay. Smell of sweat, as I removed his harness. I flung myself around his neck, while he shook and chewed the hay. I'm going home and it's Christmas and I'm happy. I've never been so happy in all my life. I love you and everybody and everything and I hope it snows and the pond freezes over and, please God, there'll be berries on the holly, and the postman will come every day with lovely parcels in coloured wrapping and cards from everyone. My aunt Betty, the confectioner, will send a beautiful cake in a box with white paper straw, and all the spaces between cake and box will be filled with sweets. Maybe, Santa Claus will come again, and we'll have a wonderful time, pulling crackers and drinking tumblers of lemonade.

The pony's shoes rang metal to metal on the flint-hard road, as we drove home. The grass along the margins was salted with frost. We wrapped the rug around our legs. When we spoke, the words steamed away and stiffened behind us, hanging in the still air like clothes on a line. The bare, sculptured shapes of trees were pleasing. Fields of turnips with stiff, ragged leaves. Birds flitting through transparent hedges. Rough-haired cattle nosing through hay which a farmer was spreading from a farm-cart. A crisp nip stinging my nose and ears. The car jogging and lurching along with a swing, a dip and a sway.

My mother had a bag of sweets. They were for eating, she said, and we hadn't to bother about the others at home, because she intended to get more for them as we passed through the village.

She doled out bits of news as they came to her. Dan Morgan's brother, Padge, had replaced me on the altar—no need to tell me what my father thought of that. Father Donnelly was hoping that I would give him a run through the Latin when I got home.

Mrs. Rochford's son, Pius, had been caught mitching by the Brothers and been expelled—he had spent a month helping a milk-man deliver his round before he had been caught. He was now apprenticed to a garage, and his mother had let it be known that it was merely a matter of time until he became Managing Director of Fords. Mick Rennick's threshing had been the poorest in memory—only twenty sacks of barley off a ten acre field. Ted Reville had come and spent the night, sleeping on a form in the kitchen and they had lost another pig.

Ned Rafter was brushing the mud off his boots and leggings, when we drove into the yard. He came to hold the pony's head as we got out.

"Begod," he said, "you've grown a power, John, boy. Ain't he, Missus?"

He was just the same, with the same flannel shirt with the thick, black stripe, his shiny trousers tucked into his leggings and the grey hair curling up around the back of his cap.

"I mind, well," he said, "it was a Tuesda' morning, the third of September and we starting to draw in the wheat from the Big Field, when you drove out of here, and I said to the Boss down there in the shed and we piking up the sheaves that you'd come back one day a priest or, maybe, a bishop."

He chuckled to himself as he led off the pony to unyoke him and put him in the stable, where his feed of mangolds, oats and hay was waiting for him.

The house was much smaller than I had remembered it. It was darker, too. But the kitchen smelled, as it always had smelled, of woodsmoke and fried bacon. My brother and sister were very shy of me and I of them. We circled around each other like dogs meeting—not saying much, but stealing glances at each other when we thought we were unobserved.

My father was hearty when he came in. He told me I'd soon be as big as himself, which wasn't really very big, as he was just average size and almost as broad as he was long. He put his arm around my shoulder and gave me a squeeze. Then he filled his pipe and, while my mother made tea, he sat and smoked meditatively, looking me over in a quiet way and dropping odd bits of farm news, as one might drop grain to fowl. I picked them up gratefully and a sort of desultory conversation went on until tea was ready. Then we all sat in.

There was meat and cake in honour of the occasion. Tom, I felt, was already calling an end to the truce that had been silently observed since my arrival. I knew by the air of exaggerated politeness with which he buttered his bread, and the way he held his knife and fork between his fingers like a pencil that he was satirising my school manners. He said "please" in a very refined way, once or twice, instead of his customary "plaze", then looked over at Moll and giggled. But she gave him no comfort and was very particular to smile at me when our eyes met, to show where her loyalty lay.

After tea, when the fragile mood of reminiscence and reunification had been shattered by the passage of sharp words between my father and mother over the question of the Lamb of God, my father knocked the ashes from his pipe, striking it angrily against the hob, put on his boots, lit the lantern and, taking Tom with him, went out to bed down the animals for the night. When he came back, he laid his boots by the hob and, without saying the Rosary, padded upstairs in his stocking-feet to bed.

After an argument, I never remembered the things actually said, but the tone of voice, the angry gesture that marked the end of amity remained with me. It was a small argument, as their kind of argument went, but it fell on my excited, anticipatory, homecoming mood with a bleak chill.

"Ridiculous, losing his temper like that," my mother said, as she swept up the crumbs and threw them on the fire, where they blazed in a lazy way. Though I loved my mother and would not tolerate any criticism of her, I felt—and was miserable because of my disloyalty—that she had rather precipitated the thing by making an issue of it.

The shadow of my father's peevishness was over the rest of the evening and, though we rallied somewhat when my mother made a fair division of the sweets she had brought, for me, at least, the joy of homecoming had been blunted. Tom sat in his corner, chewing his way rhythmically through his share and whittling in a bored way, throwing pieces of stick carelessly from him, picking up other pieces, examining their potential, making a few lazy strokes with his knife before spinning them away again.

Moll and I shared our sweets, trading hard for soft—she disliked toffees because they stuck in her teeth. She bit lightly on all hers and passed the hard ones to me. I did the same and gave the soft ones to her. We had always done that and it was nice to feel that nothing had changed.

"You remember that jig-saw," Moll said, as we chewed, "the one you got for your birthday. We never finished it. Will I get it now?"

"Yes," I said, feeling more cheerful, "where is it?"

"I'll get it."

Moll was off, racing upstairs in the dark with a flashlamp. She was down again in a trice with the big box in her hand. It was the first jig-saw any of us had ever seen. It had taken Moll and myself days before we could get even two pieces to match. But, once we had the hang of things, we had got most of it together, but, always, something happened—Tom broke it up or my mother got tired of it, lying around on a sheet of newspaper and put it away—before we could complete it.

"We'll finish it, for sure, this Christmas," I said.

"Yes," Moll said, her eyes bright with enthusiasm, "we'll keep at it and really finish it this time."

"Make it on the big tray then," my mother advised. "You can put it away safely when you are finished with it for the day and no one will break it on you."

"Childish old stuff, that!" Tom said, trying to raise a row.

But we paid no attention to him. Moll went to get the big tray with the roses on it from the parlour—the tray that was used to carry plates of meat from the kitchen to the dining-room at threshing time or to carry the good delph to the parlour when we had important visitors, like the cousins of my father who came home from America and annoyed my father by patronising him and telling him that things were done much differently—and, of course, much better—in the States.

I opened the box and spread out the pieces on the table and began to arrange them right side up. The picture was called GULLIVER AMONG THE LITTLE PEOPLE. It showed a huge Gulliver in red coat and black, tricorne hat, with black knee breeches and buckled patent shoes, standing with legs astride, while underneath passed columns of tiny infantry and cavalry in battle array, with the walls of a city in the distance no higher than his shins. In a way, Gulliver reminded me of my father, towering over us all, though, from the picture, it was obvious that he was no threat to the little people, rather the contrary, as he looked down at them in a solicitous way and seemed careful not to move his feet, in case he dislodged some townsfolk who had climbed up on his shoes to get a better view.

Gulliver and the troops we had made before and most of the walls of the town, but the sky, a weak blue, shading off into grey, was much more difficult and we had never completed it.

"Will we start with Gulliver?" Moll asked. She always deferred to me in things like that and was happy to fall in with my plans.

"Yes," I said, "here's a buckle of his shoe," and we were off. Moll had an endearing way of picking out pieces and giving them to me to put in for her. Somehow, she was able, with a simple gesture like that, to suggest affection and unity between us. She would look at me and smile and say, "We're getting on well, aren't we?"

Even though we might be floundering away with tiny disconnected patches of a few pieces each, spread hopefully here and there, she made it all look like progress. We went on that way from success to brilliant success, our heads happily together, nodding and whispering, our fingers meeting and lingering over pieces and each other, matching and piecing, laughing and nudging, as we had always done, as long as I could remember.

Later, when we had grown tired and had put away the tray on the parlour table for the night and Tom had gone off to bed, saying, "Some of us have to do a day's work tomorrow," and my mother was getting things ready for the morning, we sat by the fire, toasting our feet. I told her about College, about my friend, Kieran Maher, who came from Dublin and had never seen a cow until I showed him one on the College farm, but had ridden on the top of double-decker buses, and went to the pictures every Saturday in the Drumcondra Cinema (the Drum, he called it), and laughed when I told him that I had never been to a cinema, and had invited me to visit him in Dublin some time, and had promised to take me to the Zoo and to the pictures—not just on Saturdays, but every day of the week, and twice a day, if I wanted.

I boasted a little about the things I had learned and how cross the masters were. I told her about making French beds and we giggled over making one for Tom, though, I told her, we couldn't very well, as we only had one sheet on our beds at home and two were needed for a French bed. Moll told me about the new kittens —two coal-black ones and a black-and-white, which the big cat— Mother cat, we called her—had carried in by the loose skin on the backs of their necks and laid on the kitchen floor. She promised to show me their nest down in the hay and to let me call the black-and-white one my own and feed it saucers of milk for its meals.

We planned to go looking for holly with plenty of berries on it, down in the moors, to put up over the dresser and between the big, ornamental dinner-plates with flowers and leaves around the rims that stood on edge along the top shelf. We would hang up our stockings behind the sofa in the parlour without telling any-one, just in case Santa Claus might come, after all, because I had heard, and Moll took my word for it, that he would come to anyone who believed in him, and it was as easy to believe in him as to believe in God, because no one had ever seen God either, yet took His word for it that He was there. I told Moll that I had a theory that God and Santa Claus were one and the same person and that Faith was all that was needed—Faith and keeping out of sin, which got harder as you got older, and that explained why Santa Claus stopped coming to bigger children. Though Moll remembered Mrs. Cousins saying that Santa had given *her* a new baby, and everyone knew that Mrs. Cousins wasn't very holy, because she was always criticising people, even Father Donnelly himself, whom she accused of being greedy for money, when everybody knew that he would give his last penny to a poor person, and often had, and, sometimes, was without a fire in his grate or a blanket on his bed, because he had given them all away to some tinker-woman who came knocking at his door with a naked infant in a shawl—and a drop on the end of its nose.

But Santa Claus never did come and, when we crept into the parlour on Christmas morning, there was nothing in our stockings, except a fistful of clinkers from the kitchen fire which Tom, who had discovered our secret, had put there. He came in after us and made rude noises at our discomfiture, and, all through the day, kept asking—in the presence of my father and mother, so that we couldn't get a chance of having a crack at him—"What did Santa Claus bring today?"

Poor Moll was in tears with him and, even though she had been given a doll's pram by my mother, was in poor spirit until the following day, when Santa came, after all, because I had persuaded her to have another try, and, just before going to bed on Christmas night, when she was having her ears washed at the dresser, I had crept up and put an orange, an apple and a round tin of boiled sweets, which my aunt Nelly had given me before I left, into her stocking. We divided them, of course, and made great show of eating them before Tom as we worked at Gulliver. But Moll, who was always too soft, relented and gave him some and, for a time, all three of us worked away together, picking out pieces and fitting them together. But Tom soon tired—when the sweets were all gone—and went out with the dogs to see if he could raise a rabbit. So it was a good day, really, and made up in some way for the disasters of Christmas day.

The disasters began when my mother and the others went to first Mass and my father and I were left to mind the house. The traditional Christmas dinner of Turkey and Plum Pudding was unknown in our house—or in the house of any of our neighbours either. We had traditions of our own, though, since going to College, I would have been glad to be rid of them. One tradition was that we should have a rice pudding with lots of raisins and sultanas in it, baked to a crisp brown on top in the bakepot over the open fire.

The rice was simmering in a saucepan and we had been given instructions to stir it frequently and to make sure that it didn't boil over or burn.

"All right, all right," my father said testily, as my mother repeated her instructions, "we heard you the first time. You don't think us fools or anything that we couldn't look after a little thing like that? John'll mind it and I'll be here all the time myself. If you were as sure of being in time for Mass as you are of having this well looked after, you'd have nothing to worry about."

I sat by the fire, watching the lid of the saucepan gently breathing. It gave a soft ploof, now and again, when a bubble expanded around the brim and burst in steam. Sometimes, I stirred it and, when I thought the grains were whirling too briskly or the milk swelling dangerously, I pulled the sauce-pan back.

My father was at the window, bent over his shaving gear, his shirt-sleeves rolled up, intent on his task. Simple things like shaving or fastening the buttons of his shirt-sleeves could become complicated nightmares when tackled by my father. He laced his boots from right to left, beginning at the top and working downwards. He used a hairpin to fasten his back-stud and the knot on his tie was as nothing to the knotting of his arms in the making of it.

He had lately changed from his old cut-throat razor to a new safety razor, because he felt his hand was not as steady as it used to be, and after nicking himself regularly for years he became more and more concerned that, unless he gave it up, he would have one fatal slip of the hand and end up in a bath of blood on the floor. Every show of blood was fatal—or almost—to my father. He would bellow like a stuck pig and stagger about the kitchen with his face clasped in his fist, asking, "Is it bad? Is it bad?" And on the first sight of himself in the looking-glass he would moan, "I'm destroyed, teetotally and mortally destroyed!"

I knew from the muttering coming from the window that things were not going well with him. His lathered face, like a circus clown's, glared at me from the looking-glass he had propped against the window. He opened the razor and held the blade up to the light, turned it over and screwed it in again. He pulled it down his face and I could hear it, rasping and tearing.

"Dammit, boy," he shouted, "will you come here and give me a hand."

"That's an old blade," I said, taking it out and examining it. "It's all gapped. Look!"

"Get me a new one then!" he said impatiently.

I got a new blade from the tin box on the dresser, where he kept his shaving things, his pipe and plug and penknife and his Woolworth glasses.

"Put it in for me," he said. "Your fingers are nimbler than mine."

"Now," he said, when I had it in, "you might as well finish the job and shave me. My hand is a class o' shaky."

He sat down, facing me, his chin held high and indicated with his finger where I was to begin. He had several days' growth on and the twisted, white stubble was like angry wire. The only kind of lather he ever used was common soap and the blade could expect little help from that. He held himself in a tense way, as if he expected to be assaulted and cut to ribbons, which was very inhibiting. If there was one thing—apart from death and damnation—I dreaded more than having to shave my father, I cannot think of it.

My first stroke down his left cheekbone was successful enough. The blade sheared through with a pleasing crispness, leaving a smooth track after it. I repeated the stroke and soon had him shining and soft as fresh butter round as far as the mouth. Then, dipping the razor in a mug of steaming water before every stroke, I did a similar job on the other side.

"Easy, now, on the rest of it," my father cautioned, tipping back his head sacrificially and exposing the wizened skin, stretched like crumbling parchment across the gap of his gullet. Shaving it would be like negotiating a glacier full of hidden crevasses. I began tentatively, stretching the skin taut with my fingers and making short, light strokes.

"Dammit, you're choking me," my father shouted, as my fingers pressed into his weasand. I jumped with fright, the razor slipped and, down where his adam's apple, sharp as a tidal reef, made fair to shear through the skin, a red worm began to wriggle. My father sprang up with a howl of agony and sent me sprawling backwards on the floor.

"I'm pumping blood. My throat is cut," he roared, grabbing up the looking-glass to survey the damage.

My father's threshold of pain was always very low. The amount of noise he made gave no clear indication of the extent of the injury. A pulled hair was agony to him. The prick of a pin sheared through his sensibility like the drop of a guillotine.

He splashed water on his throat and dabbed himself with a towel, looking with greater and greater alarm at the series of blood-flecks, rising like islands out of the blue sea of cloth.

"The rib-leaf," he shouted. "Quick, dammit, boy, before I bleed into a weakness!"

I rushed out into the yard and began to search for the plant with leaves like ribbed fingers, which my father had been told by his father and he by his father before him—and so on back into the mists—would stop bleeding. Whenever we cut our fingers or gashed our legs, we held a few leaves over the wound until the bleeding stopped. And stop it always did, whether because of some property inherent in the plant itself, or, like us, because it daren't disobey my father, we could never determine. All we knew was that it worked. After a few minutes, the blood-flow stopped and back we went to our game. Sometimes, when the cut was more severe, we chewed up a few of the leaves and bound them round the wound. Immediately, the sting disappeared and when, a few days later, he bandage was removed, we were never surprised to find that it had healed.

I rushed back with the leaves and my father applied them to his throat. He held them there, his face set for martyrdom, the droopy ends of his moustache ludicrous with lather.

"You nearly done for me," he said angrily, making no distinction between accident and diabolical design. He lifted the corner of the leaves impatiently, then pressed them gingerly back again.

"It's still at it," he said in a voice that found conspiracy everywhere.

"The rib-leaf will stop it," I said ritually. "It always does."

"If it's not cut to the bone," he said darkly.

I was fairly sure that there was no bone, but I knew enough not to remind my father of that.

When he looked again, the bleeding had stopped, but he continued to hold the leaves in place just in case.

"Do you want me to finish you?" I asked.

"Finish!" he said sarcastically. "Don't you think you've gone near enough to that for one day! Any finishing that's to be done I'll do it myself."

He turned to the looking-glass and began to lather himself again very carefully.

"Dammit, the water is cold," he shouted. "Bring me over that kettle."

I was lifting the kettle from beside the fire, when I remembered the saucepan.

"The rice!" I said in anguish. "We forgot the rice!"

I poured out the water for him and rushed back. The lid of the saucepan had slithered over to one side like a cap on the head of a drunken man, and down the sides of the saucepan white streaks, like distant waterfalls, browning at the edges, were beginning to harden and come loose like transparent paper. I pulled back the saucepan and lifted the lid. The rice was the colour of brown sugar and almost as dry.

Without saying a word to my father—of whose further anger I was terrified—I poured water from the kettle into the saucepan and began to stir with a spoon. The rice at the bottom was dark brown and came away from the side in wedges with a sucking sound. The whole lot was a burnt mess. I stirred and stirred, my brain racing in desperation. I kept the lid partly on to prevent my father from smelling the burning.

"Was—was the water all right for you?" I said over my shoulder to distract his attention, making sure to keep myself between him and the saucepan.

"Ugh!" he grunted.

I looked over at him. He was bent over the glass, completely preoccupied, razor lifted for the stroke.

"Are you minding that rice?" he asked.

"It—it—boiled—a bit," I said cautiously.

"Pull it out then. Pull it out."

"All right."

A desperate thought struck me.

"I have to go out in an awful hurry," I said, putting on my lavatory-going voice and clutching my stomach. "I've a terrible pain. Will you keep an eye on the saucepan till I get back? I can't wait another minute."

"Off with you," he said crossly. "Don't do it here."

"The rice?" I asked.

"Dammit," he said, "I'm not that helpless that I can't mind a bit of rice."

It was all I wanted to hear. I rushed off, my hands supporting my stomach and groaned loudly, as I passed the window, for my father's benefit. I sat in the lavatory for a long time, counting up to a hundred slowly and then beginning again. When I got to five hundred, I came out, climbed over the garden wall and crept up to the front window of the kitchen and peeped in. My father was still shaving. His back was to me, his head lower than his behind, as he splashed water from the basin on the form in front of him over his face.

I climbed back over the wall again and took my time going round the gable of the house. I counted another leisurely hundred and then, because I was beginning to shiver, went in, stepping it out briskly, as I came past the window and in the door.

My father was putting on his coat. His shaving things were still spread out on the window.

"You were long enough about it. Are you all right?" he said gruffly.

"Yes," I said.

"Clear up those things for me then. Wash that razor and dry it well, mind!"

"Right!" I said.

I looked casually over towards the fire and asked, "How's the rice?"

"Dammit, in hell!" my father swore, "I never thought of it."

I went over to the fire. The rice was as I had left it, except that it had boiled again and the water was gone. I made a great fuss in dragging it from the fire.

"Well? Is it all right?"

"It's burnt brown," I said. "It's destroyed." There was vindictive accusation in my voice.

"You'd no right to go off and leave it," he said, throwing the blame back on me.

"You said you'd look after it," I reminded him. "I had to go."

"What a time you picked for it then," he grumbled, as if the motion of one's bowels was something that one could control by an act of will.

"You said it would be all right," I reminded him, marvelling at my own daring. My conscience was easy about what I was doing, because, if it hadn't been for his rumpus over the shaving it would never have happened. I was angry, too—though, being young and defenceless, I couldn't indulge my anger—when I thought of our great treat spoiled and the upheaval and unpleasantness there was bound to be when my mother came home, and all because of a silly old cut that wouldn't disturb an infant.

"Throw it out, be damned, and let that be an end to it," he said.

It was far from the end. My mother and the others walked round the gable of the house as I was spooning it out on the dunghill, and there the recriminations began. I retired to my room, sick and miserable, to get ready for Mass and left them to it. Tom and Moll were angry with me for ruining their day and I was angry with everyone. I heard their voices coming up and knew, without hearing, how it would all go. They would snipe at each other from carefully prepared positions—rice and children and Christmas long forgotten—fire a few more tactical shots in their perennial feud, then retire into an impenetrable silence, leaving an aftermath of hopelessness for us all.

There was more rice, but my mother said it was too late to put it on—unless we cared to wait till night for our dinner. My father and I went off to Mass, walking on opposite sides of the road to show our disunity and not speaking to each other. I ground my teeth at the hypocrisy of his greetings—effusive and hearty—when a neighbour went past, crunching on his bike over the frosted potholes. I wished he would spare some of his civility for us, and wondered what the outcome might be if I really had cut his throat. The thought came to me again when the choir was singing the *Adeste* and I knew that I, too, was a hypocrite for being at Mass and entertaining such parricidal notions.

Dinner was a miserable affair. Something had gone wrong with the steak when we were away—no one dared ask what. It was dried out and curling at the edges like the sole of an old boot lying in the sun. My mother slapped his down in front of my father, as if daring him to protest. We children sat, wriggling uncomfortably in our seats, waiting for the thunder to break out of the dangerous silence that brooded over us. I looked around at the decorations that Moll and I had put up—the holly with red berries that we had tramped the land to find, the string of balloons we had bought in Mr. Wadding's and hung from the ceiling, the

red, smiling Santa Claus that Moll had cut from a chocolate box—
and the tears were not far away.

I thought of my friend, Kieran Maher, at his Christmas dinner
in Griffith Avenue, Drumcondra, Dublin, and was glad that he
could not see me eating my Christmas dinner of potatoes and
butter—the steak abandoned, the pudding a heap of excrement—
my father and mother sitting like hanging judges in judgment on
each other at either end of the table and we, like grain between the
millstones, being crushed to silent powder.

Kieran Maher's father would surely be wearing a paper hat and
making jokes as the turkey came steaming to table, all browned
and basted. Kieran's mother would laugh as he carved it and
heaped the plates full of stuffing and passed them round. There
would be glasses filled with sparkling wines for the adults and
fizzy drinks, all coloured bubbles, for the children. His father
would pour whiskey over the pudding and set it alight, as fathers
always did in books. He would smoke a thick cigar afterwards, and
sit, dozing, in an armchair before the fire, while the children sat
on the carpet with their toys, passing round sweets and pulling
crackers, the tiniest ones of all creeping over their father and
pulling his ears, while their mother sat smiling over them all with
indulgent solicitude.

After dinner, when my father had gone to bed to sleep off his
churlishness, and my mother had tried to salvage our day by cut-
ting the Christmas cake she was reserving for tea and serving it
with tumblers of lemonade, we sat around the fire and I read a
Christmas story from the OUR BOYS for Tom and Moll—a
happy story of snow and homecoming, of greetings and presents
and boisterous harmony—and tried to construct from the sad
rags of our own ruined feast something nearer to the heart's
longing. We asked ourselves all the riddles we knew and got
pencils and paper to try our hand at the puzzles, and for a while
forgot our misery.

Then it was time to do the evening's work—to milk the cows
and feed the calves, to separate, to fodder and feed and bed down
for the night. Ned Rafter had the day off, my father was in bed,
so we did it all ourselves, while the grey evening turned black and
the first stars shivered with frost. I did the separating. The ring

of the machine, the hiss and twist of the steaming milk as it curved
into the bucket and built up a head of froth, the smell of warm
milk, and my shadow climbing and unclimbing the wall in the
muzzy light of the storm-lamp as I turned the handle—the
repetitiveness of it all, the sense of encapsulation within that
singing sound and that half room full of half-light was as soothing
and restorative as sleep after a day of turmoil.

When the work was finished, we went in to find a fire lighting
in the parlour. This was to be the great treat of our Christmas day
—to sit at the fire in the parlour and drink lemonade and play
games. Normally, the fire would have been lighted after dinner,
but, because of the misfortune earlier, it had been forgotten until
Tom remembered and got permission from my mother to light it.

The room smelt damp and musty. How could it be otherwise,
as we never used it, except briefly for half an hour or so when
unusual visitors came—like the Augustinians in the spring to
bless what we called "Thraan Water", which we afterwards
sprinkled on the crops, especially the green crop, because it had the
property of getting rid of pests like leatherjackets.

There was a big sofa there with collapsed springs, and two arm-
chairs with embroidered cushions, and a set of hand-carved oak
chairs with cane bottoms, which my father had bought at a priest's
auction and considered too good to sit on, set around an oval
mahogany table on a single massive foot. My mother was always
saying that we should use it oftener—perhaps light a fire there
every Sunday and sit and play cards—but we never did. It was a
mournful, funereal place, I always thought. A contradictory place
if you considered it. It would take the death of one of us to bring
it to life. Then the friends would gather there to sit around stiffly
in the accepted attitudes of mourning and whisper with exaggerated
politeness, awkward and uneasy in the face of the mystery of death.

We drew up the armchairs and sofa towards the fire and sat
sprawling in the unaccustomed softness, grinning at each other
and testing new positions and trying to cram a lot of memorable
living into the few hours we would be there. On some dateless
day in the vast boghole of the year it would be something to look
back on and remember—a touch of grace in the grim squalor of
our lives.

The biscuits and lemonade made the thing perfect. My mother sat in one of the chairs, reading *The Holly Bough*. Her dark hair had veins of silver through it. I liked the soft abstraction of her face as she read. Sometimes she looked up and smiled and we pressed her to have biscuits or lemonade, but she only smiled again and shook her head gently and went back to her reading.

After a while, tiring of the luxury of the sofa, Moll and I set to work on Gulliver. We finished his head and tricorne hat and part of the sky behind it. Tom came over and found a few pieces for us—the buckle on his belt and what remained of the walls of the town. Tom was all right as long as he could work on a part to himself, but when we had finished the hat and could match no more of the sky and came to help him find some roofs inside the walls, he resented our help and went back to the fire.

My father was up again and stirring about in the kitchen. When I was sent down for more blocks for the fire, I found him sitting morosely with a ring of porter bottles around him, drawing on his pipe and staring into the fire.

"We're all up in the parlour," I said. "Are you coming up?"

"Get me the corkscrew, will you," he said. And, when I had found it in his box of things on the dresser and handed it to him, he asked, "Isn't the kitchen good enough for yous?"

I didn't know what to say to that. I began to pick up a bundle of blocks from the pile by the fire.

"We're making a jig-saw," I said at length, "and we had lemonade. There's a nice fire up there."

He twisted the corkscrew into a bottle and drew the cork with a plonk. He held the bottle tilted slightly, as the head rose and dribbled down the side and dropped with a hiss into the ashes. He held it up, in the gesture I knew so well, and looked around before drinking, and I knew he was thinking of his friends whose health he had so often drunk, and I knew what he was going to say, before he said it.

"It's a cold thing to be drinking on your own," he said.

"We—we're drinking lemonade above," I said diffidently.

He looked at me and something like a smile flickered momentarily on his face.

"Go up with those sticks and bring down your bottle and we'll drink it together."

"Would you like a biscuit, too?" I asked.

"Bring some for yourself," he said.

When I came back, he had the bottle finished and another open. He held it up and looked at me very gravely and said, "Your health, son! And a Happy Christmas!"

"Happy Christmas!" I said and we both drank.

CHAPTER EIGHT

ANOTHER year. Another September. Another me—lording it in the junior alleys with insolent skill. How I loved the game of handball that lifted me out of the ruck—all those games of blood and bitterness in our own yard bearing sweet fruit in due season! The crack and snap of the half-solid high against the wall, the frantic race of feet in pursuit of the unattainable, the ball rolling dead with another ace safely stowed away. The hard-ball, like a round stone covered in pigskin, with which no one dared face me, for fear of bloodied knuckles and bruised fingers. The trick was to take it soft and swing with it, so that it left the curve of the palm like a bullet to ricochet and reverberate around the walls.

A new crop of boys to moon over the railings and drop their tears into the putrescent gardens. I was fourteen, in my third year. I was at the head of my class in Latin and Greek, having a number of dull books with a fancy college crest and my name on the flyleaf to prove it. Strange things were happening to my body. Like a rank weed on a dunghill I was shooting up. My wrists projected six inches beyond my cuffs. My hands were big and bony as a man's. My head looked top-heavy and my features were coarsening—losing their epicene softness—the man in me, hard, angular, struggling to burst from the chrysalis.

There was a war on in Europe and we were neutral and there was no white bread. We had ration books. Father Creame sent long, windy notes to our parents about missing coupons, full of phrases like "rationed commodity or commodities". Hitler was the comic bogey-man, but Rockfist Rogan, R.A.F., had the situation well in hand in the pages of *The Champion*, which my friend, Kieran Maher, got from home every week. Names like Patton, Montgomery and Eisenhower were beginning to impinge on our consciousness, but—apart from rationing—it was all very remote, like famine in India or tales of slave-trading along the Ivory Coast.

I had friends now, had found my place, the world opening

before me like the mists lifting on a summer morning, and I, a rabbit, emerging from his dark burrow into the promise of heat and soft pasture. No more tears now when I left home to return. No more weak leaning on my mother. She went home easier between the tall hedges, a flower of victory burgeoning in her mind, the pony clip-clopping, the car a-tilt and a-sway, her face settled into a quiet serenity, to write me warm letters of approval at my progress —letters which came to me greased and, sometimes, indecipherable from the pound of butter around which she wrapped them every week.

Her news was simple. They were getting in the potatoes, which were dry and abundant. Ned Rafter, complaining bitterly about the ephemerality of leather, had bought his first pair of new boots in five years. There was to be a Mission in the parish for the last fortnight in November. Tom had a sore throat.

Thus innocently, at the end of a letter, I got word of something that was profoundly to affect the lives of all of us in the months ahead. The following week there was further mention of Tom's sore throat. The week after, he was in bed, tossing about in fever, sweating profusely, complaining of fleeting pains in the joints. Tom, who had always disdained sickness and swaggered around with his shirt open to the waist, defying the frosts of winter. Dr. Reilly had been called in and diagnosed Rheumatic Fever.

With Father Creame's permission, I went home during the free day at Hallowe'en, borrowing my uncle Ned's bicycle to hurry down and returning again after a few hours in the gathering gloom, the night closing menacingly about me as I walked the last five miles back to College.

Tom's bed had been taken downstairs to the parlour for easy nursing. He lay there, wrapped in lint with the overpowering smell of Oil of Wintergreen pushing back the mildewed mustiness into distant corners. There was a fire burning in the grate—bringing Christmas in November—making me realise, as nothing else could, the gravity of his illness.

"He has to lie completely flat," my mother explained, "with only one pillow. He has to avoid all exertion."

It was dinner time when I arrived. It was affecting to see her feeding him from a spoon as if he were a baby.

"You'd better go below until I've finished," she whispered. "He hasn't got used to it yet. And he doesn't like anyone seeing him so helpless."

Later, she explained the full extent of his helplessness. He had to be washed and fed and have all his bodily functions attended to.

My father sat below, morose and silent.

"He could be crippled for life, you know," was all he said. "It can affect the heart."

"It's a wonder to me," Ned Rafter said, peeling a potato in his precise, methodical manner, "how a young lad like that can have rheumatism. He should 'a been brought up to wear hay in his boots and change it every day. There's nothing like it to keep out the damp. There's a power o' herbs in hay.

"Do you know what I'm going to tell you?" He looked across to my father expectantly, waiting for his attention.

My father neither heard nor heeded him.

"It's one o' the sins of the Irish, boy," he turned to me as a weak substitute, "that they let the old folk take their knowledge of herbs with them to the grave!"

After dinner, I sat for a while with Tom in the parlour. "How are you?" I asked.

"I never knew what it was to be sick till now," he said, his voice querulous, unsure, not at all like the old Tom.

"What kind of day is it?"

"Frosty," I said. "You remember the way we used ride the bicycles through the potholes to hear the ice crunch? It's that kind of day."

Then I thought of how Tom was no longer able to do anything like that and wondered if I should have said it.

"Are you not able to move at all?"

"I can move all right, but I'm not supposed to."

"You're as well to be in out of the cold," I said, not knowing what else to say.

"You know, I lost dozens of rabbits," he said. "I could have made a fortune this year, they're so plentiful."

He had often risen at five in the morning to attend to his snares and traps. He knew all the best runs, and, where I would have difficulty in catching one, Tom could catch a dozen and consider himself only moderately successful.

"Ned sets a few for me. He's a good sort, Ned. But he don't have the time to do it right. He's too busy now, himself and my father."

"Say your prayers that he'll be all right," my mother urged as she saw me off at the gate. "If Tom doesn't get out of this completely there's trouble in it for us all."

On the way back, her words kept pace with the rhythm of the pedals. Trouble for us all. Beneath the surface of the words, hidden somewhere under her worried frown and the disturbed weaving of her hands, was her real meaning. Moll might have been able to tell me, but Moll was not there. She had begun her first term in boarding school and had not been able to get home.

Had she meant that Tom was going to die? He was the only brother I had and we had never been close. It was not right for brothers to be like that. It was my fault as much as his—mine more than his. Tom was basically an uncomplicated fellow. He fought and he forgot. It was I who was the moody, reserved one, weeping over my injuries behind closed doors. People liked Tom. He flamed and then spluttered out. It was I who smouldered and was consumed inwardly by a secret flame.

My mother's next news was that while the doctor was hopeful of Tom's progress, his convalescence would be slow and tedious, and the danger of permanent damage could not be ruled out for a long time. Meanwhile, my father was getting more and more difficult and was talking ominously of removing me from college. Against him my mother was prepared to fight tooth and nail.

It was to this grim prospect of family discord that Moll and I returned for our Christmas holidays.

"Christmas always seems to go wrong for us," Moll said.

Tom was lying as I had left him. The very wallpaper now reeked of his sickness. The mantelpiece had started to come away from the wall with the heat of the unaccustomed fires. It was strange to see his face so pale and his hands and finger-nails so clean. The fever had abated and his pulse, the doctor said, had returned to normal. But he was still very weak.

"It will take months before he's even out of bed," my mother said.

"And most of the ploughing still to do, and all the spring work coming up," my father grumbled.

"He wants you to stay at home, you know," Tom said as I fuelled the fire for him.

"What use would I be?" I protested. "I can't plough. I'm no good with the cows. You know that. He was always saying that I was no good on the land, wasn't he?"

"It's different now though."

"I'd be no better than a yard boy and Dan Morgan or anybody could do that."

"That's what I told him," Tom said.

I swivelled round on my heels to look at him and laid down the shovel in the fender. Had I heard him properly? Was Tom really signalling that he was on my side? The very suggestion was so novel that it startled me.

"Do—*you*—think—I should stay at home?" I asked slowly.

"You're getting on all right at school, aren't you?"

His voice was gruff, slightly embarrassed, because we had never spoken so intimately before.

"Yes. It would destroy my chances. I wouldn't like to leave now."

"Don't then! Stand up to him!"

I put away the coal and came over to sit beside him.

"Listen," Tom said, "I'm here on the flat of my back a long time and nothing to do but think—and listen. I hear everything that goes on down there. I hear them arguing. Mostly about you. But I'll tell you this. They were arguing about the same thing long before I got sick. He's only using me as an excuse. If I was on my feet this minute, they'd still be arguing about the same thing. You stick to your school, boy. It's the only thing you're good at. That's what I do be thinking and I lying here, counting the flowers on the wallpaper. I made up my mind about it that evening after you coming to see me. It was a long way to come without anybody asking you to, and I kept wondering why you did it and if I'd 'a done the same for you . . ."

It was a long speech for Tom. He stopped, embarrassed. We were both embarrassed at the indecent intimacy of such revelation. There was silence between us while I tried to digest its meaning.

"I was—worried about you," I said at length. "I—I suppose I thought you were like a tree or a rock and nothing like this could ever happen to you."

"Hey," Tom changed the subject, "d'you ever smoke at all? I'm killed for the want of a fag since this happened. Only for Ned I'd be destroyed."

"I'll get you some," I said, anxious to nourish this new alliance between us.

"I tell you what I'll do, too. I'll set your snares for you and look at them every day and do anything else you want me to."

"Get me the fags first, anyway. That's the main thing," Tom said.

"Tom and yourself are getting very thick these days," Moll said, as we walked together to the village.

"Tom's not bad," I said. "This sickness has changed him a lot."

My father began his attack a few days later.

"Tell me, boy," he said, "are you doing any good in that college at all?"

"Look at the prizes he won. All those books for coming top of his class," my mother rushed to my defence.

"Dammit, hasn't the child got a tongue of his own?" my father flared.

"Leave him alone," she said. "We were through all this before."

"Let this be the end of it then. He's staying at home and that's all about it."

"I can't leave now with my exam coming up," I pleaded.

"You'll do what your father bids you."

"No!" my mother shouted. "I won't stand for it."

"He'll do it for his brother's sake."

"Leave me out of it," Tom challenged from the parlour. "He's not to do anything for me. If you make him do it, it'll be for your own sake and not for me."

"Yes," my mother hissed. "Tell John the real truth. Tell him it's for your own sake. Because you don't want to pay a man. Because you don't want the expense of him in school. Tell him the rows we have every time one of his bills has to be paid. Tell him who paid the bills for his first year—I did out of the fifty pounds poor Aunt Ellen left me. Tell him you're afraid of his learning anything because it'll help him to find out the kind of father he has. Tell him that you want to keep them all in the same black hole of ignorance you were reared in yourself. Tell him you begrudge him his chance and want to pull him back into the same pit of muck and misery you've buried the rest of us in."

As usual when she was really roused, my mother had gone too far. With an oath, my father flung the bucket he had been holding into the fire, scattering sparks and flaming embers out to the dresser. Then he was off, booting the dog before him, rushing through the feeding hens outside, leaving squawks and feathers to settle behind him.

Later in the evening, when Jem Roche drove into the yard, he went off without a word to anybody. I heard the car again in the middle of the night and the banging of doors. The kitchen in the morning full of drunken bottles and dribbles of puke, my father appearing at noon in his stocking-feet, a beat-up wreck, faltering to harbour in the chimney-corner.

Not a word more about me for the rest of the holiday. But I knew he hadn't given up.

I went back to College, eager for what it had to offer, apprehensive of having it snatched away from me. I saw it as my mother had seen it all along, the road to salvation for me, the key to my escape. With all its austerities and rigours, it was infinitely preferable to what I had left. The harshness and rigid discipline, even hunger itself, were tolerable because they would end one day. But, once drawn back into the hopeless morass of home, there would be no escape.

Hunger now was a gnawing, insistent force in my life—hunger of the body, hunger of the affections, hunger of the senses. The first was the worst, but when it was satisfied—and in college it rarely was—the others became more clamorous, nipping sharply, making me aware of vast, unexplored tracts of my being.

Mealtime was an animal scramble to grab and stuff as much as possible before someone else did. There was seldom enough of anything and, if there was, it was usually—like the potatoes that could be cut in halves and stuck together again—unpalatable. A certain number of brown loaves was allocated to each table, and when these ran out, it required a great deal of persuasion to

convince Sister Benedict that more was needed. Father Creame
and herself were constantly preoccupied with waste. Crumbs on
the floor, uneaten (because inedible) soapy potatoes that went
back, cold and purple—like the faces of dead drunkards—foul
dishes of soup with floating, greasy scum like the surface of a
polluted pool, left aside in disgust, these were proof—if proof was
needed when nutritional experts had decided that our diet was
adequate—that our requests were frivolous. The notice-board
always had its share of admonitory homilies, exhorting us to thrift
and temperance.

Sometimes, Father Creame took over from Black Jack at meal-
time. He intoned Grace with sonorous self-righteousness, blessed
himself with pontifical gravity and, while we stood and watched
weakening spirals of steam curl up from our cooling dinners, began.

"Now, men, listen carefully. I'll say this once and I'll say it no
more. I will not tolerate grumbling about meals. And I will not,
I repeat I WILL NOT (by this time he was shouting) tolerate
sinful waste. Perfectly good food is being thrown on the floor or
sent back uneaten.

"Now, men, I am here today to see that there is an end to this
kind of thing. I intend to deal sternly with those responsible.
Remember, that at this very moment countless millions are dying
in India for lack of this very food which some men are criminally
wasting. Wilful waste makes woeful want is an old saying, and I
must ask you to consider this. What you so thoughtlessly cast
from you today you will most certainly need tomorrow. God is
not mocked!"

For the rest of the meal he walked among the tables, taking up
discarded potatoes and sniffing at them, insisting that they were
edible and standing over the culprit until, mouthing and writhing,
making nauseated chopping motions with his front teeth and
gulping with oscillating eyeballs, he swallowed them down.

At the end of the meal, he gathered all the uneaten food into a
dish and held it up triumphantly when the bell had captured our
attention.

"Has everyone finished?" he asked. And, when there was no
reply but an uneasy murmur, he continued, "If there is any man
who requires more, let him put up his hand."

There were no hands.

"I take it, then, that you have had enough."

A hostile silence, as we reflected that to be finished and to have had enough of the fare provided was not necessarily the same thing as having fully satisfied our hunger. And seething anger that, because he intended to browbeat us, there was no chance to point out the distinction to him and no chance—supposing someone were rash enough to try—of making him acknowledge it. Silence, then, and a wary watchfulness.

"Now, men, look here. I have in my hand sufficient potatoes to feed at least twelve people. To throw these out would be wilful waste. I am asking Sister Benedict to serve them mashed tomorrow and to reduce the number of potatoes cooked by a similar amount from now on. The fault here is not too little food but too much.

"Good day, gentlemen, and let no one presume to make complaints about inadequate food to me again."

However badly we fared on our feet, to be confined to bed was to be absolutely starved. Sister Benedict's practice of medicine was very simple. If a boy had a temperature, his illness was acknowledged and he was allowed to stay in bed. But, as he was sick, food —apart from slops (that awful soup, cold, weak tea and aspirins with, perhaps, a saucer of slimy carrageen at dinnertime)—was considered inadvisable. No doubt, it was intended to discourage malingering.

On first news of an illness, she appeared with a rattle of beads, her thin lips sewn into tight disapproval, to demand, "Why aren't you up like everybody else?"

Her next question, as she shook down her thermometer, was, "Have you your exercise done?"

It was her conviction that boys only stayed in bed when they had something to escape from or someone to dodge.

"Open your mouth. Close your lips but not your teeth."

She popped the thermometer in and grasped the patient's wrist in her cold, cloistered hand to check his pulse. She took a watch on a leather strap from the front of her habit and squinted at it over the top of her spectacles. The remote, starched, inhuman chill of her offered no comfort, no sympathy. To be sick at all was an offence. Even to be suspect of shamming illness a heinous crime.

The slow, calculated look, as she weighed the evidence, the mouth a bloodless line, the hands returning the thermometer to its case.

"Nothing much the matter with you. A slight—very slight—temperature, that's all."

Then grudgingly, "You'd better stay in bed—but, no reading, mind!"

Her fingers searching under the pillow for books.

"And no malingering!"

Later she appeared with a dose of cascara—her panacea!

Once, when I had caught a chill after a heated game in the alley on a drizzly afternoon, I passed the temperature test and was confined to bed for three days. By the night of the second day, I was so famished that I crept out of the dormitory at midnight, when everyone was asleep, and felt my way down to the kitchens in search of something to eat. With eyes grown accustomed to the dark I tried the doors of all the presses and cupboards, some of which were locked, until I opened one and got the delicious smell of bread.

I pulled out a loaf and, sitting there in the warmth of the huge Aga cooker, I tore it apart with my hands and ate it dry—the full two pounds of it—stopping only to drink from the tap at a marble sink, big as a horse trough, beside the window. I did my best to clear away all the crumbs and leave no trace of my crime but, as I didn't dare put on the light, for fear of detection, I made an imperfect job of it. I closed the press again, and with bulging stomach crept back up to bed. I had considered taking another loaf with me, but I could think of nowhere safe to hide it, and to be caught in possession was a prospect too frightening to be risked.

The loss was discovered next day. News of it filtered in to me in the dormitory. I lay there, half in fear and half in exultation, thinking of the stories I had read where some vital clue, picked up at the scene of the crime, led to the unmasking of the culprit, examining my pyjamas for missing buttons or pulled threads, expecting at any minute to be dragged out for interrogation, and, as the day passed, with a growing elation at having challenged the system and got away with it. When I heard that Father Creame had blustered about, demanding confession and threatening reprisals,

I felt that I was safe. It meant that he had failed to solve, and no longer expected to solve the crime. But I was horrified when I heard that he had imposed bread rationing for a day as punishment on the whole school. Everyone was to get three slices of bread and no more for breakfast and tea the following day.

It would be comforing to my conscience to be able to report that I confessed and saved everybody. But I did not confess. I spent the rest of the day and night tossing and twisting in misery. I knew confession was the only decent thing. But I was too cowardly. The thought of Father Creame thundering like Jehovah, as he drew the long, polished ashplant from his trouser leg and held it mercilessly over his head for the downstroke, unnerved me. Even worse—if anything could be worse—was the fear of expulsion, the realisation of my father's wishes and the terrifying prospect of being buried alive in the inhospitable soil.

The dormitory that night was sparking with revolt. A strike was discussed, but, like most school revolts, it came to nothing. It only needed Black Jack to come flashing his torch and telling everyone to stop talking and go to sleep for it to peter out. There was a small crumb of comfort for me in the fact that no one blamed the thief. Their sympathies were with him. They refused to consider his offence a theft at all. There was even talk of a mass raid on the kitchens to show their solidarity with him.

Still, the following day, there was much grumbling about the unfairness of it all. Hunger shortened tempers and I was the cause—in some measure, at least—of more than one bloody nose. The most unpleasant aspect of the whole affair was that Father Creame had found a weapon that he was to use against us with increasing severity again and again.

CHAPTER NINE

IT was a relief when Sister Benedict evicted me and I went back to class. There was too much time to think in the lonely dormitory. The picture of Tom at home in his bed and my father stumping crossly about the farmyard kept cutting through the sounds of college life—cheers from the alley, the commanding call of the prefect's whistle. I was suspended somewhere between the two, needing desperately to submerge myself in one to drown the intrusion of the other.

But there was to be no escape for me—even after the resumption of class. On my very first evening in study, I was called from the study-hall about 8 p.m. to a fracas at the front door, where I heard with sickening horror the thickened voice of my father raised in argument with Father Turley. He was battering with his fists at the door, while the priest barred his way and said quietly, but firmly, "If you insist on creating a scene, I must ask you to go away."

"I want to see my son, dammit," my father pounded with both fists. "I've every right to see him and I'll stay here till Doomsday unless you let me in."

"If you are quiet and reasonable and stop the noise, I'll let you see him for a few minutes."

"Why didn't you say so then? That's all I wanted. It's hardly too much for a man to ask to see his own son."

Then, seeing me, standing in shame, my head bent, my face aflame, he roared, "Get your things, boy. You're coming home with me."

"This boy isn't going anywhere tonight," Father Turley laid his hand in a friendly and protective way on my shoulder, "or any other time either until the matter can be discussed in a responsible and (with heavy emphasis) sober manner."

"Sober!" my father ranted. "Who's not sober? D'you hear that, Jem? He says we're not sober!"

Jem Roche, who had been hidden by the door, now came into

view, sticking his head over my father's shoulder to swivel his hot, irresponsible eyes over Father Turley and myself, a wicked leer of recognition on his face when he saw me.

"Sober?" he cackled. "If we were any soberer, we'd blow away like dust in the wind. We haven't enough in us between us to moisten the bill of a wren."

"That's what I'm telling him," my father said.

"The driest, soberest, most Pioneering funeral I was ever at," Jem went on. "I never before seen the dead put away with such devotion and piety. The last of us there to have a drink was the corpse—and him three days stiff."

A few boys, returning to the study-hall from some errand, stopped to look at us curiously. I first became aware of their presence when Father Turley waved them impatiently into the hall. I saw that Kieran Maher was one of them. He looked at me in a friendly, but inquiring, way and passed on. Jem Roche raised his hat to them in an exaggerated gesture, and bottles clinked in his overcoat.

"It's Foley's old fellow," I heard one of the boys whisper, before the door closed behind them.

"Are you the head man?" my father was asking Father Turley. "I want to see the head man."

"Always ask for the head man," Jem Roche advised. "This is no job for the boy in the yard."

Their loud voices grated like iron on my sensibility. In my head I willed them to silence, wished for an apoplectic fit to fell them, a kind hand to shake me free of my nightmare and tell me it was all a bad dream. But there they were, belligerent, disputatious, irrepressible. My father, his face flushed, the blue veins, like arterial highways on a map, losing themselves in the swamp and scrubland of his moustache. Jem Roche, his hat on the Kildare side, his forehead glistening, a fleck of froth at the corners of his mouth, ready at the slightest urge of his wayward temperament to burst into song, dance a jig or floor a roomful of men, all in the name of good fellowship.

"I have sent for Father Creame," Father Turley said. "He will be here presently. In the meantime, I must ask you to lower your voices and step into the staffroom."

He indicated a door behind him, and stood aside to let them in. They pushed by him at a trot and, Jem Roche in the lead, opened the first door that came to hand, which happened to lead to the study-hall and in they staggered.

There was an unnatural silence inside while Father Turley, his arm turning like a windmill in a storm, beckoned them out.

"Look at the poor lads," I heard Jem Roche say, "up to their eyes in the books."

"Hey, Jem, Jem!" came my father's foghorn whisper, "I think we're in the wrong place."

He raised his voice, addressing the study-hall at large.

"We're looking for the head man."

The startled silence was breaking into fragments of whispers, titters, laughter, guffaws.

Father Turley rushed in, called for silence and half-guided, half-pushed my father and Jem Roche out again.

"As big as men, some of them," my father marvelled. "It's on the land they should be."

It seemed to me that there was nothing further they could do to humiliate me. My shame was changing to anger. I caught my father's sleeve, as we followed Father Turley and Jem Roche into the staffroom, and pulled it savagely.

"You're drunk," I hissed. "You're disgracing yourself and me and all of us. Go home for God's sake and leave me alone."

"You're coming with me," he said.

"Now, gentlemen, gentlemen," Father Creame blew in behind us, bringing authority with him like a well-trained dog on a leash, "what is all this disturbance about? This is not a bar-room, gentlemen, nor a house of ill-fame. We have rules here. We observe discipline. We have a code of behaviour. We have standards. I tell you once, gentlemen, and I'll tell you no more. We do not lower these standards for anyone. State your business, if it is on business you have come. If not, I must ask you to leave, or I shall send for the police."

"You're the head man." It was a statement, not an enquiry.

My father spoke with approval as a man of authority himself.

"This is John Foley's father," Father Turley said. "He insisted on seeing you."

"And who is this other—person?"

"Education for the sons of the middle classes," Jem Roche mused, following some train of thought of his own. "Pon my oath, a noble calling."

"Master Foley, who is this person?"

"Mr. Roche," I said. "A—friend—of my father's."

"My sound John," Jem Roche said and lifted his hat to Father Creame, who liquidated him with a look and turned back to my father.

"What is your business?"

"I'm taking this boy home," my father said. "He's wanted on the land."

"Is that in the boy's best interest?" Father Creame asked.

"What's that got to do with it! He's wanted and that's all about it."

"Are you telling me," inquired Father Creame at his most magisterial, "that the welfare of this boy is of no importance, that you are prepared to sacrifice his career for some short-term benefit to yourself? Have you no thought of his needs?"

Of course, my father had. He was the best, most considerate father any boy ever had. His friend, Jem Roche, could prove it. His children had always had full and plenty, and good shoes on their feet, when others had gone barefoot. I was a lazy inconsiderate boy, who was no good on the land, but must be made do his part now that my brother was laid up, without any hope of his immediate recovery and the very real threat of his permanent incapacitation. And much more on the same theme, with frequent appeals to Jem Roche for moral support, all of which was freely given, with a deal of handshakes and backslapping and mutual congratulation.

I sat there, listening to it all, a sick knot in my stomach. It was strange to hear Father Creame championing me against my own father. It was not a role I had previously thought of him in, and ironic, in view of his obsessive investigation of my crime a few days previously.

He listened patiently to my father's tirade, probing him with questions. Could he provide a doctor's report on my brother's health and future prospects? My father couldn't. Did my mother approve. She didn't. Had he sought any advice in the matter other than his own convenience? My father hadn't. Skilfully digging a trench around him like that, he soon isolated my father from all prudent counsel and left him sinking knee-deep into the shaky-bog of his own bluster.

Then, just as skilfully, he threw him out a rope and hauled him to safety, generously giving him an opportunity to recover his self-esteem.

"When you decided to send this boy to college, you did a good day's work. Don't undo it all now before he has a chance to prove himself."

My father, who was like a flame that had burned fiercely and blown itself out, was beginning to sober up. The certainties of intoxication were being slowly eroded and what had seemed a good idea earlier in the evening was souring into embarrassment. Respect for the clergy—one of the strongest threads in the weave of the peasant mind—was returning too with sobriety. For the first time since his arrival he was silent and prepared to listen to someone else.

"Now," Father Creame continued in the tone he used when addressing the school on some hanging matter, "as it is obvious that you seem unaware of your son's scholastic potential . . ."

"His what?" My father looked at him, slackjawed.

"His scholastic potential," Father Creame steamrolled on, "a review of his progress since he came here is in order."

He took a key from his pocket and opened a steel filing cabinet in the corner.

"Master Foley," he turned to me, "kindly wait outside while I discuss these confidential matters with your father.

"You, too, if you please," he said to Jem Roche.

He opened the door politely and stood, waiting for us to go.

"What's my business is Jem's business," my father said.

"I will discuss this boy's affairs with no one but his parents."

"Quite right," Jem said amiably, "whom God hath joined together—or whatever the Good Book says."

Then, in a loud whisper to me, as we went out;

"He's a tough nut, that head man. What's his name?"

I stood outside, wondering what was going on inside, wondering, most of all, what Father Creame could possibly find to say in my favour. I was still furious with my father. I was determined to write to my mother and tell her everything. She would know how to deal with him. It was the only weapon I could think of to use against him.

Jem Roche had wandered off, looking for a lavatory. I heard him downstairs, opening the ponderous door of the refectory. I didn't dare go after him, in case Father Creame came to call me in again and found me absent. Jem had discovered the kitchens. I heard conversation, and laughter from the girls. Then the whiplash of Sister Benedict's voice, hunting him out, and Jem's indignant roar, "Christalmighty, woman, I wasn't going to jump on any of them. I only lost my way."

I heard him fumbling up the stairs again, as the door opened and Father Creame called me in. I hoped that, whatever he did, Jem Roche wouldn't go into the study-hall again.

"Well, Master Foley," Father Creame said briskly, "I have some news for you."

"I don't want to go home," I said sullenly.

"Your father has reconsidered. He now sees the wisdom of letting you sit for your examination. He has agreed to defer any action until after your Intermediate Certificate in the summer. By then, I trust, the situation will have clarified itself further. Have I your word for this, Mr. Foley?"

"Let it be so," my father said, refusing to look at me.

"Very well! Now, Sir, I will bid you . . ."

The door opened and Jem Roche stuck in his head.

"Is there a convenience handy?" he asked.

"Mr. Foley, I will bid you goodnight. I must ask you now to say goodbye to your son and to remove yourself and this—person from the precincts of this establishment within five minutes."

He swept out, casting one disdainful glance in Jem's direction and curling his nostrils as if he had smelled rancid butter.

"It's easy to see why they made him head man," Jem said in admiration.

My father looked at me and I looked at him, each waiting for the other to speak.

"Well," he said at length, half defiantly, half appeasingly, "you have what you want now after all."

I said nothing.

"So it wasn't the worst thing in the world us coming here, was it?"

"They'll all be laughing at me." I was bitter, unforgiving.

"Never mind, boy," he said in a conciliatory tone. "Maybe we shouldn't have come. But it can't be helped now."

He put his hand in his pocket and took out some money.

"Here's a few shillings. Buy yourself something."

"A couple of bob more for the young fellow." Jem Roche dived into his pocket.

I took the money distrustfully, and stood, shifting from one foot to the other.

"Maybe," my father began tentatively, "maybe, it would be better not to say anything to your mother about all this."

I didn't speak. Events had moved too fast for me. Emotions were churning around inside me. It wouldn't do to anger him, make him change his mind.

"What she don't know can't hurt her," Jem urged.

"Well?"

"You—won't go back on your word?"

"On my dying oath!"

"All right!" I said, gracelessly.

"Good man! We'll forget the whole thing."

Easy for them to go away and forget, but what about me!

"I'm bursting for a piss," Jem said.

"All right, all right, we'll be off now," my father said.

I followed them out to the door and watched them go. Jem Roche stood and urinated in the middle of the lawn.

"Not a word now, mind!" my father warned.

"No! Goodbye."

He put his hand in his pocket again.

"Here's another couple of shillings. God bless you, son!"

I watched him go, an old man ashamed of himself now, the drink and the outing gone sour on him.

I turned back to face the ridicule of my companions. Luckily for me, a diversion had been created in my absence. I slipped unobtrusively into a study-hall seeded with rumours of a new outrage. Another theft—the kind that everyone condemned—had just come to light. A boy's case had been rifled. A food parcel which he had just received from home, containing a cake, a pound of butter, a box of chocolates and a ten-shilling note had been taken.

Father Creame's first move was to use the theft as an excuse to ban all further parcels, which he looked on as a slur on the good name of the college. His second was to initiate an investigation more thorough than any he had ever attempted before.

Next day, the whole school was assembled in the study-hall and, with his ash-plant ominously drawn, he strode in to confront us. His lowering face and corduroyed forehead told us what we might expect.

"Now, men," he began, flexing the ash-plant and testing its spring, "you know why I'm here."

He looked about with sharp jerks of his head, as if to single out the culprit by sheer force of will and hypnotise him into confession.

"A mean and despicable theft (he emphasised the adjectives with a savage intensity)—mean and despicable, I repeat—has been committed. A boy's case has been broken open and the following items stolen."

He drew a slip of paper from his trousers pocket and consulted it.

"Item one. A rich fruit-cake.

Item two. A two-pound box of chocolates.

Item three. A pound of creamery butter.

Item four. A ten-shilling note.

"Now, men," he began to stride back and forth purposefully at the top of the study-hall, "while I abhor the practice of parents sending unnecessary food-parcels—as if this were some sort of prisoner-of-war camp—(some covert glances and face-making towards the back where I was, at this)—and for that reason have already banned all further parcels, it is my duty to uphold the right of private property and to let it be known with all the vehemence at my command that I will not rest until I have rooted out the thief from our midst and punished him with the severity he deserves."

He paused to let his words sink in and came to rest on the top step of the rostrum.

"Do you follow me, men?"

We nodded dutifully.

"Now," he continued, "I call on the person, or persons, responsible to step forward and confess their crime in a manly way. I can promise them that an honest admission of guilt now, and a solemn undertaking to make restitution and never commit such a crime again will predispose me to lenity."

He stopped again and swivelled his head slowly around, waiting. The tension was palpable. Boys held their breath. I could hear my heart thumping in the silence. There was a feeling of drama and excitement. I felt as I sometimes felt at a moment of crisis in a story, alert, expectant, the thrill of danger making my hair stand —and somewhere at the edge of my being the heartening thought that I myself was not involved.

"I am waiting, men!" Father Creame said.

No one came forward. No one stood up. No one moved.

"Very well!" he roared, bringing the ash-plant down with a crash on the desk-top. "I should have known that the despicable perpetrator of this mean theft would never have the moral courage to confess. I now call on anyone who has knowledge of the crime, anyone who knows something or has seen something suspicious, to come forward and do his duty."

There was still no move.

"I refuse to believe," he roared, "that among one hundred and thirty boys there is not someone who can throw light on the matter. If, through misguided loyalty, you are shielding a criminal, let me cite you the law on the matter. In law you are an accessory— whether before or after the fact, or both—and are liable to the same punishment as the criminal. I exhort you, men, to come forward, while there is still time, and bring this reprehensible creature crawling into the light."

No one moved. Boys were getting uneasy. They shifted and coughed.

"You are forcing me to do something I have no wish to do," Father Creame thundered. "You are forcing me to penalise everyone for the crime of one, or, at most, a few men."

We looked at each other glumly, guessing what was in store. But no one stepped forward to help Father Creame.

"Very well!" He rapped the ash-plant on the desk three times and waited dramatically.

"From tea this evening, until further notice, bread will be strictly rationed. Three slices per person will be your allotted portion."

There was an audible groan. He rapped on the desk for our attention.

"You have brought this punishment on yourselves. In my book, non-co-operation is the same as insubordination. Your punishment, men, is just. And let me remind you that I reserve the right to impose further penalties, should such a course seem to me to be justified. I am telling you once and I'll tell you no more that I shall crush ruthlessly—I said ruthlessly, men—any attempt at undermining the fabric of this institution."

He strode down among us, tapping his heels with the ash-plant, staring along the desks and breathing heavily.

"You," he said, pointing the stick menacingly at a thin boy with lank, pale hair from second year, "what do you know about this?"

"Nothing, Father!"

"Your name, man?"

"Fintan Cogan, Father."

"And you know nothing of this theft, Master Cogan? Answer, man!"

"Nothing, Father."

"Or," he said, and my hair lifted at the words and the blood made my cheeks burn, "or about the loaf of bread that was stolen from the kitchens last week?"

"No, Father. Honest to God, Father."

Father Creame stopped beside me and turned back to face up the Hall.

"Let no one imagine," he said, "that I have forgotten last week's theft. Last week we found we had a thief in our midst. This week— just a few days later—we find we have another. I refuse to believe that this college is so steeped in knavery that we have two separate thieves. It is my considered opinion that both crimes were committed by the same person. There is the same surreptitious stealth about both crimes, the same low, animal cunning, the same voracious greed."

The edge of his habit was touching my shoulder. I could feel it move with me as I twitched in terror. I eased myself in from it before it brought the trembling message of my guilt to his notice. I put up my open palms to hide my face and stared down at the scored wood of the desk.

REM. B. CHADWICK—7TH. SEPTEMBER 1944.

"I will not rest until I unmask this villain," Father Creame roared. "I shall be in the staffroom for the remainder of the study period. I shall personally interview every boy in this school, beginning with the Juniors. I shall find the culprit—be assured of that—and, when I do, I intend to make an example of him before the whole school and then expel him. Like a rotten apple in a barrel he must be removed before he infects the whole school."

He strode out, whacking his ash-plant fiercely against his habit and making the chalk fly. Father Turley, who was waiting outside, slipped in and started the procession out to the staffroom. Every time someone came back the whole study-hall looked up expectantly and watched him back to his place and the next person out, before returning to a half-hearted study again.

I waited my turn in unease. Father Turley let me out to the lavatory the first time I asked, but, when I put my hand up again shortly after, he shook his head, then strolled down to inquire, "What's wrong with you tonight?"

"Nothing, Father."

"No confession to make, for instance?" and he looked at me quizzically.

"No—no, Father," I stammered, "I—I drank a lot of water."

"Let this be your last time then," he said.

Father Turley always made me feel uneasy. He had a way of looking at me that suggested some intimacy between us that I neither wanted nor understood. During his geography class he had a habit of drawing his hands over our shoulders, when he stood behind us, that some boys seemed to like, but which I found disconcerting. Sometimes, too, especially in my first year, when he was bending over me to look at a map I had drawn, he pressed his cheek to mine and let his fingers wander over my neck and hair.

More than once, when the seat was vacant, he had sat in beside me and put his arm around me to explain something and his hand was inclined to stray while he talked and develop a will of its own, opening a shirt button and creeping in and down over my bare skin until, alarmed and troubled, I pressed hard against the desk and he withdrew with a queer, apologetic sort of smile. I liked him, really, except when he got too familiar like that, because he could be very considerate and generous and was never vindictive like Father Creame.

But he could be moody, especially when he suffered from migraine, which he frequently did—and more than ever lately. He would appear, tense and nervous, and sit on the rostrum with his hands clasped to his head while we did written work. Now and then, he would raise his head infinitely slowly with his fingers to look at us with a wan face and appeal for silence. The very scratching of our pens was sometimes too much for him and he dragged himself off to bed until the attack had passed.

Next day, he was around, cheerful as ever, laughing and making dubious jokes about squiggles on our ill-drawn maps, which he would equate with "certain parts of our anatomy". He never said what parts, but we all giggled as if we knew—and, no doubt, we did. But I, at least, wondered why he said things like that.

His worst feature was that he had sucks. To be a suck, one had to endure a certain amount of what we called "mauling". Since I did not like mauling, I had forfeited my right to be a suck, but I knew, from delicate overtures that he made me at times even yet, that the position was still open to me. Sucks were called to his room and given sweets. They were tucked in at night. Sometimes, he sat on their beds, when the light went out, and talked to them in whispers for a few minutes.

Once, in my first year, I had been summoned to his room and given sweets. He was sitting on his bed in his shirt-sleeves without his collar and looked more human than I imagined a priest could ever look. He sat me on the bed beside him and fed me toffees. He put his arm around my shoulders and squeezed me and told me I was a nice boy and that he liked me and would look after me and that I was to come to him whenever I was lonely. He made me cry he was so nice and gentle.

He dried my eyes and pressed his cheek against mine and said that he was sometimes lonely too. Then his hands began their strange wandering and I got very agitated and he did, too. When I jumped off the bed and said I wanted to go, he apologised for frightening me and gave me more sweets to take away with me. He asked me to pray very hard for a special intention of his and when I said I would—wondering what his intention could be—he made me kneel down with him and say three Hail Marys to Our Lady. He asked me to say them every day for him and then he let me go. When I looked back, there he was, his old cheery self, laughing and waving from the doorway with his habit and collar on, no longer so human—or so strange. I was not invited to his room again.

He never played handball or hurling or football with us like Father Hogan or Father Coffey, but he would often come to watch and urge us on. He was lenient with the smokers—senior boys who had written permission from home and were allowed an official smoke three times a day—and would often give them an extra smoke after late study at night before going to bed. In the shop which he ran, he could be persuaded to grant a little credit and he never approved of Father Creame's punitive rationing policy, though he could do nothing to modify or change it.

When I came back from the lavatory the urge started to build up again. All I could do was hold myself tight and wait. I had no confidence in my ability to keep my secret from Father Creame. One searching look from those sharp eyes of his and my very soul would be stripped bare.

"Come in, man," he shouted to my timid knock on the door of the staffroom. He was sitting behind a table with the ash-plant laid out in front of him. He had a little black notebook open in front of him and he was thumbing through it.

"What is this?" he asked abruptly, holding it up for me to see.

"A—notebook—Father," I faltered, my mind full of thoughts of the Inquisition and all kinds of subtle mental and physical torture. His start, so strange and unexpected, completely broke me down and I could feel my legs weakening.

"What's in it?"

"I don't know, Father."

"Sit, man, sit!" he bellowed.

"Your name?" he asked, as if the events of the previous evening, when I had stood there with him in the presence of my father and Jem Roche, had slipped his memory already. It was just a trick of his, I knew, to disconcert me and indicate that I could not count on his previous good will.

"John Foley, Father."

"Now, Master Foley," he said in a threatening tone and leafed slowly and with a quiet menace through the notebook, "I'll tell you what's in it. Here I have a record—a full and well-documented record—of all the activities, good and bad, of every boy in this college."

He stopped at a page and read.

"Foley, John," he paused dramatically, stabbing his finger at the page, and stared at me.

"It's all here, Master Foley—like the book of the Recording Angel—your virtues and your crimes writ large!"

I trembled and looked down at my fingers, knotting and unknotting in my lap. He began to read out items, slurring over phrases, skipping bits, mumbling quietly, but every now and again shooting out a few words that hung over my head like a sword.

"Let me see, let me see ... SLACKER AT GAMES ...especially team-games. Competent—handball . . . but . . . BROKE WINDOW IN STUDY-HALL WITH HANDBALL . . . Mmmmmmmm! . . . Academic record—satisfactory ... Hm! ... Discipline ... good ... generally ... FOUND IN COMPANY OF BOYS SMOKING!!"

"Are you a smoker, Master Foley?"

"No, Father," I said eagerly, pleased at being able to tell the truth.

"Show me your fingers."

I held out my hands for inspection. He examined them, turned them over and seemed satisfied.

"What were you doing in the company of boys breaking the rules then?"

"I was sick in bed, Father, and they came in."

"Be more careful of the company you keep, Master Foley, or you will find yourself in trouble," he said severely, as if I had had any choice in the matter. Father Turley had come in and found them smoking in the locker-room and been angry with me because I had been unco-operative.

He looked at the notebook again.

"Mmmm . . . Mmmm . . . UNPUNCTUALITY . . . rising in the morning . . . in the classroom . . . training sessions . . . CAUGHT TALKING IN THE STUDY-HALL . . . SEVERAL TIMES! . . . READING COMICS . . . RECEIVING FOOD PARCELS . . ."

He struck the table with his fist.

"Is your food inadequate, Master Foley?"

"No, Father," I lied.

"Then why does your mother send you a cake of brown bread and a pound of butter almost every week?"

"I—I—like the bread she makes, and—and—she—keeps sending it," I stammered, "and—I don't like anything—except country butter."

"You will write immediately and tell your mother to send no more parcels."

"I have written, Father. She won't send any more."

"I'm glad to hear it," he said.

"Now, Master Foley," he continued in a more reasonable tone, "your record—all things considered—is not a bad one, as I had occasion to tell your father yesterday. I want you to keep it that way."

"Yes, Father," I said, amazed at the tolerant attitude he was taking to my vices.

"Now, I want you to look me in the eye and tell me what you know of this theft."

I lifted my face to look at him. His eye was so stern and terrifying, his face so inflexibly set against wrongdoing, that I faltered and let my eyes fall.

"Look at me, man!"

I raised my head and his eyes burned through me.

"Well?"

"I know nothing, Father."

"Did you take it?"

"No, Father."

"Do you know who did?"

"No, Father."

Please God, I prayed, don't let him ask me about the loaf of bread. I'll put the price of the loaf in the Poor-Box and never do it again—even if I'm going to starve. Punish me, if you like, by making me die of hunger in the middle of the desert or at the North Pole, when I grow up, but, please, don't let him find out and half-kill me and then expel me.

"Have you seen any boy or boys eating cake lately or bringing butter to the table?"

"No, Father."

"Think carefully, man, before you answer."

"Yes, Father. I didn't see anything."

He looked at me in his skewering, inquisitorial way, for a solid half minute, before he said slowly, "I believe you, Master Foley. You may go."

I rose, knocking over the chair in my eagerness. As I picked it up and turned to go, he said, "I want you to promise one thing, Master Foley. I want you to keep your eyes opened and your ears to the ground and to report back to me anything suspicious that you may see or hear. Is that clear?"

"Yes, Father."

"It is everyone's duty to help in this investigation."

"Yes, Father."

"Send in the next boy," he said by way of dismissal.

He was leafing through the notebook again, as I eased my way out and clicked the door shut behind me.

CHAPTER TEN

ALL evening the investigations went on, boys coming and going, anxious on the way out, grinning and winking at their friends, as they came back. I could not concentrate on my work. A voice was singing in my head, telling me I was free, not under suspicion, my record—all things considered—not a bad one.

It seemed an appropriate time for my Game. My mind swung around to it in the slow, lazy way it had, the thought suffusing my consciousness in a warm glow of anticipation. It was like opening a secret door into a private garden and closing it behind me, shutting out everything and everyone. Something to retire to, something to do when I was elated—as I was now—or, as so frequently happened, when I was depressed. I waited, getting more and more impatient, for the bell that would signal the end of study and time for bed. When it went, I drifted off in a dreamy way to the lavatory, deliberately slowing the pace to tease myself and prolong the pleasure. Once inside with the door locked, the Game began.

It was a strange and mysterious game that had come to me out of sleep one night, in my bed at home, during my twelfth—or it might have been my thirteenth—year. I awoke to a pleasant tingling between my thighs. My legs were jerking in a frantic way and then a most wonderfully sweet and intense sensation of pleasure spread through my loins and all over my body. It was like a lovely, happy dream, but I knew it was real, because Tom sat up crossly in his bed and shouted, "What's all the kicking about? Will you stop making noise and go asleep!"

I did go to sleep. Almost immediately, it seemed to me. In the morning, I wondered if it had really happened. I wouldn't ask Tom about a thing like that. But I waited, and it happened again—a beautiful, exciting sensation of release. It was so wonderful that I began to experiment to see if I could induce it at will. I threshed about wildly with my legs, but nothing happened, except that Tom awoke again and reported in the morning that I had been kicking the bedclothes all over the place.

It was quite a while before I stumbled on it by accident one night. My penis, which did strange things when I was asleep, was now doing them when I was awake. I stuffed it between my thighs, because it embarrassed me to have it behave like that, and felt a strange and tingling sensation. I began to move my legs— slowly, so that Tom would have nothing to report—and felt it build up, until, Tom and everything forgotten, I pedalled madly, like a racing cyclist, my heart pounding, elated, triumphant, because I knew it was within reach. And then, it burst with a rainbow shower of sweetness all over me, and I lay back, happy, happy, happy with my beautiful, new Game.

Afterwards, I sometimes felt sad and lonely. I was aware of a void somewhere in my life—a longing for something, I didn't know what—a desert emptiness across which I was stumbling, in the hope of meeting. . . . What? Though the image and the location might change, one thing never did. I saw myself as an individual, alone, not wanting to be alone. But isolated, islanded in an infinity of space, with the chilled dread that I was moving away from, instead of towards life.

It was like eating a plum and tasting some of the bitterness of the stone at the end. But mostly—at the beginning especially— it was a thrilling experience, an exciting, secret world on the magic borderland of sleep.

Once—her presence in some way giving spice to the Game—I had played it when Moll was with me. We were lying on the grass by the Pool down in the bogs, after splashing about in the shallow water—brown where it slid over smooth stones—dressed only in ragged knickers, castaways of Moll's which she had saved for this purpose. We were wearing the knickers, not for the sake of decency or modesty, but, because we had observed on our yearly trip to the sea that the best people wore bathing suits, and we liked to pretend that we were on our holidays at some exclusive resort.

It was a warm, drowsy day. Smell of spearmint and crushed grass and peaty water. A trickle and gurgle through the stones. Bees in the purple bells of the foxglove. White, feathered clouds drifting high. Moll was teasing me in a gentle way, drawing a stem of white clover across my face. The scent of it was pleasant and its touch was soft. I lay on my back, my eyes closed, and gave myself up to lethargy. Sometimes her hand brushed my face, warm, alive. I put out my own hand and ran it in a light, tickling way up her arm. The contact was pleasant, intimate and in some way exciting. I felt a languorous warmth rippling through me. My body was preparing itself for the Game. I began to move rhythmically. Contact with Moll seemed to refine all my sensations, giving them an exquisite beauty and depth, sending quivers of pleasure shooting through me. My body seemed to expand and fill the universe. At the peak, I pulled her on top of me and our flesh seemed to fuse in showers of stars and a white heat like love.

It all happened so quickly that I was almost as surprised as Moll was.

"You hurt me," she said, "and you tore my togs."

"I was hugging you," I said, "don't you like me hugging you?"

"You did it too hard."

"I didn't mean to, Moll, you know that. I'll hug you soft, if you like."

"All right!" Moll was always quick to forgive.

"Don't you like me hugging you?" I asked.

"When you do it easy."

I knelt up and put my arms around her. Her cheek was soft against mine. Her hair smelled clean and fresh. I felt very gentle and protective towards her. I gave her a slight squeeze, before she broke away from me, laughing.

"You're funny," she said. But she said it in a nice way, a friendly, appreciative way that pleased me.

We lay down again, our outstretched hands touching. Moll had kicked off her torn knickers and flung it on a branch to dry. I noticed her body, as if for the first time. It was very nice and smooth, rounder than mine, almost as big, the flesh beautifully distributed.

"Moll," I said on sudden impulse, "it's nice bathing without togs, isn't it? We'll throw away those old knickers and not use them any more."

"Whatever you like," Moll said. "Mine's in ribbons anyway."

"We'll pretend we have nice new togs," I said.

"Yes," Moll laughed and flung up her legs, "look at mine! Blue and white stripes."

I ripped off mine and flung them on the bush with Moll's. "Look at mine! Red, with a silver buckle on the belt."

We laughed and rolled over and over until our bodies met, and we lay there, laughing and spluttering with our arms around each other.

Moll pulled two blades of grass and stuck one of them into my mouth.

"Wouldn't it be nice," she said, "if you and I could go away and live together where it was always summer. We'd lie in the sun . . ."

"In our togs!" I said and we laughed.

"And talk, and there'd be no more school . . ."

"Or fights . . ."

"Or them . . ."

"Or anybody . . ."

"Or anything . . ."

"But us!"

"Together."

"Always!"

Whenever I played my Game after that, the day at the Pool was my starting point and Moll's presence—and lately her imagined participation—the spice to my imagination. I had often thought of telling her about it, but the knowledge that she could never enjoy the ecstasy of it herself always restrained me. She was made differently from me—a difference that I was now finding intriguing and exciting beyond anything in my experience—and, though I could think of intimate ways (and inflame my imagination in the thinking) in which she could contribute to my pleasure, I could not think—and was saddened by my inability—how I might help her to achieve the fulfilment that I got out of my Game.

There was no seminal flow—as I have since learned to call it—in those early days. It had begun to come lately, a glutinous, pale secretion that puzzled and worried me. I was afraid that it was the marrow leaking from my bones or some other equally vital substance without which I might shrivel up and die. I watched myself anxiously for days after the first discharge, wondering when I would notice the decline and which of my faculties it would strike first.

But nothing seemed to have changed, no weakening of the limbs, no decay. Nothing that I could see or feel. But I knew that there were terrible patient diseases like cancer that hid themselves away in the flesh for years, burrowing into the cells, gnawing through the tissue like worms in wood, until one day, without warning, the whole structure would collapse in a heap of dust, and, intermittently, I was afraid. But never enough to abandon my Game entirely. I knew that, sooner or later, I would have to ask someone about it. But whom could I ask! And, in the meantime, it was my pleasure, my consolation, my secret delight— as soothing to the spirit as the answer to long prayer.

The interrogation continued next day. Senior boys were called out in turn during the morning class. By lunch-time it was over and the thief had not been found. Everyone was uneasy and rebellious. Wherever groups were gathered there was only one topic of discussion. Anger with the thief was growing. Everyone was hungry. Those with money had sent out with the day-boys for rolls or penny baps. But Father Creame had all the day-boys searched when they came back, and the bread was taken off them. The Seniors went round threatening their own form of reprisals against the culprit and against anyone who was withholding information unless they confessed immediately. Everybody was envious of the odd boy, here and there, who had a small appetite, and went round boasting that he wasn't the least bit hungry.

Big Tom Traynor, whose appetite was huge, spent most of the day holding his belly and groaning. But before tea he carried off a neat coup which made him the admiration—and the envy— of the College. It was one of those drizzly September days that improve and capture the last heat of Summer late in the day. After class, Black Jack ordered everyone to bring his overcoat, and took us for a walk out to Hunter's Rock.

There was mist standing off the river when we set out and a luminous circle of vapour scarfing the sun. By the time we got to the Railway Bridge, it was gone and, when we came to the place where the river turned right sharply to meet the road again, overcoats were off and everyone was panting and wiping his face with his handkerchief. We stopped there to sit on a wall, and then were off into the fields to stave off the hunger with blackberries and sloes, and even the sticky, unappetising haws.

I found a field of greencrop and initiated Kieran Maher and four other city boys into the art of eating raw turnip. Often, at home, on our way from school we had nipped in over a ditch and pulled a likely turnip—about the thickness of a man's fist—bashed it this way and that against the iron bars of a gate or a sharp stone to get rid of the clay and open it for eating, then bit into the sweet, juicy heart as we strolled along, holding it by the leaves and waving it about like a torch. I helped prepare turnips for the others and we lay in the sun, eating.

When the whistle went for the return, we raced back to retrieve our overcoats—heavy as lead—from the pile where we had dumped them. There were groans, as we flung them across our shoulders, or bundled them up loosely to carry them awkwardly like armfuls of hay.

Big Tom Traynor was there, looking everyone over speculatively and offering to carry back an overcoat for anyone who would give him half a slice of bread from his ration at tea-time. Several boys of a delicate, weedy kind were taking his offer and one big arm was already well loaded down.

On the way back he puffed along like a stout coat-rack, his face a boiled beetroot, his glasses fogged with effort, sweat trickling from them like rain down a window-pane. Three miles back, across the bridge and through the town to face the final barrier—The Hill—so steep that there was only a footway, up which one scrabbled and clawed as up a mountain-side, or long flights of steps to draw the chest in like a concertina and leave one gasping as one stumbled in through the little green door into the College yard and collapsed in a sodden heap on the steps down to the alleys, shattered, windbroken, gulping, heaving, faint almost to syncope.

Big Tom had five slices of bread for tea as well as his own three and the eyes of everyone were on him. He had them piled in a tidy heap in front of him. Every time he took a new piece, he held it above his head and all eyes were raised, as if we were in Church for the Elevation of the Host. He finished them all, too, while the rest of us rounded up stray crumbs with our fingers and spooned the tea-leaves from our cups.

He never repeated his triumph. All the weaklings were immediately canvassed by their best friends and their future leavings—for years ahead—were bagsed. There was to be no repetition by anyone of Tom's inspired coup.

The tension and the frustration grew. An edge of bitchiness fanged through the corridors and yards. Friendships were hammered into hatred. Suspicion bred like worms in the carcase of our hunger. In such an atmosphere it was too much to expect that my father's visit would be charitably ignored.

After tea, I walked into the Recreation Hall in search of Kieran Maher. As I stood, looking around, a group of Fifth Year boys, sniggering in a corner, fell ominously silent and turned towards me. One of them, a squat, belligerent fellow, with the reputation of being a "hard man", thrust himself forward.

"Would you," he said, in broad parody of uncouth, peasant speech, "be anny chance be lookin' for de head man?"

His companions guffawed. I turned on my heel to go. Hickey, the squat boy, raced to the door and stood with his back to it, barring my way.

"That was your old fellow the other night, in the Study-Hall, wasn't it?"

"What if it was?" I said quietly. I wasn't afraid of Hickey or of the others. But I didn't want any row with them, especially not in defence of my father.

"Nothing," he grinned, "nothing. Only (he appealed to the others over my head) they were a right looking pair of bogmen, lads, weren't they?"

They laughed again.

"Listen!" I said, angered by their ridicule. "I don't have to defend my father to you or anyone. I never asked you about your father, did I? For all I know—or care—you mightn't even have one."

It wasn't a very inspired attempt at insult, but it had the effect of putting Hickey himself on the defensive.

"Take that back, you scum of a drunken bogman," he shouted, "or I'll push your face in."

"You take back what you said."

"I wants to see de head man," he mimicked.

His criticism of my father hurt me. What hurt me most was the fact that the way he saw my father was exactly the way I had seen him so often myself.

"You're a bloody snob, that's all," I shouted.

The recognition that if he was a snob, then I had been a snob, too, all those years, was no comfort to me.

"You think," I continued, my anger getting the better of caution and good sense, "that because a man doesn't pronounce his words properly, because he sometimes gets drunk and makes a fool of himself, that that's all there's to him. What do you know of my father? What's your idea of a good father anyway? Some stuck-up toff of a Bank Manager that plays golf at the week-ends and talks as if he had a mouthful of hot potatoes? Maybe that's the kind of old fellow you have. Well, if it is, you can stuff him."

I had sometimes imagined that it would be pleasant if my father had been a Bank Manager and wore a ring on his finger and knocked back a few civilised drams of brandy in the club-house with collar-and-tie citizens, instead of guzzling like a caveman in Wat Wadding's bottling store with the lame black-smith and Jem Roche.

"Leave my old fellow out of this," he shouted.

"If you have an old fellow at all," I repeated recklessly now that things had gone so far.

He lashed out suddenly with his fist, hitting me on the side of the face. The blow hurt, but it took some of the pain out of my anger. In a queer way, I felt obliged to him for hitting me. It was taking the quarrel on to more acceptable ground. I could stand up to blows, but criticism of my father left me defenceless. It was too easy. I had been doing it myself all my life. Now, Hickey, by doing it too, was forcing me to see myself as I really was. It was not pleasant seeing myself as another Hickey.

I was clumsy and awkward with my fists, had never had a real fight, except with Tom, the last being years before, and, even with him, it was mostly standing at a distance, like two warriors from the Táin, casting stones and abuse at each other as a preliminary to more serious engagement. We rarely got beyond preliminaries and the few times we did we had bit and clawed and kicked each other like savages, until Ned Rafter booted and cuffed us apart as he might a pair of mad dogs.

I lowered my head and went for Hickey's belly. My fist sank in with a soft plop and he deflated like a balloon. He brought his knee up into my groin in a vicious jab. I grabbed him by the hair and battered his head against the door.

"Fight fair!" his friends shouted. It seemed to me that Hickey was more in need of such admonition than I was.

It was ironic that I should be fighting in defence of my father. I wondered if I was fighting for him or for myself. Had I really meant what I had said in his favour? If I hadn't, I was just a hypocrite.

We were locked together, our arms about each other like Roman wrestlers. Hickey was trying to get his heel behind mine to throw me. I could smell the sour sweat of his body as we grappled.

"Come on, bogman," he challenged, confident from the searching test his muscles were giving me that he was stronger than I was.

It was true—unpalatable as it might be for me, his severest critic, to acknowledge—what I had said about my father. There *was* more to him than the sum of his faults. He had courage, more courage than I had, strength, determination. He had, by his patient labour and skill, built up a good farm out of nothing. He was loyal, generous, too, in his own way. I had always known these things, but had never felt them deep in my blood as I was feeling them now.

We rolled over and over on the floor and came to rest against a wall, Hickey sitting astride me, holding my wrists with one hand, pummelling me with the other.

"Snob!" I shouted with a kind of exaltation, "stinking, rotten snob!"

I was shouting at myself, as much as at Hickey, exorcising the devils that had possessed me for so long.

I didn't care any longer what Hickey thought. He was nothing to me. His opinion could not hurt me. In a way that would have bewildered him had he known it, he was doing me a favour. He was battering into me—or, more precisely, because it had always been there in the dark opacity of my subconsciousness—he was battering *out* of me an acknowledgment of my father's basic humanity.

I gave a sudden heave upwards and unseated Hickey. With legs and arms locked we rolled about the floor. I grabbed his greasy, black hair again and forced his head back. He put the heel of his hand under my chin and pushed. We both let go at the same time and shot apart. His friends helped Hickey up and he came at me again. I put the ping-pong table between me and him.

"Get away, you snob," I said. "My father may be all the things you think he is, but he's no snob. There's nothing worse than being a snob."

Hickey didn't relish being labelled a snob. It was odd to see him on the defensive.

"Hey, cut that out," he roared.

He knew that, if I said it a few more times, the curious crowd that had gathered about us, as we fought, might latch on to it. Some wit might hang a nickname, like "Duke" or worse, about his neck and he would be greeted with it derisively wherever he went.

Blood was trickling from my nose into the corner of my mouth. My body felt as if it had gone through a threshing drum. But I didn't care. I was more at peace with myself than I had ever been before. I felt grateful to Hickey, didn't hate him at all, was sorry, already, that I had called him a snob. I stood there, wiping my nose with a handkerchief, a ridiculous urge to laugh making me twist my face into a painful grimace.

"Call it quits," someone shouted. "You've had enough."

I dropped my arms and the laugh I had been trying to control burst out. It was a hysterical sound, over which I had no control.

Kieran Maher stepped out of the crowd and gave me a friendly tap on the back.

"Come on," he said. "Let's get out of here."

"Listen," Hickey called after me, "I don't give a damn what your old fellow does, or what he is. But mind you don't call me names like that again."

"As long as you don't give me reason to," I said.

"Jeez," he explained to everyone, "I was only having a bit of fun."

"Forget it then," I said without rancour.

"Hey," Kieran exclaimed in admiration, as we looked down over the railings into the sombre gardens, "you were mad in there. I never saw you like that before."

"Tell me one thing, Kieran. I want the truth, mind. Were you ever ashamed of your father?"

"Now and again, I suppose," he said, after some thought, "when he'd done something silly—came home a bit jarred, made a scene in public. Once or twice, maybe, in my life."

"Don't ever be," I told him solemnly, as if I were come hot from heaven with the revelation. "He's the only father you'll ever have."

Kieran laughed.

"Hickey's made quite a philosopher out of you," he said. "You'd better come and wash that nose and try to stop the bleeding."

CHAPTER ELEVEN

NEXT day, Father Creame was on the warpath again. In the course of the morning, we were called individually from our classrooms and ordered to open our trunks and cases, which were stacked in the Boxroom, and turn out everything they contained on the floor, while Father Creame stood suspiciously over us, raking through bundles of clothes with his ash-plant.

When my turn came, I found him there beside a pile of slim paperbacks with garish covers, rumpled and smelling of cheap hair-oil, which he had confiscated in the search. There were Mills & Boone romances, racing stories by Nat Gould, Cowboy Stories, copies of Ring Magazine and The Wide World Magazine and Photographic Magazines with nice—but bare-looking—girls on the covers.

"Well, Master Foley," he said in a tone which, I felt, was not completely hostile, "have you anything to declare?"

"No, Father," I said, not really sure of his meaning, "I didn't see or hear anything."

"Your case, man," he said, "open it!"

I opened it and turned out the contents, which were few—a pair of brown shoes, needing repair, my silver napkin-ring in its square cardboard box, a couple of handkerchiefs, the stone Moll had given me, a box with needles, thread, buttons and darning wool, things for polishing, a few old letters from my mother, and very little else.

Father Creame picked up a green Autograph Book and opened it.

"Kieran Maher, Griffith Avenue," he read out. "This is not yours!"

"He gave it to me, Father," I said, blushing at the thought that must be in his mind.

"Is that the truth, Master Foley?"

"Yes, Father. He's my best friend. It's an old one. He got a new one for his birthday—a bigger one."

"Very well."

I felt weak with relief. There was a trickle of sweat under my armpits. He turned a few pages.

"There's nothing offensive here, I hope."

I said nothing, because I wasn't sure what he could mean. He read:

"Remember me on the river,
Remember me on the lake,
Remember me on your wedding day
And send me a piece of the cake.

MOLL."

"Who is this—person (he made it sound very distasteful) who signs herself Moll?"

"My sister, Father."

He handed it to me.

"Very well! You may put them back."

All through the day the rumours flew. A boy in Leaving Cert. had run away and when his trunk was forced the missing things had been found. Later, it was revealed that he had been sick in bed all the time and his case empty. Another boy was locked in Father Turley's room without food or water until he confessed that the two-pound chocolate box (empty) found in his trunk was the stolen one. Maggie Tulloher, the kitchen-maid, had taken the things and given them to one of the Seniors, who had—under severe grilling—admitted all to Father Creame, and, furthermore, admitted to having carried on an affair with her—kissing and smooching in the Coal Hole—and both would have to be married, for the sake of decency, on account of their intimate and compromising relationship. None of which proved to be true.

During tea—another rationed reprisal—a boy from Fifth Year, named Denis Wheeler, was called out. He was a big, surly fellow, spiteful in his ways with the Juniors, offensive in his language, the leader of an unruly element among the Seniors. His nickname, The Bike, had grown up in the curious manner in which most schoolboy nicknames evolve. He had something in common with Kehoe, the boy who had frightened me out of my football boots. He was in the habit of making free with younger— and smaller—boys' things, picking up a hurley here, a jersey there, for the duration of a match and returning them—if he bothered to return them at all—torn or splintered or abused in some way. Because of this he had been dubbed Free-Wheeler, which suggested a bicycle. So, The Bike he became and The Bike he remained. No one would be sorry to see The Bike convicted and expelled.

Excitement grew when Matt Guerin, the owner of the stolen parcel, was called out. Matt, the son of a rich shopkeeper from Cork, had the same kind of pale, puffy features as a flour miller. His podgy hands, dimpled like a baby's, were forever on their way to his mouth, slipping in sweets and toffees and biscuits and thick wedges of rich fruit-cake. He had a limitless supply of money and was continually sending out with day-boys for more grub. His nickname was Baby Beef and he was regarded as mean. Once, I had come across him dumping a whole cake in the Coal Hole, after allowing it to turn into a putrid mess of green mould in his case, rather than share it with anyone. He had no friends except a few toadies who flattered him for the sake of the odd crumb which he threw their way. I didn't like him very much, but I was prepared to tolerate him because he minded his own business and was not a bully.

After prayers and Benediction, Father Creame, wearing his executioner's mask, was waiting for us in the Study-Hall. With him, like a cut-down corpse, was Wheeler, all the bravado and toughness drained out of him like wind from a balloon, a sad, sagging hulk of a fellow, desperate with fear. Father Creame had a new ash-plant, longer, more terrible than any he had used before. He was flexing it lightly with his two hands, testing its suppleness. When we were all in place, he rapped on the desk for order. The silence was painful.

"Stand forth, Master Wheeler," he roared.

Wheeler shuffled forward two paces and stood with his head lowered.

"Now, men," he continued, "Master Wheeler has a confession to make."

Wheeler, who seemed to be in a comatose state, moved his head sluggishly from side to side like a sick animal, lifted it up slightly, so that I could see his pale tongue licking the dry spittle from lips that were almost blue. Then his mouth began to move like the mouth of a fish when it is landed, but no sound came.

Father Creame drew back the cruel ash-plant and slashed forward and down at his behind. The sound, as it struck, was sharp as the crack of a whip. Wheeler did three things simultaneously. He straightened up, leaped forward and clasped his behind.

"Your confession, man!" Father Creame bellowed.

"I—I—I. . . ." Wheeler's mouth twisted and writhed and the sound choked off into nothingness again, though the lips were still twitching and, down in his throat, his Adam's apple was trembling.

The ash plant cut mercilessly down again.

"I—I stole. I STOLE!" Wheeler screamed.

"Go on!" Father Creame was inexorable.

"I stole the parcel from Guerin's case. . . ."

"AND," Father Creame thundered, "AND. . . ."

". . . And I'm sorry . . . and . . . I'll make restitution."

"AND. . . . Come on, man, your apology."

". . . And I apologise for the trouble I caused and—the—lies I told . . . and—and . . . everything."

He looked out towards us in an appealing way and dropped his head again.

"Now," Father Creame began solemnly, as if he were conducting a religious ceremony. "It is my duty to punish you for this heinous offence and to banish you forever—forever, I said—from this College. You will leave here under disgrace. I have already written to your parents to acquaint them of your expulsion and the reasons for it. Your name will be struck from the school records, so that no trace of you may be left to sully the good name of this establishment. Go, like the outcast Cain. You are not fit to associate with decent, God-fearing people."

Then, turning to us, he continued.

"Men, let what you are about to witness be a warning to you that the rules of this College are not to be flouted lightly. Let everyone who contemplates wrongdoing in his heart see himself in the place of this wretched thief. This, men, is the just reward for insubordination. This the decreed penalty for crime."

He turned again to Wheeler, who seemed to have shrivelled

up and fallen in on himself progressively, as the speech went on. Every word seemed to have battered and dented him, until he looked as insubstantial as a collapsed bladder.

"Hold out your hand, man!"

Wheeler extended his right hand, the palm upwards, the arm bent, a look of intolerable strain on his face, a trembling rigidity in the arm, as if it were holding a fearsome weight.

All through Father Creame's speech I had been watching Wheeler and was so shocked and frightened by the change I saw in him that, though I never liked him and had often been bullied by him, and knew that he was a wicked boy to steal, and deserved punishment, I felt an overwhelming pity for him. It was intolerable to have his weakness exhibited like this for our edification and terrorisation, a betrayal of his human dignity to flay him before our eyes. I did what I had not done for years. I wet my trousers in my agitation.

"Oh, God," I said, "don't let him break down or scream, or I will, too."

Already I could feel the tears in my eyes. My stomach was threatening to heave and there was a taste of vomit in my mouth.

"Straight, man!" Father Creame shouted.

He raised the ash-plant and brought it down with all his might. There was a gasp. The force of it brought Wheeler's arm down. His left shoulder rose and he almost stumbled. He recovered himself with a dreadful shaking of the hand and held it out again. His eyes were almost closed, his whole face concentrated in agony. The ash-plant fell a second time with a sickening thud into the meaty part of his hand behind the thumb.

"Keep it straight, man!" Father Creame shouted, his face flushed with the strain.

"Take this . . . and this . . . and this . . . and this."

The ash-plant rose and fell so fast that it was a sweeping blur. It struck Wheeler on the wrist, the palm, the fingertips, the thumb. His face was a twisted scream of pain, but no sound came.

"The other hand!" Father Creame drew up the loose sleeve of his habit and prepared to continue.

Wheeler, his right hand quivering and fluttering by his side like the wing of a stricken bird, held out his left hand. His face had the pallor of death. His nose was pinched and blue. I was afraid he was going to collapse. But he held on, rising and falling under the successive blows—terrible, sweeping lashes—Father Creame straining on tiptoe and bringing all his massive weight down on the stroke. Six more, and when he had finished Wheeler stood there, nursing his swollen hands under his arms and swaying about like a drunken man.

"Your right hand, again!" Father Creame stood over him, stern and inflexible.

"Let this be a solemn warning to you all the days of your life."

Poor Wheeler looked at him like a beaten hound at his master. He was near to exhaustion. But Father Creame was not to be moved.

"Your hand, man!"

It was like a second crucifixion to watch it all over again. Only this time it was so much worse, because his hands were shaking lumps of raw meat. I could not look any longer. I sat there, my hands over my eyes, counting the strokes, quaking lest he break down or cry out, saying, "Oh, God, it's wrong, it's wrong. Don't let him break down. Let him have that much to take away with him."

I felt a great hatred of Father Creame and all authority rise in me. I began to think how noble a thing it would be to commit some crime deliberately, so that he might flog me and kill me and then be up for murder and die roaring with the hangman kicking him into eternity.

Stroke followed relentless stroke, until the sound of wood on flesh became unbearable, an obscene ritual of hideous torture to appease some barbarous deity, Moloch, Baal, Huitzilopochtli.

When I looked again, it was over. Wheeler stood there, staring dully at his poor, ruined hands. His knees were bent and almost touching. But there was a stubborn set to his haunched shoulders. He had not broken down. A silence like death was over the Study-Hall. When boys' eyes met, I noticed them drop away, as if they had been partners in a shameful thing. Wheeler was still looking at his hands—uncomprehendingly, like a man after an accident, staring curiously at his mangled limbs. Father Creame brought down the ash-plant on the desk.

"Get out!" he roared. "Pack your case and leave this College, first thing in the morning."

Wheeler shuffled off like a punch-drunk boxer. When he reached the door he had difficulty in getting his hands round the knob. A boy stood up to open it for him, but Father Creame bellowed him down, and we had to suffer the further embarrassment of watching him trying to manoeuvre it open with his forearms. When he had opened it and dragged it to after him again, Father Creame struck the desk—more lightly this time—and spoke.

"Now, men, let that be a lesson to you!"

He pushed the ash-plant into the slit at the side of his habit and came down from the rostrum.

"One final thing," he said. "Bread rationing continues until the end of the week. This theft is a reflection on you all. No one came forward with assistance. No one co-operated in the apprehension of the thief. You must purge yourselves of this contempt. All of you must suffer, because some of you are undoubtedly accessories. You may call it rough and ready justice, men, but justice it is—until such time as you learn to do your duty.

"That will be all," he dismissed us with a slight nod of his head. "Continue with your study." And off he went, striding in that juggernaut way of his and slamming the door behind him.

I was feeling sick, and when I thought he was safely off the premises, I asked Father Turley to let me out. I went to the lavatory and retched and spat bile but could not be sick. Then I went to the dormitory and changed my trousers. On my way back down, I heard water running in the Washroom and looked in. Wheeler was there holding his hands, blue and raw like butchers' meat, under the tap. He looked at me indifferently. I felt that I should say something that would convey to him that I did not approve of what had happened, that I felt for him and was appalled at the savagery of his punishment. But I had no words.

"Hel—lo," I said lamely.

He looked at me with fierce hatred and spat into the washbasin.

"Fuck off, you rotten bastard!" he hissed, "and leave me alone."

I closed the door in a hurry. Tears came unchecked. I rushed back to the lavatory and vomited my guts all over the seat.

CHAPTER TWELVE

SUMMER again. The Intermediate over. A load of irrelevance off our poor, muddled minds.

Tom was out of bed now, moving around again, sitting, strangely for him, during the afternoon of a busy day, watching the rest of us making hay. His skin was still pale and girl-like, his long wrists and bony hands projecting yards beyond his cuffs. Chewing grass coolly in the shade, while the rest of us sweated.

Dan Morgan, who had been hired to take his place, reminisced, as we worked, reminding me of how we had stood together at Bible History, and asking me—because rumours of the War had seeped even into his sluggish brain—what part of England Germany was in.

"Your father seems to have changed his mind," my mother had written in a surprised tone, shortly after his visit to College. "He came back last night after a funeral and said he was letting you finish your exam. He's gone off now to see if he can get Dan Morgan to take Tom's place on the land. Tom is much improved. Work hard like a good boy. Your future depends on it."

I went over to where Tom was sitting and took a drink from the water-bucket.

"You've the life!"

"I'm fed up with it," he said.

"Enjoy it while you can, boy. It won't last much longer."

Dr. Reilly was pleased with his progress. He had told my mother he was reasonably certain that he would make a full recovery and that there would be no damage to the heart. My father, whose judgement in the matter we were still awaiting with trepidation, kept his counsel and said nothing. Sometimes, over meals, I saw him looking at me speculatively and I wondered what he was planning.

He was getting old, my father. His kidneys—never good— seemed to be getting worse all the time. He rose several times at night, often waking me with his stumbling about. In the fields, where he rarely appeared any longer, except to bring the three o'clock tea on fine days, he would scarcely have arrived when he was hurrying over to the shelter of the hedge or through a gap into a neighbouring field. Thenhe would reappear, flushed and short of breath, to sit with his back against a haycock and breathe wheezily, like a squeaky bellows, while we drank the sweet tea and ate thick cuts of brown bread, so hot that the butter had melted into them.

Then, because he was ever an impatient man and hated to see anyone sitting down on a fine day when there was work to be done, he would grab a pike and set to worrying a pile of hay that Ned Rafter had gathered in with the rake, and shame us into rising with our mouths still chewing. And, when he had us all bent into the work again, he would lay aside the pike and gather the tea-things together and put them into the basket and amble off, stopping as he passed to pull a few stray strands from a cock or tighten a rope. Sometimes, he would sit at the gate watching us and, perhaps, pull out his pipe and make a clumsy attempt to light it. And then his bellow would resound over the resonant afternoon and I would run, damp from the heat and uncomfortable with hayseed, to fill it for him and hold out the lighted match, while he drew shallow breaths and pressed the red top down with the matchbox. After a few puffs, he would put it indifferently away and cough and spit mucus into the grass and say, "It don't taste the same any more."

His drinking habits were changing, too. Sometimes, after a moderate drinking session, he returned and rushed out suddenly in the middle of a meal to get sick, and afterwards took to his bed for a day. More and more a bottle of stout became his drink and he avoided spirits, except on the odd occasion—seed-time, harvest-time—when he went in the pony-and-car (never the Croydon, which was not used for business) to Wexford.

It was a ritual with him to leave the pony in a yard down on the quays and begin the day with a glass of whiskey in John Parker's near the Bull-ring. Then he was off to Stafford's to see about seeds or with a little bag of barley for bushelling. Afterwards we had dinner—lunch they called it—in Love's Café, always the same,

Roast Beef and Rice Pudding. Nothing else interested my father. The girl who took our order would shout in through the hatch, "Roast Beef and veg.—two gents." and when we had finished, he always asked me if I'd had enough and insisted on the girl bringing more, because he believed in getting value for money, and 2/3 entitled us to the best. I liked being described as a gent. The food was always good. I could think of no greater luxury than dining in Love's Café—the name was an added touch of romance. Jack Keating, the vet. who came from out our way, had his dinner there every day of the year, which seemed to me to be the epitome of gracious living.

My father always slipped the man in the yard a shilling for himself, when we went back to yoke the pony for the journey home. Jimmy, the man's name was. He smelled of porter and had a greasy, dirty complexion and wore a greasy sailor's cap and a greasy suit, very shiny at the elbows and seat, with irregular-shaped stains on it that smelled like train-oil. He wore rubber boots with the tops turned down and walked with a roll. He told me once that he had spent his life sailing the world and had rounded the Horn in a windjammer, when the waves were fifty feet high and men had to lash themselves to the mast for fear of being swept overboard.

Sometimes, after work in the evenings, my father got out his blackthorn stick and ambled through the fields, stopping to cut sharply at purple thistles, leaning on a gate to inspect a field of corn, giving an affectionate scratch to the backs of cattle that interrupted their grazing momentarily to look up at him with mildly curious eyes.

I liked to go with him, because he was always gentle then, stopping to peer at young blackbirds in a nest, careful to rearrange the foliage and preserve their secrecy before he left, talking of crops and yields, his weather eye on the islands and the clouds riding high.

One evening, as we sat at the edge of a turnip-field, looking at the tiny seedlings glistening in the sun like lines of green sequins on brown corduroy, my father spoke to me, his voice tinged with a curious regret.

"Did you never take to the land at all, John, boy?"

The question startled me, because I had just been thinking how beautiful and peaceful it was, how I loved that gentle fall of land away to the Saltees, floating like delicate seabirds on the blue horizon.

"I—I do like it—in—a whole lot of ways," I said lamely, wondering how I could ever explain to myself, let alone to him, how I could love the country in all its moods and at the same time hate the tyranny of the soil.

"Look at those turnips," he said. "Wouldn't it do your heart good to see them! Look at the way they push themselves up, lifting lumps of clay ten times their own weight in a mad rush for their little bit of life."

"They're grand," I said.

Lines of words along a page—ideas springing just as magically to life—affected me in the same way as turnips did my father, but would he ever understand that?

"Walking of an evening through your own field of corn," he said. "The head shooting out and your whole year's work coming to harvest around you. That's no mean thing, boy."

"Yes," I agreed, "if the weather doesn't come and ruin it all."

"Never mind the weather. That's God's will."

"I do be wondering," he continued in a thoughtful way, "when I see clerks and fellows standing behind counters, parcelling up pounds of tea or suits of clothes, what kind of life that is for a man."

"Somebody has to do it, I suppose."

"Tilling the land is a man's job. There'd be nothing without the land."

It occurred to me, then, that if I was ever to reach him, it would have to be in some terms that he understood—terms of the soil and cultivation.

"A man's mind is like the land," I said.

"What do you mean, boy?"

"It's something God gave us to cultivate."

He looked at me in a peculiar way. But he was listening. "Land lying idle is not much good, is it?" I said.

"No good at all, boy."

"A man's mind isn't either. He has to till it, to sow something in it, to make use of it."

"If you put it like that," he said.

"Some land is better than other kinds, more fit for cultivation. Some will grow only rushes."

"Don't I know it!"

"People are like that, too."

"I daresay."

I sensed he was getting bored because I wasn't coming to the point.

"Not every field will grow the same crop," I began again.

"True," he said. "Take wheat for a start. . . ."

"People's minds are like that, too," I hurried on, seeing light at the end of the tunnel. "You grow different crops in them. Some people have the kind of mind that makes good farmers. Some are better suited to be doctors, or priests, or teachers—shop-boys even," I ended hesitantly, making a concession to his prejudice.

He looked at me slowly, not unkindly.

"Yourself, now! What do you think you'd be fitted for?"

"I—I don't know," I admitted helplessly, conscious that the initiative was slipping away from me again.

"You wouldn't want to be a priest, would you?"

"I don't think so."

I knew that I didn't. But I thought it would be injudicious to rule it out entirely. No countryman would dare put himself into the position, where it could be urged against him that he had prevented his son from becoming a priest.

"You think you're not right for the land?"

"Yes."

He tapped his stick thoughtfully against his boot and did not speak for the length of time it took a spider to climb a stalk of grass beside me and launch himself down to earth again on his silvered string.

"That priest said you had a good head on you."

I waited for him to speak again.

"He said you worked hard. Do you?"

"I—think so."

"A man should always work hard and do the best he can—even if he's only cleaning out a henhouse."

"I like studying. It's the same as the land to you. I like it better than anything else."

My father laid his hand on my shoulder to help himself up.

"We'd better be getting back," he said.

"Did I ever tell you your uncle Nick, God rest him, went for a while to a Latin school and had a notion of being a priest?"

"No."

"He had then. But times were hard and nothing could be done about it."

"Was he a scholar?"

"He was in his own way. He read the paper every day and followed the Mass in Latin with the priest."

"I don't think I'd be fit to be a priest," I confessed.

"Never mind, boy. Keep to your books and be whatever you can. It seems to be the only way for you."

We walked back silently in the still evening. Already the first dew was light on the grass, moistening our toecaps to dullness. There was a new easiness between us, an understanding that had no need of words to define and circumscribe it. Inside me, rising like a lark on a bright pillar of air, my spirits soared and sang. The sky out over the islands was still warm with memory of day. A croak of crows, tumbling home to roost, passed overhead, buoyant in the free drift of air. And, over all, the elemental singing in my head. My father had recognised my individuality, my right to be myself, to carve my own destiny out of the unique piece of life that was me.

He said nothing more about it beyond indicating to my mother, when I had gone to bed, that he had no further objections to my return to College. My mother was surprised—and grateful—at his unforced acquiescence, and for the rest of the holidays there was peace in the house.

When the time came for me to go back, he saw me off with a quiet approval that hadn't been there before, and I felt that a new era had opened in my life.

My status in College had changed, too. I was a Senior now, entitled to sleep in the Senior Dormitory, to eat at one of the

Senior tables. I was under pressure from no one, bullied by no one, free to develop myself in my own way. I found courage to speak at College debates. I took a small part in the school play. A sharp eye, developed from my skill at handball, made me a useful enough reserve goalie on the hurling team. I was beginning to enjoy life.

CHAPTER THIRTEEN

Iт was blowy October weather with leaves flying, when Father Turley went out of his mind. He appeared at lunchtime one day, at the window of his room off the Top Dor, overlooking the alleys, naked to the waist—or even beyond; at that height it was impossible to see—and waving a cane. He lunged out like a fencer, weaving and bobbing, and shouting at the top of his voice, as we abandoned our game and craned our necks to look up at him. His words were swept away before they reached us four storeys below.

Flinging his cane aside, he began to throw things down at us, slippers, shoes, books, the pillows off his bed. Then he threw out the bedclothes, the wind catching the sheets, bellying them out, like sails, as they floated over our heads down into the dismal gardens, where they collapsed and died for want of air.

Father Hogan, who had been playing a game of handball, threw on his habit and ran off, tying up his cincture as he went, to find out what was wrong with him. A few minutes afterwards he appeared at the window, from which Father Turley was now flinging chalk in fistfuls, and began to reason with him. But the chalk kept coming, until Father Hogan caught him by the arm and drew him back and pulled down the window and locked it. What happened after that none of us could say, because the whistle went and we were hustled back to our classrooms prematurely.

All afternoon, speculation was rife. Everyone remembered incidents, insignificant at the time, but now, in the light of hindsight, signposting, like beacons for those of us with wit to read, his progress along the road that led to madness. He had a way of scratching his head very lightly, with his fingers crooked over his ears like talons, and grimacing, when he thought no one was looking. He sometimes did it at study, and it was amazing now to find how many boys just happened to look up and catch him in the act.

He had been surprised in the Washroom, strutting before the mirrors, stamping his heels and clicking the fingers of his upraised hands like a Spanish dancer. The boy who surprised him said that, on his entry, Father Turley had brought the palms of both hands together in a smart slap, at the same time clicking his heels and shouting, "Ole!" before pushing past him without a sign of recognition.

Everyone knew that he sometimes talked to himself in his room at night. Now some—more inventive than their neighbours— began to recall snatches of his conversation, wild and whirling such as it was, and shake their heads over their own failure to appreciate its full import at the time. There was even someone to insist that his most active bouts of soliloquy had occurred when- ever the moon was full.

By teatime, over which Father Finn presided, it was reliably reported that he had been taken away in a straitjacket to the mad- house at Enniscorthy. But, during late study, Father Creame himself—to allay any further wild speculation—came to announce, in his uncompromising way, that Father Turley had been taken to a Nursing Home with a suspected brain tumour and that he was being held under sedation there until the morning, when he was to be taken to Dublin for further tests and a possible operation, that our prayers were solicited and that a special Mass for his recovery would be read in the morning. Father Finn was to move into his room and take over as Dean.

Father Finn was a little, old man with a bleating voice who had been Rector in the good old days before Father Creame and his regime of grim rectitude. He was a gentle and kindly man with wisps of white hair blowing out like thistledown over his ears, and an expression of benign goodwill on his face, which was wrinkled and rosy like an apple in autumn. But, for all his meek- ness, he had an air of authority about him. A direct look from his mild blue eye, out over the top of his spectacles, was enough to quell a riot or to bring a rowdy Refectory to order. In study he padded around, pausing to have a word here and there, quietly promenading with his hands clasped behind his back, hovering near a group of dissidents until, with shamefaced looks, they returned to their work, never actually saying anything—not for him the dramatic announcement—but leavening the lumpen mass of us with his indefinable moral ascendancy. Because he expected that boys would do the right thing, because—without ever saying it—he gave the impression that he understood that most boys, most of the time, want to do the right thing, they generally did it when he was there.

The most strenuous part of the job—supervising recreation, organising games—was taken over by Father Hogan or one of the younger priests. These were an energetic lot, who togged out for games and took their knocks with the best of us. They played handball or threw snowballs or joined whatever activity happened to be in progress when they came on the scene. In class they were industrious, though rarely—since few of them were qualified to teach their subject—inspired teachers. Their discipline, though firm, was not oppressive, a thing which could hardly be said of Mr. Cuffe, under whose ferule we groaned.

Mr. Cuffe taught us Greek and Latin from the beginning of Third Year on. He was nothing if not a perfectionist. He was also a realist. After the kindlier cultivation of Mr. Ronan, who was not without hope that some of us might acquire a respect—perhaps, even, a love—for the culture of Greece and Rome, it was a wintry transplantation into the inhospitable soil of Mr. Cuffe's classroom.

He began from the premise that, as no one could possibly have any interest in these dead languages, it was his duty to beat the rudiments of their grammar and syntax into us. As a teacher, he was a very good carpenter. We were the raw timber, and it was his duty to saw and plane and chisel, to mortice and nail and hammer us into perfect replicas of classical scholars. So long as we could write after the manner of Caesar or Cicero or inveigh in the style of Demosthenes, could remember that T cubed, C squared was a mnemonic of the First Punic War (Ticinus, Trebia, Trasimene Lake, Cannae and Capua), could sing out without omission or faltering the many rhymed rules of grammar and exceptions, he was—I dare not say satisfied; he never was that—he was content to withhold the full weight of his punishing cane from us—for the time being.

From his coming to his going, it was, "Hold out your hand

(CRASH! BANG!)", with him. He would stride in, a big sandy-haired Kerryman with coarse freckled face, dressed like a lion-tamer in jodhpurs, his cane smacking ominously against his gleaming brown leggings. He would lean on the desk and look us over with his frosty stare.

"Hickey!" he would roar, "the translation."

And, when Hickey bogged down in a quicksand of "ahs" and "ehs" and "ands" and "buts", it was BANG-BANG, and on to someone else, until the translation was flailed from us like grain from a sheaf of corn.

"Tabula Rasa!" was his cry then.

This was a signal for a clean sheet of paper and a series of sentences, based on the construction used in the text, which we had to translate back into the original Latin or Greek. Again, to be less of a Latinist than Livy, to falter over a quaint turn of Attic Greek was to incur his wrath and to invite the sharp cut of his cane.

Censure was the only currency of his despotic empire—praise an unknown coin. The sole reward of merit was a grudging silence—and sometimes, not even that. With five marks short of the full 400 in Intermediate Latin and seven in Greek, I thought I had done well. His only words to me on the subject had been a sour inquiry as to what stupidity of mine had lost me the full marks.

I had missed an Intermediate Scholarship by a similar small amount. The loss would not have troubled me, except for one thing. Father Creame had promised that anyone who got a scholarship would be fed rashers and eggs for his breakfast for a whole week. It was tantalising to sit in the Refectory and watch my friend, Kieran Maher—who had got a First Class Scholarship—and three other boys, sitting out at a ceremonial table in the middle of the room, scoffing greedily, while the crisp smell of bacon teased my nostrils. I was fifth in a class of thirty-one, but that was poor consolation.

My mind, I had always felt, was slower than those of the leaders, as a countryman's walk is often slower than a townsman's. Given my own time, I was not bad at working a thing out for myself. Father Creame was of the opinion that I might, eventually, get a university scholarship or gain entrance to the training college for national teachers. I didn't know whether I really wanted either of those things. I wasn't particularly worried. It all seemed far away still. All I did know was that I had no vocation for the priesthood. The more we were urged to consider such a vocation—and it was the only career guidance we were ever given—the more convinced I was that I was unworthy of such a high calling.

At our annual retreat in November, shortly after Father Turley's skull was successfully trepanned and his tumour removed, our minds were gently turned in that direction again. Our spiritual director for the retreat was a bustling roly-poly Pickwick of a man with bald pate, gleaming glasses and cherubic smile. He spoke with a very attractive lisp and was full of apposite anecdotes, which, like spoonfuls of treacle, sweetened his dose of doctrine.

"Let me begin, dear boyth, by telling you a fthory . . ."

The inevitable talk on the religious life came. But what we were all waiting for was his homily on the Sixth Commandment. Sex— or, at least, girls, and what one did when in their company—was the great new thing in our lives. Since Christmas, when I had persuaded him to get me a photograph of her, I was in love with Kieran Maher's sister, Nuala. I was forever pestering him to write to her and mention my name. Whenever he got letters from home, I was always disappointed if there was none from her. He gave me the odd letter she wrote—full of her school pals and never any mention of me—and I cherished them as if they were Holy Writ. I carried her picture in my wallet and sometimes at night in the dormitory, when boys boasted to each other of their girl-friends, I would seize on a silence to moan, as if in sleep, "Nuala, Nuala, I love you, Nuala!"

In the photograph she looked very beautiful, red-haired in a green dress, under an apple tree in bloom, laughing into the camera with white, even teeth. Moll, who was now a boarder in the convent at the other end of town, wasn't as enthusiastic as I expected her to be, when I showed her the photograph.

"She looks stuck-up—or something," she said, and was out with me for most of the day. Later (it was during the Easter holidays) she came along and rubbed her head against my sleeve, when I was reading, and asked if I'd like to play a game. She would pretend to be Nuala and I could kiss her if I liked. Moll was queer and intense about it and, though it was nice and I loved her, we were quarrelling again before night. Things seemed to be breaking up between us, at least cracks were appearing, though why they came or what they signified, I could not explain. All I knew was that I felt that it was so, that I was sorry and puzzled about it.

I was only aware of it at odd moments. Next day, we played one of our old games. We went down into the shed and climbed up on a bench of hay, high under the roof and there took off each other's clothes—with a thrilled shiver of excitement on my part, at least— and rolled about in the sweet hay and laid hands on each other, until Moll drew her fingers along my thighs and whispered, "It's time for your game, isn't it?"

She had teased me into flame and kissed me at the peak and kept her arms around me when I was still again, and said, with her lips on my chest, "Didn't I make you feel nice? Don't you like me best of all?"

"Yes, Moll," I said and stroked her hair. "I like you best of all."

"And always will?"

"Always," I said.

"Your heart is thumping," she laughed. "I can hear it."

Then she was up again, tossing hay and standing on her head and laughing as she dressed in my clothes and I in hers and we laughed at the strange figures we made, and exchanged clothes again and climbed down with a warm, secret understanding that lasted for the rest of the day.

I have forgotten now when I told her of my Game, or how much she understood of it beyond the fact that I enjoyed threshing about and she could help my enjoyment by kissing and fondling me. When I played it alone I thought of her, but, often lately it was of Nuala I dreamed. Or tried to dream, because it was Moll's trim little bottom I saw and her crescent breasts, whose nipples she liked me to touch. But the face was beginning to be Nuala's.

"Thex," Father O'Kane said, his glasses glinting, as he beamed down on us from his high seat on the rostrum, "ith a gift of God. In the married fhtate ith right and reverent uthe ith thacramental."

Fifth and sixth years had been specially assembled for his lecture. Afterwards, he would be in the staffroom for those who wanted to consult him privately. He spoke very frankly and understandingly on friendship between boys and girls and the correct behaviour to be observed. He spoke more obscurely on temptations to immodest actions, on sinful habits and the necessity of continuous struggle against the erotic stimulus of pornographic films and literature. He spoke of the temptations inherent in an all-male society such as the one in which we found ourselves—again in a way which I only vaguely understood. He spoke of the need for adequate sex instruction and urged those of us who understood these things imperfectly, or needed guidance, to come and see him privately.

Because I had been troubled by some of the things he said, and because, though I had since childhood observed the casual coupling of animals, I had never thought or been told—except in the most vague and smutty schoolboy way—about the origin of human life, I went to see him. I was like someone with bits and pieces of a jigsaw puzzle which he has never been able to assemble fully to form a complete picture.

Father O'Kane was very gentle with me. He smiled at me and lit a cigarette and puffed and removed a piece of tobacco from his lower lip and smiled again and asked, "Will you ath the quethionth or will I?"

When I hesitated, he smiled again and said, "Well, I'll begin, and if I'm not on the right track you can thop me."

Under his careful prodding, I told him my age and my background, and whispered, "No," when he asked if I fully understood the facts of life. Then, beginning with a seed and a garden, which I understood very well, he took me through the life cycle of plants and flowers. He spoke about the beauty of life and nature and natural processes.

"Human life, too," he said, "beginth with a theed."

As he talked on about the seeds of life and how the potential for making them lies dormant in the body until puberty, and then comes into production like a factory in which the power is switched on for the first time, and how the seed is stored in the body until needed and the excess is drained off naturally during sleep—a process which need not worry me, because it was perfectly natural —I was getting more and more agitated, because the terrible truth was beginning to strike home to me. When he went on to

explain that any voluntary act to cause a spillage of seed was
gravely sinful and a habit which, once formed, was very difficult
to overcome, my whole life seemed to collapse around me—a
ghastly sinful lie over which the devil, under the guise of my Game,
had taken complete control.

I could feel my face getting hotter and hotter. I covered it with
my hands to hide my shame and confusion. I was an evil, filthy
person, squandering the inviolable seeds of life for my own selfish
pleasure. I was as bad as that man, Onan, in the Bible, of whom
Father O'Kane was talking. God would condemn me too and I
would burn. I put my head down between my hands and, try as I
would, I could not control the anguish that raked me. I could feel
my shoulders heave and my hands get wet. The shame and horror
of it! The priest must already have guessed everything and would
presently denounce me for the unspeakable sinner I was. How
could I ever look him or any decent person in the face again! If
only God would strike me dead at once and save him—and me—
the embarrassment!

I hadn't noticed that Father O'Kane had stopped speaking or
that he had got up, until I felt the gentle pressure of his arm about
my shoulders.

"There! There!" he said, "it can't be that bad now, can it?"

The gentleness of his voice released the last spring of restraint
in me. My whole body racked and heaved. It was as if all the
innocence and purity of childhood were being washed out of me
in a flood-tide of self-knowledge, and, when it ebbed, all that was
left was a frightened and despairing adolescent. It may have lasted
only a few moments, but, when it was over, my childhood had
gone for ever.

"Would you like to tell me about it?" Father O'Kane asked.

"I never knew!" I said. "I never knew!"

"You didn't?" he hinted delicately.

"That it was wrong," I said, and started to heave again.

He tightened his grip on my shoulders.

"Poor lad! Poor lad!" he said.

"I didn't know," I said again.

"It wath no thin then," Father O'Kane said.

I said nothing.

"You can't commit thin," he said, "without full knowledge. You didn't know. Therefore, for you, there wath no thin."

"But I did—that," I said dully.

"Would you like to tell me about it?"

I made several attempts to speak but each time was overcome with shame.

"You don't find it eathy," he said sympathetically. "Let me thee."

He searched around for a way to help me.

"It began accidentally, didn't it?"

I nodded, still unable to speak.

"On waking at night, maybe?"

I nodded again.

"It wath pleathanth?"

I nodded, feeling unspeakably ashamed now of the pleasure it had given me.

"God meant it to be pleathanth," Father O'Kane said.

He went on to explain that the use of this faculty was reserved by God for those in the married state; that the pleasure attached to its performance was His way of ensuring that life continued; that self-love of the kind I had unfortunately fallen into was a perversion of real love; that it was sterile, opposed to life; that, now, since I knew of its evil, I should avoid it like the plague.

I wiped my eyes and nodded again.

"Feeling better?" Father O'Kane asked solicitously. He gave my shoulders a squeeze and resumed his seat.

I wasn't feeling better, but I nodded. My head felt like an over-blown balloon. Somewhere inside, my mind, like a caged animal trying to escape, turned around and around desperately.

Father O'Kane had said that as I was ignorant of what I had been doing, there was no sin. But I no longer felt clean. I was old, soiled, experienced in sexual perversion. All the white innocence of my First Communion day gone.

Then he said something that laid an even worse burden of guilt on my shoulders. He asked if anyone else—any boy or boys—had been involved with me in these perverse acts.

Moll! My God! I had been corrupting and perverting my own sister without even knowing it.

Under his skilled probing it all came out, like venomous pus from a wound. Wishing that a mountain would be piled on me to hide my shame, that some cleansing fire would consume me utterly, I let him drag the whole sordid story from me. When it was finished, I was drenched in sweat and limp with exhaustion. I felt old, worn and inexpressibly evil.

"You are not to be blamed," Father O'Kane said. "You didn't know."

But his words were no consolation to me. I thought of Moll, so innocent and affectionate, Moll whom I loved—and had corrupted. To do things like that with girls, as he had explained, was dreadful. But to do it with one's own sister! What pit in hell could be hot enough for crimes like mine!

Although he insisted that there was nothing for me to confess, to ease my guilt and terrible remorse of conscience, Father O'Kane agreed to hear my confession, there and then. He put on his purple stole. I knelt down beside his chair and he, with his hand laid kindly on my head, led me again through my dreadful litany of igorance and desire. He asked me if I was sorry for my sins—in so far as anything I had confessed had been sinful—and if I was determined never to do anything like that again. With a fervency and vehemence of feeling, such as I had never felt before, I assured him of my contrition and my absolute resolve to amend my life.

For the rest of the retreat, I went about abjectly, my mind dark and despairing, getting no consolation from my prayers, remembering all that I had ever heard at missions and retreats about hell being filled with sexual sinners and about the incalculable consequences of the sin of scandal which, like a stone thrown in a pool, spreads its influence ever outwards, continuing on, even after the death of the scandal-giver, right up to the crack of doom, corrupting and dragging down millions, yet unborn, into the bottomless pit.

CHAPTER FOURTEEN

ANOTHER Christmas.

"You're different," Moll said to me, as we lay in the hay—far apart, fully dressed. "You never want to play with me or tell me secrets or laugh. What's wrong with you lately?"

"Nothing," I said.

"You don't even want to come up here any more."

"It's childish," I said.

"I like it then," Moll insisted, "and so used you."

"It was all right when we were children."

"You'd think you were a hundred!" Moll said and threw a wisp of hay at me. It landed on my chest and I left it there.

"Is it that one in the photograph? Did she let you down or something?"

"That's all finished long ago."

"Aw, Johnsy," Moll said, sidling over to me, "won't you tell me, please?"

She took up the wisp of hay from my chest and let it drop in strands on my face. I lay there with the hay over my face and did not answer her.

"I'll kiss you if you like," Moll offered.

"No!" I said, sitting up. "No! You musn't ever again."

"I will if I like," Moll laughed and flung herself in her tomboy way on top of me.

"No!" I shouted. "You mustn't. It's a sin." I flung her roughly from me.

"Aw, Johnsy," Moll complained, "what's wrong with you at all?"

"It's wrong," I said, determined now to get it all off my mind and tell her everything. "What we were doing was wrong. It's a sin. A mortal sin. We musn't kiss or see each other."

"See each other!" Moll laughed. "What's wrong with seeing each other?"

"With nothing on," I said. "That's a sin."

"Why? What harm is that?"

"It's a sin now, and that's all. A priest told me. You must go to Confession and tell everything we did, and you must say it was all my fault and that you'll never do it again."

"I will in my eye!" Moll said.

"You must," I said earnestly, "or you'll go to hell and so will I for leading you astray."

"Aw, go on," Moll said, "you're only codding me, aren't you?"

"I'm not, Moll. Honest to God!"

"Your Game? Was that wrong too?"

"Yes."

"Aw, Johnsy, you liked that, didn't you? Is that why you're so fed up?"

"You must tell the priest everything, Moll. Promise me."

"And tickling me—there—was that wrong too?"

"It was all wrong."

"And putting each other to bed in the hay?"

"Yes."

"And you coming in and getting me ready for bed at night? That was nice. Was that wrong too?"

"All wrong, Moll. Terribly wrong!"

"And we can't ever do it again? And never see each other—like that—again?"

"Never!" I said.

"What's wrong about it?"

"Only married people can do things like that," I explained.

"My father and mother are married and they never did anything like that," she said.

"How do you know?"

"I know!" she said stubbornly. "They don't even sleep in the same bed. If I was married to you, I'd always sleep with you and kiss you and play your Game with you—and everything."

"Brothers can't marry their sisters," I said crossly.

"I never want to marry then," Moll said.

"Moll," I stared at her earnestly, "will you promise me to go to Confession?"

"If you like," she said.

"Good girl!" I felt lighter than I had felt for a long time.

"The nun said Adam's sons married their sisters," Moll remarked thoughtfully.

"You should become a nun," I said to get her mind away from dangerous things like that.

"I don't want to become a nun," she said. "If Adam was your father, would you marry me?"

"I don't know," I said. "It's a silly question anyway."

"Aw, Johnsy," Moll protested, "can't we pretend anyway! Would you marry me?"

"Yes," I said to please her.

"Yippee!" Moll threw herself on her back with her feet up in the air.

"Moll," I said, "you musn't do that any more."

Moll sat up and smoothed down her dress.

"That one in the photograph was stuck up, wasn't she?" she said.

"I don't care what she was," I said.

"You wouldn't want to be doing—our things—with one like her, would you?" she asked.

"I don't ever want to do things like that with anyone again," I said vehemently, "because it's wrong."

"You never told me what's wrong about it anyway," Moll said, her mind turning off on a new track.

Picking my words carefully, I told her the facts as I had learned them from Father O'Kane. Moll was very interested and laughed at the funny way the seed of life was made and where it came out. I hushed her and told her not to laugh at sacred things like that. She said she didn't mean any harm, but insisted it was funny all the same.

Then she got serious again and told me about the day, nearly a year before, when she thought she was going to bleed to death and my mother had told her that it was nothing to worry about—only a thing that happened to girls—and it had been happening to her ever since and a girl in school had told her that it had something to do with having babies. I told her what Father O'Kane had told me about the female producing the ovum and the way it joined with the male sperm to make a baby.

"So," Moll said thoughtfully, "if you and I were married, we'd be able to make a baby!"

"You mustn't say things like that!" I was horrified.

"'Twould be fun all the same," Moll laughed. "Much nicer than an old doll."

"It's wrong even to think about such things," I said.

"Don't you wish my father was Adam all the same?" Moll asked.

"Everything to do with things like that is a sin," I told her, "so you musn't say any more about them."

"'Twas a lot nicer when we knew nothing," Moll grumbled.

In my own thoughts I agreed with her. The burden of sin was a very heavy one. It lay in wait for me behind the most innocent-looking fancies, like a snake coiled in a basket of fruit. My mind was forever on the retreat from seductive images. Going to bed and waking were hazards. Dreams, too, in which I played my forbidden Game.

"Come on in and we'll make your new jig-saw," Moll said. "We're still allowed do that, I suppose?"

"I'm sick of jig-saws," I said. I was determined not to be pleased with anything.

"We could collect eggs and smash them," Moll suggested hopefully.

"No," I said.

"We could look in the Long Moor for holly with berries."

"Putting up holly is only childish," I objected.

"Aw, Johnsy," Moll said, "is there nothing you want to do?"

"I wish I was dead!" I said.

But in the evening I cheered up. Tom, who had fully recovered and was stronger than ever now, suggested that we should go into the pictures, as he often did lately on Wednesday and Sunday nights. Someone from up the country came with a projector in a van on those nights, and young and old trooped into the Parish Hall to sit on hard forms and enjoy the vicarious thrill of romance and dangerous living.

On our way into the hall, Tom met some of his friends and left me standing there. He had more in common with them than he had with me. They were all fellows with roots in the land and understood each other. Cattle, fairs, handball, local gossip—they could stand at the crossroads and discuss them for hours. I was just an exotic weed on the periphery of their lives. They were uneasy with me and I with them—my white hands and college vocabulary an affront to their manhood, their honest earthiness jarring on my sensibility. I was afraid they might think I despised them when I didn't.

Perhaps, even then, they were beginning to fear me—not for what I was, but for what I might become—a priest, perhaps, someone with power over them, like Father Hoare, whom everybody saluted and deferred to when he came home on holidays, though they had no particular regard for his brother Eddie, who had lived amongst them all his life. Father Hoare had only to voice an opinion—however fatuous—on farming to be listened to obsequiously. Apart from Eddie—saved only by his blood and ignorance from the suspicion of blasphemy—nobody questioned his total infallibility on any subject that he cared to pronounce on.

I sat a little apart from Tom and his friends and watched the people coming in. It was something to do while I was waiting. Then a girl passed up and I was no longer waiting. The evening— life—began to unfold like a new creation full of infinite possibilities. She sat down on the form two rows ahead of me. Her hair was black and long and ringleted. It swept down over the collar of her red coat, a glistening cataract. I had caught a glimpse of her face as she passed me. A pale, serene face, very beautiful. She sat alone and I would have given my life, my soul, to be sitting beside her, even for one hour. A subtle, exciting girl-scent came back to me and I could feel the blood rushing through me with a skip and a bound. My imagination was trapped in the dark maze of her hair.

When the lights went out and the film began, I followed the sway and tilt of her head and thought of myself, sitting beside her, holding her hand in the dark. What the picture was, whether it was good or bad, I have no recollection. She lifted her head back to laugh from time to time, so it must have been amusing.

When the lights went on again, while the reel was being changed, she looked around, as if searching for someone. She was even more beautiful than I had imagined. I smiled in a timid way, as her eyes passed over our row, but she showed no sign of acknowledgement and turned back again. I sidled in towards Tom who had stepped back across the forms to speak to someone.

"Who's that girl up there?" I asked, as casually as I could, wondering if he noticed the tremor in my voice.

"That one," he said, "your one in the red coat? That one is so stuck up she wouldn't look the same side of the road as you."

"Who is she?" I asked.

He looked at me in his teasing, maddening way. Since his recovery, we had been inclined to relapse into the old antagonistic relationship—though never as completely or as virulently as before.

"What d'you want to know for?"

"No reason," I said and felt myself blushing. Tom had a way like that of seeing right through me. And he was never one to spare my feelings.

"You needn't be thinking you'd get any place with her," he said. "Half the country was after her and she'd talk to nobody."

"I was only asking," I said.

"Helen Murphy is her name," he said grudgingly. "One of the big Murphys" (he said "big" in a particularly scathing way).

"They live out in Doonashee—The Dower House. It used to belong to the landlord's agent. Forty rooms. Half in ruins. Tumble-down walls all around. Nettles and ivy—and big notions!"

"I know the place," I said.

I had often cycled past it on summer evenings through a green, leafy cathedral and stopped at holes in the boundary wall to admire the great sweep of avenue and the peeling Georgian house, looking out over a tiny lake choked with weeds.

"Your one follows the hunt," he said. "Riding breeches, black coat, cap and all!"

"Oh!" I said.

"She's away in school most of the time. Dublin—or some place. Her old fellow isn't worth a damn. Cuts down the timber and sells it. Knows no more about farming than a pig knows about manners."

Helen! I said the name to myself as the lights went off again. A beautiful name. Helen of Troy. My Helen. A name full of romance and wonder. She wouldn't look at me, of course. Living in a big mansion like that and riding to the hunt with people like the Major Bloodworths and that mad, dashing—very dangerous—Freddie Thimblehead, son and heir of the Honourable Mr. Thimblehead of Screen Hall.

When the film had finished and the credits were coming up, I noticed Helen slipping from her seat and leaving the hall. On a sudden impulse, I left after her. Outside it was darkish, with clouds scudding. Somewhere behind them was a faint brightness as of the waning moon. I watched as Helen mounted her bicycle and set off for Doonashee, the light from her dynamo flaring and falling. I sprang on my bike and followed her, looking around furtively to see if I was being observed. The sound of the National Anthem was still coming from the hall and there was no one in sight.

I cycled along behind her, my heart beating wildly. I felt like someone starting on a great adventure, Jason or Theseus—or Oisín following the golden girl, Niamh, to Tír na nÓg. There was no one on the road but ourselves. It was so quiet that I could hear the squeak of her pedals ahead of me. The road wound sharply downwards, turned left around a hump-backed bridge, and then went straight up. I came around the bridge very fast and almost struck the back wheel of her bicycle, as she dismounted to walk up the hill. I pulled up with a squeal of brakes and got off too.

"Oooh!" she exclaimed in alarm.

"I—I was almost into you," I heard myself say foolishly.

She made no reply, but started to push her bicycle very briskly up the hill. A bit further on I caught up with her again.

"It's a fine night," I said.

It was too dark to see her face, as she turned to look at me, but I could see that she had turned.

"I—I saw you at the pictures," I said, when she still did not speak. "Did you like it?"

"It was all right," she spoke for the first time in a low voice—low and sweet—a very beautiful thing in a girl.

"I was sitting behind you," I said.

"I—don't know you," she said after a while. "I don't know many people around here."

I couldn't make out whether her tone was asking a question or was meant to be a dismissal.

"I don't either," I said, "but I know you. You're Helen Murphy, aren't you?"

"Yes," she said.

Her every word was music to me. Tom had said that she wouldn't speak to anyone and she had already spoken several words to me.

"I'm John Foley," I said. "I live out at the other side of the village."

"Oh!" she said.

"You're away in school, aren't you?" I asked.

"Yes."

"So am I."

"Oh!" she said again.

At the top of the hill we mounted and cycled on again. I had exhausted my conversational powers and didn't know what to say next. I couldn't tell her that I was madly in love with her. But that was the only thing I wanted to tell her and even I knew that such a declaration would be premature.

It was Helen who spoke first and, when she did, she said something that greatly embarrassed me. I was glad that it was too dark for her to see my face.

"If you live at the other side of the village," she said, "what takes you out this way?"

"I—It's—a nice—night," I stammered. "I like cycling."

"Oh!" she said.

We were coming to a high, crumbling wall and I knew we were near her house. There was something I wanted to say to her, but every time I tried my courage deserted me. We came to the gate-lodge with its big, iron gates.

"Well, goodbye," Helen said casually, turning in.

"I'll open the gates for you."

I sprang off the bicycle. I opened one of the gates. It swung back with a dry grating that caused a flutter of crows in the trees over-head. Helen wheeled in her bike and prepared to remount.

"Wait!" I said.

She paused with her foot on the pedal.

"W—W—Would you—Would you—come to the pictures with me some night?" I asked, my tongue dry with excitement.

She was a long, long time—an eternity—in answering.

"I wouldn't be let," she said slowly.

My heart fell over a precipice and smashed on the rocks below. Then it rose again and soared into the heavens. She hadn't said no.

I had the flashlamp of my bicycle in my hand and was waving it about in my excitement. Its light must have fallen on my face, because she said:

"I remember now. I saw you behind me."

My heart floated, skimmed away and there was music everywhere.

"Would you meet me some evening?" I asked.

She hesitated.

"You wouldn't have to ask anybody. Just a few minutes out here. You could come down as far as the gates for a walk and I'd be here."

I was surprised at the boldness of my suggestion.

"I—don't—know," she said. Then a great rush of blood to my ears, as she concluded, "I'd like to."

A flood of feeling surged through me and I blurted out everything.

"I saw you," I said, "and I followed you home, because I wanted to tell you that you are beautiful and I'm sorry I frightened you, and, if you're cross with me, tell me to go and I'll never trouble you again—but I'll always think you're beautiful. Please let me see you again. Any night you say, I'll be here. Or, if you can't come to the pictures with me, maybe you'd let me see you home when they're over. I could meet you out the road, if—you'd —like that."

"All right!" she said.

I felt like a knight in a fairy tale whose destiny it was to win the princess.

"How about the Sunday night after Christmas?" I heard myself say as in a dream.

"Yes," she said.

A hesitancy then while we thought of something to say next that wouldn't be anti-climactic and banal. Helen was the first to break the silence.

"I must be going," she said. "See you on the Sunday then."

"Sunday," I said.

"Goodnight—John!"

"Goodnight—Helen!"

She started to move off.

"I'll write you a letter," I said, my mind full of poetic things I was going to say.

"All right," she said.

"I'll give it to you on Sunday."

"That'd be nice," she said.

"Will you write too?"

"Yes."

We said goodbye again and lingered again and said goodbye yet again, before she mounted and pedalled off round the curve of the avenue. I watched her out of sight, then stood for a while in ecstasy under the gaunt trees, before clanging to the gates again and disturbing the crows, which turned noisily in their sleep, indifferent to my song of love.

I caught a stone and flung it up amongst them and they roused again with a raucous croak and a flutter and flap of dissent and I laughed at their tired response to life, when there was so much to be up and shouting about and cheering for, because it was a wonderful world, this globe of ours, circling among the stars, with God brooding in love over it—and over Helen Murphy and me— and life was no sometime-thing, but an infinity of loving and knowing and being happy together always.

Light with love, I leaped into the saddle and pedalled back. The only sound as I passed through the centre of the village was the endless flow of water from the fountain, a continuous liquid bubbling, as it fell into the full trough and slipped over the side and ran away into a drain.

There was a skitter of laughter as I passed the cross, and ironic shouts. I knew it was Tom and his friends, but I didn't care. I slowed down and let them overtake me.

"Did you lose your way or something?" Tom sniggered.

"I was talking to Josie Moran," I said, knowing he would like to have been and, obviously, hadn't.

This set the others guffawing and we pedalled on, calling and whistling, a green gabble of raw youths, with most of the needs and none of the assurance of manhood. They were all very

curious to know where I had been and how I had fared, but I had
no intention of telling them. I left Tom talking to them at the road
gate and went home.

I drank the milk laid out for me and ate the bread, chewing away
in a dream over the red embers, and then went upstairs to bed,
stepping lightly in my stocking-feet, smiling to myself in the dark-
ness that closed round me like the black hair of Helen.

On the Sunday evening after Christmas, I was very careful
about my dressing. I polished my shoes again, though they had
been clean since morning. I oiled my hair, doing my best to tame
the unruly wave that kept tumbling over my eyes. I brushed my
overcoat and made sure I had my best handkerchief. I checked the
money in my pocket and hoped I would have enough to buy her
a tiny box of chocolates. I had a letter in my inside pocket.

Dear Helen,

It was rude of me to follow you home, as I did, but I was
desperate to meet you and knew of no other way of getting
introduced to you. It was nice of you not to mind and to make
a date with me. I've never had a date with anyone before—
and never want to with anyone except you. I can hardly wait
to meet you again. It was lovely talking to you. I've been
thinking about you ever since, day and night. You looked
lovely with your black hair and red coat. I would like to have
a photograph of you, please.

I wrote a poem about you, but it wasn't very good. It
didn't say what I wanted to say about at all. I'd send it to you
only you might think it silly. It might be too, but the way I
felt was not silly. I think of you all the time and I hope you
think of me sometimes. Will you agree to be my girl-friend
and I'll be your boy-friend? I'd like to write to you when I
go back to College, but we aren't allowed to get or send letters
like that. Maybe I'll write every day, and give them all to you
when we get our holidays again. I hope tomorrow night
comes soon or I'll die of impatience. When it does come, if it
lasts forever, for me it will hardly be long enough. Until we
meet—and always.

Love, John.

It was a silly letter—like all my attempts to put my feelings into words. It didn't say what I had in my heart at all. I was clumsy at expressing myself. I hoped she would overlook the inadequacies. I wondered for a long time over writing the word "love". I had never written it before. I wondered, too, if I should have put my full name, in case she had forgotten it. But "Love—John Foley" would be ridiculous, and "Love John (Foley)" even worse.

The name "John" didn't please me, either. I would have preferred something classical to go with Helen, a name like Paris or Alexander. "Love—Alexander" sounded interesting. It was virile, potent. There was conquest and glory in it. John was a monosyllabic nonentity. I wondered, too, if I shouldn't have asked her to write to me in college and pretend she was my aunt. It had been done before, I knew, and boys had got away with it.

She wasn't there when I went into the Parish Hall, and she hadn't arrived before the picture started. Every time anyone came in, I strained my eyes in the darkness and craned my head. But no Helen. When the lights went on for the change of reel, she still hadn't come. The evening slowly curdled on me. Something had happened. She hadn't meant what she had said at all. She had only said it to get rid of me. What interest could a girl like that have in me! The box of chocolates I had bought was a hard mass in the inside pocket of my coat. The letter I had taken such pains over, the romanticising of a fool. Perhaps it was not her fault, whatever it was that kept her away. I would keep my side of the bargain anyway. I would cycle out to Doonashee, and perhaps she would be waiting.

Just before the end I left. It was a dark, cheerless night, with a moistness on the wind. It was veering south-west for rain. The flash-lamp picked out circles of the red road surface, made of peculiar stone from the mountain that bled when it rained. I stopped to listen a few times, in case she had been there and I had missed her. But there was no sound, except the indeterminate noises of the night, a sighing of the hedges, animal shufflings, and then, far away, the cry of curlews, looping sadly over the moorland.

I stopped under the gaunt trees by the gate-lodge and flashed my light up the avenue. Nothing but fallen twigs, and at the edge, clumps of buff grass, bent and dead. Away in the distance, I could see the lights of the Dower House. Somewhere inside was Helen. Thinking of me? Or not thinking of me at all? I would have given a lot to know. When I was cycling out, I had some hope that she might have skipped out for a moment to explain why she didn't come, or that she might leave some sign or signal, a note under a stone or tied to the gate that would explain everything. I searched around but could find nothing. I flashed the light on the gate-lodge. The windows were grimy, opaque with dirt, without curtain or shutter. The place seemed to have been vacant for a long time. I listened for the sound of her feet on the avenue. Nothing. The lights of a car came sweeping in the distance. I clambered through a gap in the wall, dislodging loose stones, and stood there, my heart pounding, until it had passed. She was not going to come.

I had no watch, but I must have stood there at least an hour, waiting and hoping, feeling more and more despondent. In the end, I climbed out and, taking my bicycle, walked tearfully away. When I had gone half a mile, I turned and cycled back again and flashed my light and called, "Helen! Helen!" hopelessly into the indifferent night. Then I remounted and went back to the village.

My grief was abysmal. I loved her and would always love her. Nothing could change that. Whatever change had come over her feelings, I would act as if nothing had happened. I would do everything I had promised to do. I had written her a letter and I would post it. I got three penny stamps from the machine outside the Post Office and shoved the letter in the box, and went home morosely.

In bed, I kept going over every aspect of the affair, my mind turning in tight circles, closing in on itself. I tossed back and forth, unable to sleep, raking through the debris of my evening for some crumb of hope. There was none. I was loveless. Alone, as I had always been.

Somewhere in the dead of the night, I came out of the heat of sleep into the middle of my Game, and with a despairing cry of anguished ecstasy, comforted my loveless body, until the bitter harvest of wasted seed was reaped and I turned to the wall, shattered, doomed beyond all hope of salvation.

CHAPTER FIFTEEN

On Tuesday the postman came with a letter. The envelope was pale blue and smelled faintly of violets. I rushed to the privacy of the earth-closet to read it. The first thing that tumbled out was a photograph of a girl, standing knee-deep in grass, patting the neck of a pony with a white blaze on his forehead.

HELEN!

Dear John,

    Thank you for your lovely letter, which came today. I am sorry about Sunday night. I was getting ready to go when visitors arrived—friends of Daddy's whom we hadn't seen for a long time—and Mammy insisted that I stay at home to help her cater for them. I could think of no way to let you know what had happened. I hope you didn't think it was intentional. I was looking forward to meeting you again and was very disappointed when I had to stay at home. It was a boring evening, sitting listening to talk of long ago and wondering about you and what you would think when I didn't turn up.

    I'm sending you the photograph you asked for. It's not very good, but it's the best I've got. I'll try and get a better one for you later, if you like. I would love to have one of you too and the poem, please. No one ever wrote a poem for me before. I would love to have it. I'm sure it's very nice. You said if I could come down to the gate-lodge some evening, you would meet me. Could you come on Thursday? I will be there at eight. I hope that suits you. I won't be able to stay long—I'll say I'm taking the dogs for a walk—but even a few minutes would be nice.

    I'm very sorry about Sunday night. I wanted very much to see you again. I hope you can make it on Thursday. I will be there without fail.

Love, Helen.

P.S. Please don't forget the photo and the poem.

LOVE!

She said "Love". She said she loves me! Helen LOVES me! She loves ME! HELEN LOVES ME!

The concept was so great, so magnificent, so beautiful, so wildly wonderful that my mind could not grasp it all at once. I sat there, sniffing in the fragrance of her words, looking at her photograph, kissing it. I turned over the back and there it was again, that magic word, potent as a talisman. "To John, with *Love*. Helen."

Life began for me again. After the double tragedy of Sunday night—that loss of love, human and divine—I had gone about like the irrevocably damned. Now, there was hope again. I would confess and be forgiven. Love would be restored. And, because God was good and life wonderful and Helen loved me, I would never be tempted to play my soul-destroying Game again.

I was bursting to tell Moll everything, but I was afraid she might be critical as she had been about Nuala. So, though I would have loved to confide in her, I went around hugging my secret to myself, whistling in my tone-deaf, tuneless fashion, shoving my hand into my inside pocket to revel in the physical presence of Helen's letter, sleeping with it under my pillow at night.

Thursday was wet, with fine drizzle falling all day. It was a gloomy day, the light veiled and grey. Ned Rafter was sorting seed potatoes in the barn and Tom was away all afternoon with horses at the forge. It was that kind of day—a day for odd jobs, for cleaning up. My job was to sweep the loft and prepare a place for meal that was coming from the mill. I had a notebook with me, as I swept, and was writing down the lines of the poem I had written for Helen, as they came back to me. I had torn up the original after Sunday, and now I was regretting my haste. It was a conventional, trite thing. Not at all the kind of poem she deserved. But I had been silly enough to mention it, and now she wanted it and it was up to me to let her have it.

I felt I was no good as a poet. I had the emotion, but lacked the words to express it. My poem was just a series of echoes of all that I had ever read. It was not my own. It had no individual stamp. I was thoroughly disgusted with it. But Helen had asked for it. I hoped she wouldn't be too critical.

I had trouble in finding an excuse for going out on such a night, but my father came to my rescue by running out of plug for his pipe and I volunteered to get some for him.

On my way through the village, I bought the plug at Mr. Wadding's and was out under the dripping trees at Doonashee in good time. I stood in the shelter of a pier and waited. The mist came at a slant across the beams of the flashlamp, as I shone it through the bars down the avenue. No sign of Helen yet. I turned off the lamp and waited, my heart thumping irregularly, conscious of the sound of my own breathing. Drops of water fell from the branches on my neck and wrists. There was a faint brightness, no more, away in the direction of the Dower House. I listened for the rush of feet, the snuffle of dogs that might announce her coming. The rain dropped silently on my upturned face from the concentrated darkness overhead.

When she did come, she came without a sound. One moment she was not there and the next she was standing a few feet inside the gate, like a ghost, in a white raincoat. I turned on the light and called softly.

"Helen!"

"John." She answered with a musical ring in her voice that made my pulse race. I turned the beam on her. She had the collar of her white raincoat turned up and a red rain-hat over her dark hair. She put her hands to her eyes to shade them from the beam, laughed and said:

"Please, turn it off."

I turned off the lamp and for a moment could see nothing.

"Where are you?" I said.

"Here!"

When I saw her again, she was beside the gate with her hands on the bars.

"Thanks for coming," she said.

"Thank *you* for coming," I said.

I stood at the outside of the gate with my hands on the bars a few inches above hers.

"I'm sorry about Sunday," she said.

"It's all right," I said, "I got your letter."

"I got yours."

Now that we were together, I felt very shy.

"It's a bad night," I said.

For me the night was exotic, beautiful, unparalleled. But my tongue was rooted in conventionality and could compass only the banal.

"I was afraid you wouldn't be able to come," she said.

I laughed with happiness to hear her say that. It meant she had wanted me to come very badly.

"I thought it might be too wet for you to come out," I said.

"I like walking in the rain."

"Where are the dogs?" I asked, not knowing what to say next.

"Back there, somewhere," she said carelessly.

Our hands touched on the bars of the gate and each of us withdrew simultaneously. I didn't know why I withdrew. It was done before I knew I was going to do it, and then it was too late. I felt I had been cheated out of something pleasant. Helen might not have withdrawn if I hadn't. It would have been nice and romantic to hold hands through the bars of a gate on a wet evening in early January.

"You'll get wet out there," Helen said.

"You'll get wet in there," I said.

"Would you—would you like to come inside and we could stand under the porch of the lodge?" she asked a little hesitantly as if she were afraid of being thought forward.

I shone the torch on the bars of the gate and opened it. Drops shook off on my hands as it moved.

"I'll hold the lamp," Helen said.

Our hands touched again as I gave it to her. The lodge had a sort of verandah on the side facing the avenue, with the roof supported by two iron pillars. We stood under this with our backs to the door, which showed up red and peeling in the light of the lamp.

"Turn it off again," Helen said.

I turned off the lamp and the night thickened about us. Her scent was a lure in the darkness. I moved closer to it and for a second our bodies touched, then drew apart again.

"I brought the photograph for you," I said.

"That's grand," she said. "Did you remember the poem too?"

"It's no good. But I'll give it to you if you like."

"Please!" she said.

I took them out of my pocket and gave them to her.

"That's lovely," she said.

"I liked your letter, Helen."

"Yours was nice, too."

"Will you write to me again?" I asked.

"I have a letter for you here. I found a better photograph, too, if you'd like it."

Like it! I'd keep it and treasure it all the days of my life. When I could afford to, I'd have it framed in silver—or, better still, in gold.

"Thanks!" I said.

I took it from her and put it in my pocket. I would have loved to look at it there and then, but it might get wet or fall in the mud and I didn't want to risk that.

"I'm going back to school next Tuesday," she said.

"Will I see you before you go?" I asked. "I'm not going until the eleventh."

"I'm afraid we won't be able to meet again until Easter," she said. "Mammy is coming to Dublin with me and she wants to be up for the week-end. We're going on the train tomorrow evening."

I was disappointed. But she did want to meet me again.

"Would you write again—before you go in?"

"I'll write on Sunday," she said. "We'll be staying with my aunt. If you'd like to write to me there any time, my cousin would bring me in the letter."

"That'd be great!" I said. "I could get a day-boy to post them."

Then I remembered Father Creame's ban and told her that I wouldn't be let have letters from her.

"Could I send them to your home?"

"I'd rather not," I said. "They'd be asking too many questions. I might be able to work something out with one of the day-boys. I'll write and let you know."

I was disappointed that we could not write direct, but, in a way, the challenge of beating the system added spice to the romance of it all.

"I'll have to go now," Helen said.

"I suppose so," I said.

"Yes," she said, but made no attempt to move.

"I'll have to go too," I said.

"I suppose so," she said.

"Yes," I said.

I took out the box of chocolates I had bought and held them out to her.

"I had these for you on Sunday night," I said.

"You shouldn't have," she said.

She took them from me and held them close to her chest in a little girlish gesture. "You're very nice," she said.

. My heart was overflowing in a gush of emotion that came from some endless source in me, so that I knew that however much drained away there would be sufficient always to take its place.

"We'll have to be going," I said.

"It's only a week and a day since we met," she said.

"It's a long time to Easter," I sighed.

"Yes," Helen said.

I could not be sure whether she sighed, too, but I hoped she did.

"What age are you?" I asked.

"Sixteen. I was sixteen in November."

"I'll be seventeen in July."

"You're older than me," she said. She seemed pleased that I was older.

"What do you do in your spare time?" I asked.

"I ride horses. Do you like horses?"

"I don't know much about horses," I said.

"Daddy breeds them," she said. "Hunters mostly. What do you do in your spare time?"

"Nothing," I said lamely. "I go to pictures and read books. I like books."

"So do I," she said. "Ones about horses and ballet. Do you like ballet?"

"I don't know much about it," I said again.

"What kind of books do you like?"

"Stories," I said, "novels. I'd like to begin at the beginning and read my way right down to the present day. I've already read Richardson and Fielding and Smollett and Sterne—and a lot more of the early ones."

"Oh!" Helen said.

"We'll have to be going," I said again.

"Yes!"

We moved out from under the verandah and stood in the dripping avenue. I did not know how to leave gracefully. I didn't want to leave at all. The thought of parting with her, when I had only barely discovered her, was painful.

"Well, goodbye!" Helen said.

I held out my hand shyly and she took it. The press of her fingers on mine was beautiful. Her hand was soft, slender, feminine. The intimacy of such contact was thrilling. All the men in the books I had read would have raised her hand to their lips and kissed it. I would have liked to do the same, but I hadn't the assurance.

"Goodbye, Helen!" I said.

"Goodbye, John!"

Her hand was still in mine, soft, pliant, alive. "I'll write," I said.

"So will I."

We pressed hands again. Then, gently, she disengaged herself and began to back away from me.

"Easter isn't that far away," I said.

"No," she said.

She backed off into the mist, waving her hand and calling goodbye, until she blurred into it, becoming just a brighter part of it, then merged with it and disappeared.

I stood there, hearing nothing but the irregular drips, my sense of loss acute. I raised my right hand, which her hand had clasped, and kissed the fingers that had touched hers. I could smell her subtle perfume off them—a little piece of her, a precious piece, that lingered with me until I got home. Then there was her letter to read and her new photograph.

As I cycled along, I told myself soberly that I would have to learn something about horses—hunters particularly—and find a book about ballet which I could read. Then, I would be able to talk to her about these things.

When I went back to College, I showed Kieran Maher and the rest of my friends her picture. They were impressed by her beauty, but inclined to doubt that she really was my girl-friend, in spite of her signature on the back. But when I showed them her letters—all three of them—there could no longer be any doubt. As a man who was in love and had his love returned, I was accepted into the higher echelons of our status-conscious society. Kieran, being from Dublin, had, of course, plenty of girl-friends, with whom he went to dances and played delightful games, like Postman's Knock—where a lot of kissing went on—at parties in the houses of their friends.

I would dearly have loved playing games like that at a party where Helen was a guest. But the thought of other boys kissing her was enough to make me insanely jealous. I hoped she hadn't gone to any parties like that or played Postman's Knock or Forfeits, when she was in her cousin's house in Dublin.

Some Senior boys in school had a habit, which to me seemed both disgusting and stupid. They had a habit of picking out some junior, usually some weedy, effeminate thing, like a delicate, wilting flower, and pretending he was their girl-friend. On the evening of a Free Day, especially—twice or three times a term— they would gather in the dark in the Games Room, each with his surrogate girl and sit there and hold hands and talk and lie in each other's arms and—a thing I could never understand—even kiss. The thought of myself sitting there with some pale scut of a Junior, pretending he was Helen, was so ludicrous and so revolting that I was in two minds whether to get sick or die of laughing whenever I came across it.

On such nights, I would stand at the railings, looking out over the bright town and the shimmer of lighted water and dream of Helen and of the future. Or I would slip away to the Study-Hall to write her a letter, or drive myself to frustrated defeat in trying to express my feeling for her in verse that, however I tried, plodded when it should soar.

I had made an arrangement with the day-boy, who posted my letters, that Helen would seal her letter to me in an envelope, which she would then place in another envelope and send to him at his own address. He was a big, gentle fellow, who made no secret of the fact that he intended to join the Order as soon as he had his Leaving Certificate, so I felt safe in trusting him. There was no fear of him reading my letters or trying to cut me out by

starting a correspondence of his own with her. A more unlikely
pander it would be hard to imagine. I often wondered what his
family thought of all the mysterious letters coming to him in an
unknown feminine hand from Dublin.

These letters from Helen became the centre around which
my life turned. I read them and re-read them, the letter in one
hand, her photograph in the other. In bed at night, I would think
myself back under the dripping trees of Doonashee. Our hands
would meet on the wet bars of the gate and remain there in
conscious and intimate contact while we talked. I would drift off
to sleep and wake in the morning with her still in my mind. All
through the day she was there, a warm source to draw on against
the failures and defeats of the moment.

We met again once in the brief Easter holidays, and stood under
the crumbling verandah in the twilight of a March evening. The
crows in the silver-barked beeches were quarrelling over their
nests, croaking and flapping, repelling invaders, staking out their
noisy spheres of influence. Helen, more beautiful than all my
dreams, with a red band across her hair, looking at me and smiling,
as I picked a primrose and handed it to her, slipping it gaily under
the band where it shone palely, like the evening star just coming
up over Sleedagh Wood.

CHAPTER SIXTEEN

BRIEF as those Easter holidays were, there occurred during them two unrelated incidents which combined to make a third that affected us closely. Jamesy Brennan, an old drinking companion of my father's, died, and Nicky Breen, my father's cousin, having reached the age of seventy, made over his farm to his son, Mike, and applied for the Old Age Pension.

On the morning of the funeral, my father and I set off in the Croydon, the mountings and harness polished and shining, the body-work newly washed and glossy, the pony freshly clipped, currycombed and rubbed down. I was sent along in the hope that my presence would restrain my father and help to get him home reasonably early—and reasonably sober, because, though his drinking had eased off, funerals were still a hazard.

My father, freshly shaved, in his blue-serge suit, best shirt and with laboriously knotted tie kept in place by the horse-shoe tiepin and its thirteen tiny pearls, which I had often counted where it lay, as it usually did, in the blue velvet box on their dressing table along with my mother's gold locket with the pictures of her father and mother inside, was making hissing noises through his teeth—pzzoooith—pzzoooith—in an offhand, carefree way. His gold watch-chain, looped elegantly across his waistcoat, swayed gently as we moved.

Jamesy Brennan had not been a close friend of my father. They had once been neighbours—a long time ago—when my father, early in his life, had bought his first small farm at the other end of the parish, but they had continued to meet occasionally, on fair days, at race meetings or coursing matches or funerals and lubricated the old acquaintance with the odd few drinks to keep it from getting rusty. We would not be visiting the house. We would attend the Office and High Mass at the Chapel-of-ease in Kildimmock and the funeral afterwards to the old graveyard at Coolreasky.

Kildimmock was a rather meagre-looking chapel—a high

barn with a belfry—on the top of a hill with a few tall trees with
sparse branches and leaves, like moulting birds standing on one
leg and leaning away from the south-west. We tied the pony in
the shade with a lot of other animals, ponies, horses, jennets,
asses, yoked under cars of all sizes and shapes, but all looking very
plebeian beside our elegant, aristocratic Croydon. The last thing
my father did before doffing his hat at the chapel door was to look
back down the road at it and smile in a proprietorial way. He was
very proud—we were all very proud—of that Croydon.

The porch of the chapel had big, square tiles the colour of
burnt umber, with deep grooves worn in them around the Holy
Water fonts from generations of feet that had lingered there and
scraped about, while their owners whispered and exchanged
confidences. My father dipped into the Holy Water and sprinkled
himself with a flourish. I followed him at a discreet distance up the
aisle. He genuflected, hitting the ground with his knee—the
necessity of doing which was one of the central dogmas of his
orthodoxy. I did the same and followed him into an empty seat,
selected, with his unfailing sense of the nicety of things, at the
correct distance from the coffin which was laid out on wooden
trestles outside the Sanctuary gate—not sufficiently near the small
group of people (the women and girls in black, the men with black
diamonds on their arms) in the first seat to intrude on the chief
mourners, not so far back as to be part of the well-meaning ruck
of folk who went to funerals, because it was the thing to do—a
form of insurance which one took out to safeguard against going
to the grave alone. My father was a mourner of the second class,
or—to be more strictly accurate—the third class, a concerned
acquaintance come to do the right thing in the right way. He
blessed himself and breathed out a few whispered prayers that
soughed and sighed like a plaintive lament up to the timbered roof.
Then he sat up and arranged himself into a mournful slump,
until the Office was ready to begin.

The first four pews on either side had been turned to face out
towards the aisle and the coffin. These were beginning to fill up
with priests in surplices. Everyone kept a sharp eye on them. A
man's standing at the end was judged by the number of priests at
his Office and it was one of the chief duties of those who went to

funerals to make an accurate tally of the clergy present and report
back to those at home. It was the measure of a man's incompetence
to describe him as the kind of fellow who could come away from
a funeral without knowing how many priests were there.

The number of priests depended entirely on the family's
ability to pay. For the standard fee of £1 a head one could hire
as many priests as one could afford—or the diocese provide.

Father Donnelly was already there, sitting quietly reading his
breviary. Canon Codd came tottering in on a pair of walking
sticks, unimaginably frail, like a puppet spun out of glass. Big
Father Evans was there—the man who ate stirabout out of the pot
and shared his meals with tinkers and always carried his stole in
his pocket, so that he could hear a hardened farm-labourer's
Confession in the ditch of a field where they had stopped for a chat.
Father O'Connor, prim and dainty as a nun, with his white
ascetic hands and his little, narrow orthodoxy and exclusive heaven,
pushing sinners into the yawning pit every Saturday night with a
cold jerk of the Confessional slide. An Augustinian from Grants-
town with the hood of his gown out over the neck of his surplice.
An old man whom I didn't know with a rough crumpled face,
picking his nose with angry little stabs and sniffing, with his head
turned to one side. Father Keating was there, a little, fussy, hen-
pecked-husband of a man, whose housekeeper was said to rule him
—and his parish. Beside him was a Franciscan, a round, scrubbed,
rosy man, the skin of his face bursting with cheerfulness. I
wondered if it could be the same man who had come to our house
on quest and won me over with his sweet apples.

> Dies irae, dies illa,
> Solvet saeclum in favilla:
> Teste David cum Sibylla.

Two chanters intoned the solemn opening Sequence and were
answered antiphonally by the others.

> Quantus tremor est futurus. . . .

The magnificent, melancholy, awesome words echoing from
the yellow walls, the subtle cadences of the chanters who sang
well, the uneven rise and fall of the main body, many of whom
could not sing at all.

We sat and stood and knelt, following the lead of the clergy.

The whole solemn ritual, fraught with mortality, was ultimately consoling. Life springing out of death.

High Mass followed. Father Kelly, the curate, was celebrant. Deacon and sub-deacon were Fathers Donnelly and Evans. The slow swing of the thurible and the smell of incense, spreading in an aromatic cloud, had a hypnotic effect on me, making death seem something rich and strange—a pleasant oasis where one sojourned before travelling on into the promised land.

Afterwards, we stood in the long grass outside, waiting for the coffin to be taken out. My father was shaking hands with people he hadn't seen for years.

"A fine turn-out," he was saying, "eighteen priests. God be good to poor Jamesy. It would have done his heart good to see it."

I didn't like meeting strangers. They had a way of praising me to my father, as if I were a possession of his they felt obliged to admire, which was embarrassing.

"He's off in College," my father was boasting. "The land wasn't good enough for him."

"The young people wants a better life," they said, "and who'd blame them for it!"

Six men carried out the coffin on their shoulders and put it into the hearse. Sam Simmonds, the Protestant, who wore a black top-hat with a black streamer out of it, got up on the hearse and shook out the reins over the pair of blacks and the funeral moved off. The chief mourners walked after it as far as the crossroads. Then they got into the big, black sedan that belonged to Tom Hayes, the undertaker, and the pace quickened. People on bicycles, asses and carts, ponies and cars followed. My father and myself, enthroned above the throng, drifted along in elegant superiority in the middle.

In Coolreasky we gathered around the grave to see the priest recite the last prayers. The family stood on the edge with drawn faces and red eyes. I knew it must be embarrassing for them to be stared at in their grief and did my best not to look at them. But my eyes kept coming back to them, while people at the edge of the crowd talked and laughed or passed cigarettes among themselves. I wondered what they really felt, what this man in the box, whom the workmen were lowering into the hole, had meant to them. It was not the custom for the widow to be present at the graveside, so the two women in their forties—younger, perhaps, as black made people look old—must have been his daughters and the man with bare head and pale face his son, the boy—my own age—and the two girls—younger—his grandchildren. An old man on crutches, his brother, perhaps.

The girls were rubbing their eyes with white handkerchiefs—men's handkerchiefs. The boy with his head down was staring into the hole. Then there was the thud of clay, as two men with shovels attacked the yellow pile of earth backed up against a neighbouring tombstone. The boy stared down with bent head at the falling clay.

My father, who didn't like hanging about graveyards, was anxious to get away. The minute the grave was filled to ground level and the workmen crossed their shovels over the raw earth, while the priest recited a decade of the Rosary, he was up off his knees and away. The next stop would be Wat Wadding's where the mourning could continue in a more civilised manner. "Jamesy wasn't a great one for graveyards," he said to Nicky Breen, whom we found standing beside the Croydon waiting for a lift back to the village. "He wouldn't want his friends to be delaying in one any longer than they could help. We'll be there long enough, he used to say. I remember him remarking once, and he well on, that if he had to be buried some place he'd like it to be in Wat Wadding's bottling store."

"He'd be among friends anyway," Nicky Breen said.

"A graveyard's no place for the living," Mick Rennick, who had just joined us, said. "As Jamesy, God rest him, used to say, there's many a man got his death in a graveyard."

"Will we see you at Wat's?" my father asked Mick.

Mr. Rennick said he would be along later. He had to see a man about ploughing for his potatoes.

"Dear God," my father said when he had gone, "why can't Mick ever do anything in time!"

"You know Mick," Nicky Breen said cynically.

"He's one dacent man," my father said severely. He would not tolerate anyone—apart from himself—criticising his friends.

To accommodate Nicky Breen my father unstrapped the extra cushion behind the main seat and put it on the seat that faced backwards. He let the tailboard—which was also the door of the luggage compartment—open out on two slack chains, turning it into a footrest. Nicky climbed up in front with him and I got up behind.

"Well, young fellow," Nicky Breen said to me, "I suppose you have all the knowledge of the world gathered into that head of yours by this time!"

This was the kind of sneering observation that I never knew how to answer.

"Knowledge was never any load," my father said, coming to my rescue.

It was pleasant racing along and watching those we passed drop away into the distance. My father liked to drive fast and cut a dash. He had a strong, sure touch on the reins and wrists of steel. He liked to race up to a place and stop within inches of the door with a flurry of dust and the horse's four feet gathered so close together that they could fit on a dinner-plate.

Their voices, whipped back to me on the wind, seemed unnaturally loud, but with the metallic beat of the horse's hooves and the swish of the flying wheels I could make out nothing of what they were saying. Whatever it was, by the time we drove into Wat Wadding's yard and tied up the horse, a coolness had developed between them. My father, with a stubborn set to his shoulders, pushed ahead into the bottling store, while Nicky Breen hurried for relief to the stable.

"Dear God!" my father said, as I closed the door behind us, "did you hear what he's after telling me?"

"No," I said, wondering what it had been to upset him so mightily.

"He's making everything over, lock, stock and barrel, to Mike and putting in for the Old Age Pension."

He looked at me carefully to study my reaction. It was obvious that he expected the same shocked horror as he had shown himself. All I could do was look puzzled and wonder what all the fuss was about.

"My own cousin," he shouted, angry at my slowness in reacting, "to throw himself like a pauper on the charity of the parish!"

"Oh!" I said and immediately realised the inadequacy of the exclamation.

The door opened and Nicky Breen came in. He looked through the little diamond pane and pressed his finger on the bell. Then he opened the door and called.

"Hey, Wat, bring us two large Jamesons—and a bottle of orange for the lad here."

"Can you spare it, do you think, out of your pension?" my father sneered.

That was as good a remark as any to get the argument rolling again. I sat on the rim of an upturned barrel and listened to them. Though it mattered nothing to me whether Nicky Breen got the Pension or not, and I felt it wasn't for me—or my father—to decide if he was entitled to it, I was secretly cheering on my father, because I had never liked Nicky—or Mike—and was still half of the opinion that, if they hadn't actually killed old Jack Middleton, they were just the kind of pair that might have done it. His red, uncouth face and the wisps of white hair standing out over his ears, and the bald spot on top of his head—red from sun and rimmed at the hairline with dirt—disgusted me. I liked him about as little as I liked the lame blacksmith, who might be expected to shuffle in at any moment to batten like a leech on the mourners.

"Whist! Whist! You don't want the whole world to know my business?" Nicky Breen hissed, when a hand was heard on the latch of the door leading from the bar.

"When a man's business isn't fit to be known by the whole world, there's only one reason for it," my father said. "He's doing something he ought to be ashamed of."

The door opened and Wat Wadding came in with the drinks on a tray.

"Poor old Jamesy went quick," Nicky Breen said in a conversational tone.

"Aye," Mr. Wadding said in his melancholy way and stroked his nose.

"One dacent man!" my father said in a challenging tone with undercurrents that were not lost on Nicky.

"The best!" he said heartily—too heartily, "the best!"

"A great man for a day out," Mr. Wadding said.

"The likes of Jamesy are a dying breed," my father said. "Jamesy Brennan and Padge Lamport and poor Cullimore. All gone, poor fellows! And nothing but hangers-on and arse-lickers and charity-men left. No looking for public assistance for men like that. Jack Rossiter, too, and Richie Connors. . . ."

"And Peter Doyle," Mr. Wadding said.

"God be with Peter," my father said. He looked in disgust at Nicky. "It's the good men go first!"

"Like the best flowers," Mr. Wadding said.

"Aye," my father agreed, "and we're left with the buachallawns and the nettles and the thistles."

"Good luck, Bill!" Nicky raised his glass in a placatory gesture.

"Your health, Wat!" my father pointedly ignored him.

"That's life," Mr. Wadding mused. "There's always a some-thing."

"And when there's not, there's something else!" my father finished it.

Mr. Wadding and he nodded their heads gravely and Mr. Wadding went off to attend to his other customers.

"And you'll disgrace us all for the sake of a few shillings?" said my father, returning to the main theme of his objection. "The Foleys and the Breens and the Quigleys that never took a penny charity from anyone in their lives! Dammit, your father was a dacent man. It seems he was the last of the good breed."

"What the hell is it to you anyway what I do?" Nicky was getting redder in the face—if that were possible—the veins tightening like rope in his thick neck. "Mind your own bloody business."

"Right! Dammit, right!" my father shouted. "To hell with you and yours. I wouldn't lower myself to be seen in your company again. Get your bloody pension. But don't ever put your foot inside our place again. And if we meet, don't expect any salute from me. And if you're kicked out on the road by that fat son of yours and his new missus, when he gets one, don't send to me. Find your own bloody way to the Poorhouse. And when your time comes, don't expect me—if God spares me to see it—to be at your burying. As far as I'm concerned you're dead as it is.

and, by God, they'd better be thinking of getting you under, because, Goddammit!, you're beginning to stink already."

"Come, boy," he said to me, "drink up your orange and we'll be off. I wouldn't want us to be getting a bad name from mixing with the class of people that'd take the few shillings out of the pockets of the poor."

Outside in Wadding's yard the Croydon, gleaming black and yellow in the sun, was waiting, the pony tied to a ring in the wall. My father, whose kidneys were getting worse all the time, made a hurried visit to the stable and emerged with a scud of the shoulders and climbed in, while I untied the pony and handed him the reins. I turned the pony round and led him out on the street before climbing in myself. Then we were off down the street, my father in his annoyance with Nicky Breen giving the pony a sharp nip of the whip. Then the swift beat of his hooves on the tarmacadam and the hiss of the rubber tyres, the yelp of a dog fleeing our path and the swaying, floating motion high above the road.

"Dear God," my father ranted around the kitchen, when we got home and the Croydon had been safely put away, "to think of that sleeveen beggaring himself for the sake of a few shillings and disgracing us all and putting us on the one par with the beggars of the road!"

My mother who took a more detached view merely said, "If he wants to do it, it's his own business and nobody can stop him."

My father who had no time for the Laodicean, and held that those who were not for him were most malignantly against him, was greatly angered by this.

"'clare to God," he shouted, "is there to be no more right and wrong, only grab all you can, while you can, and to hell with the laws of God and man? I was brought up to believe that to take what belonged to another was stealing. And the worst form of stealing is to steal from the poor."

He looked at my mother, as if daring her to contradict him, but she just went about her business, scraping the keeler with a fork and throwing the little bits of dough left over after bread-making out to the fowl in the yard.

"I always knew Nicky Breen was as mean as dirt," she said in a placatory tone, "but we've enough to do to mind our own business."

"It *is* our business, dammit!" my father insisted.

"I don't know about your side," he continued with the hint of a sneer, "but nobody on our side ever took charity from anybody."

"Much good it'll do him, then!" my mother said unruffled.

"To think of him lining up there in the Post Office," my father lamented, appalled by the disgrace of it, "in front of everybody with his Pension Book like the rest of them, crawling to that old Martin one for his few shillings and the whole country knowing his business. And all a body had to do was look out on the street of a Fair-Day to see his cattle standing there and Mike walking into the Bank to lodge the money that he wasn't supposed to have to support his old father in the latter end of his days!"

"Would it make it any better if he was to draw it in Wexford?" my mother asked.

"Dammit, he wouldn't be seen anyway."

"Is the disgrace all that matters then?" she continued to probe. It was always dangerous when my mother began to ask questions quietly like that. My father, who saw the drift of them well enough, was up in arms immediately.

"Leave it so now," he shouted. "It's no thing for anybody to do and that's all there's to it. He'll never darken this door again as long as I live. I told him that."

"That'll be no great hardship—on him or us," my mother said lightly. "We only see him once in a blue moon as it is and even that is too much for me. I won't die if I never see him again."

"You'll see him sooner than you think then," Tom, who was standing at the table, looking down the lane, said. "Here he is up the lane in a dust. I'd know that spring car of his any place."

We rushed to the window and, true enough, there he was, lashing his clay-coloured jennet, which had its ears laid back and was leaving a cloud of dust in its wake.

"I'll soon put the run on that fellow," my father swore.

"Leave him be," my mother advised. "You'll only distress yourself and say something you'll be sorry for."

"I'll deal with him." My father's face was very flushed and he was breathing heavily.

"You'll only annoy yourself," my mother said, "and you can't do any good."

"He's tying the jennet at the gate," Tom reported from the dining-room, where he had gone to get a better view.

"Get out, childer, in the name of God," my father ordered. "Get in the cows. See to the calves. Feed the pigs. And, on your lives, don't come back in here until that fellow's gone. Do yous hear me?"

In the yard we met Nicky Breen.

"I want your father," he said roughly. "Is he within?"

He had a scowl on his face and was walking with a rush, his shirt open almost to the waist and the smell of porter off his breath.

"He's inside," we said.

His boots clattered over the stones as he passed us. Mother Cat who was lying in his way got a sudden boot and ran off with a howl. A great hatred of Nicky Breen seized the three of us at the same time.

"All the men from here to Screen," shouted Tom suddenly in the childish game we hadn't played for years.

I looked around to make sure he was out of earshot. He was stumping in the kitchen door without knock or salutation.

"All the men from here to Screen," Tom shouted again.

"Couldn't wring a penny out of Nicky Breen!" I chanted.

We laughed and went around the gable and threw clods at the jennet, which backed and tugged at the reins. When he had brought in the cows, Tom got a shovel and—Moll and I keeping watch—lifted a big, soft cowdung and put it in the middle of the spring car and covered it with the pollard bag that he had for sitting on.

There were loud voices coming from the house. We crept up under the window and tried to listen, but the walls were too thick. All we could hear was an angry bellowing as of bulls locked in combat.

I was finishing the separating when I heard impassioned shouts at the gate. I turned off the milk, let the handle fall and crept to the door. There was Nicky Breen at one side of the gate untying the jennet. My father stood in the yard, his legs spread, his old, single-barrel shotgun at half-cock.

"Get out," he was roaring, "and never come back till your dying day, or, by God, I'll blow you into kingdom-come!"

Nicky Breen turned the jennet in a short circle, and, shouting and gesticulating, jumped up on the side of the spring car and lashed the jennet in the rump with the reins. With a plunge it bolted off, jerking him on his back in on top of the pollard bag, but he grabbed the tailboard in front and righted himself again. Then there was a puff of smoke from my father's gun and a resounding roar that echoed from the empty haysheds as he fired into the air. My mother came running from the kitchen and Tom and Moll from the cowhouses and we all stood there, speechless, looking at him, while the clatter of the jennet died in the lane and the smell of burnt cordite spread across the yard.

My father flung the gun from him in disgust beside the gable and stumped into the house. When I had finished the separating and we had fed the calves and pigs, I went in. He was sitting there on a chair just inside the door with a strained look on his face. He had his right arm clasped across his chest, the fingers caught under his left arm, the hand of which he was holding very stiffly straight down by his side. My mother said he had a pain of some kind and was trying to persuade him to go to bed. He complained of being thirsty and asked me to get him a mug of water. I filled a mug from the enamel bucket on the stool under the window and held it while he sipped. He asked Moll to get a towel and wipe his forehead which was covered with sweat, although he said he felt cold. After a while he let Tom and myself help him upstairs where he agreed to lie in his clothes on the bed with a blanket thrown over him. Tom was sent to the village to get the doctor and returned to say that he was out on a call, but would come as soon as he got back.

My mother kept going upstairs to look in on my father. The last time, she tiptoed down and said he was asleep. Tom took in the gun and hid it away in its usual place under the stairs. We had our supper in silence and, just as my mother and Moll were clearing away the delph, we heard Doctor Reilly's car changing gear at Half-Ways-The-Lane and Tom ran out to open the gate.

"Well, well!" Dr. Reilly bustled in, a big man in a check suit and green velours hat, and shook hands with my mother. He had a hospital-tobacco smell and was carrying a bag that bulged open, with a roll of cotton wool and the caps of a lot of bottles and jars sticking out. My mother brought him upstairs and we stood around at the bottom, craning our necks up and straining our ears, until the door opened again, when we rushed back to the kitchen and were sitting in various attitudes of repose by the time my mother came down, followed by the doctor who was folding up his stethoscope.

"A few days' rest," he was saying, "and no more excitement. He's not as young as he was, you know. Seventy-three, he said— and all his own teeth. A good age. A good age."

My mother poured hot water into a basin for him and he washed his hands.

"Is it his heart?" she asked.

"A slight attack," he said. "Nothing to cause alarm. But keep him rested. And as for the other—the kidneys—send one of the lads here into me with a specimen in the morning. It's the kidneys we'll have to watch. Any trouble there would put a strain on the heart."

He opened his overloaded bag, took out a little bottle of pills and gave them to her.

"Let him take one of these now, and one every morning and evening. Drop in to see me in about a week and let me know how he's doing."

When he had his hands dried, he sat down and began to fill his pipe in a leisurely way. That was one of the nice things about Dr. Reilly. However busy—and he was on call twenty-four hours a day—he always had time to sit and talk. He asked how I was getting on in college and told us of the time he was doing an English exam for his general degree in Trinity and was asked about the storm in "King Lear" and had written, not about the storm of thunder and lightning on the heath, but about the "brainstorm", as he called it, which was going on at the same time in Lear's head, discussing the thing purely in medical terms, and his professor had been so taken with his ideas that he had passed him on the strength of his answering in that question alone. He talked, too, of Kavanagh's history of '98 and offered to lend me his copy, if I promised to be very careful of it. He had, he said, a pair of pistols that once belonged to Hunter Gowan, the notorious priest-hunter, which I might like to see.

When he got up to go, he warned my mother again to keep my father in bed and make him rest—as if anyone could make my father do anything he didn't want to do. On the way out he measured himself against Tom, who was now 18 and very tall, and asked him if he'd like to join the L.D.F. of which he himself happened to be Commandant. Being an ex-Troubles man, with a long history of daring adventure, he was very keen on young fellows having military training. Tom was delighted and gave no one any peace, until he was let join—as shortly he was—and our kitchen rang with the clatter of his huge boots as he went through his drill. His rifle barrel, as he swung and pirouetted, was in constant danger of sweeping a row of mugs off the dresser.

My mother made tea to bring up to my father and gave him his pill. Shortly after, he was sitting up, calling for his pipe. I brought it up and filled and lit it for him and read him bits from *The Free People*—notes from the various towns and villages, deaths, auctions, advertisements for the sale of hay, court cases, pieces that interested him from the County Council meeting and snippets from a column headed "Fifty Years Ago", over which he nodded his head in reminiscence.

In the morning early, he was roaring for us to come up and get our instructions for the day. When we came in for dinner, he was—in defiance of my mother—sitting at the head of the table, but after dinner he complained of feeling dizzy and having an inclination to puke, and went back to bed tamely enough. And there he stayed—on and off—for a week, until Dr. Reilly came again and told him he might safely stir about, as long as he kept regular hours, didn't strain himself and kept off spirits—or, better still, off all kinds of alcoholic drink.

After a couple of days, when news of his illness had got around, came Ted Reville, the cow-doctor, on a very delicate mission, his bag of medicines swinging from the bar of his bike like a cow's bloated udder, the observation of which made Tom inquire facetiously if his bike had Milk Fever.

Ted thugh-thughted, while the long ash gathered and drooped and fell from his cigarette and the sweat swelled jn globules on his bald head and joined to form rivulets that coursed down over his ears, and thugh-thughted again, as he lit a fresh cigarette from the stump of the old one and inquired solicitously after my father's health, and, thughting, advised him that a little rum punch taken last thing at night warmed the blood and made it flow more freely, and so on, delicately, through dinner and the busy afternoon, thugh-thughting and spinning out a fine web of nothing in his blind, burrowing mole's way, past teatime and into the long, blurring shadows of evening, before, thugh-thughting, alarming himself at his own precipitousness, thugh-thugh-thughting to the point.

With all the delicacy of an ambassador, fearful of his reception, but determined in the interests of peace to sacrifice his position, his honour, his very life, Ted delivered himself of the message that Nicky Breen sent his compliments, inquired solicitously, as behoved an anxious relative, after my father's health and wished it to be known that, notwithstanding anything that had passed in heat between them, he held my father in the utmost respect and was prepared to bury their differences in a pit of oblivion and nevermore resurrect it to the embarrassment of them both, and was ready, at a word from my father, to seal eternal amity and friendship between the two illustrious branches of our venerable house.

My father's reply was short and sharp. With all due respect to Ted, whom he valued as a friend, he would see Nicky Breen and all his seed, breed and generation in hell first. Whereupon, Ted mounted his bicycle and, with his udder swinging alarmingly, pedalled into the purple evening, in which his bald head hung for a moment like a luminous moon, before going under at Half-Ways-The-Lane.

CHAPTER SEVENTEEN

For most of the summer Helen was absent in France, where she had gone to study for her exam, staying with a family near Lyons. There was a son called Guillaume, whom I could, on no account, like—or trust—though Helen assured me he was very nice and about my own age. I scrutinised her letters for any excess of warmth in her references to him and was depressed for a long time at his handsome sophistication in the photograph of herself and the family which she sent me.

My own summer was rather different. There was haymaking, and long days bent under a torrid sun, shuffling on my knees down the knobbly turnip drills, my legs bound with sacking, my shirt stuck to my back, half an inch of clay under my soft, broken nails, my fingers swollen with thistle-thorns, a cloud of flies about my ears, and the sweat blinding my eyes whenever I lifted my head.

Sometimes, in the cool of the evening, I cycled over to Doonashee and circled the crumbling walls, peering through leafy openings at the house she knew so well. Sometimes, picking up a soft stone, I scribbled her name and my own in some secret place, lifting a veil of ivy that hid a smooth boulder and letting it fall back again when I had finished. Then home to write to her. THE WOODS IN DOONASHEE ARE A WONDER NOW . . .

Sometimes, in frustration, wearying of my loneliness and isolation, I sought a remote field and, stripping, rolled about in the long aphrodisiac grass, with the sun warm on my body, and played my Game with a desperate defiance, closing my ears to all inner counsel for several days in a sweet orgy of the flesh, until self-disgust and loathing set in again and I crept off in depression to join the penitential queue in one of the town churches, where I was not known.

Once or twice Moll and I had cycled to the sea. We had real bathing togs now, and were anxious to use them. Without anything being said, Moll had withdrawn to put on hers and, while we splashed around and flung strips of seaweed at each other, neither of us made any reference to the river or our visits there.

We dried ourselves and dressed apart too. It seemed to me—and part of me was sorry because of it—that something like a tacit understanding was growing between us that what was past was past and that a new, and different relationship was developing between us. We were, somehow, more wary of each other, more conscious of the fact that we were two separate entities. But often still, especially when I was depressed, I sighed for the old days, when Moll would fling her arms around me and console me.

My father was better now. He was up and about again. He was well enough to drive through the fields in the pony and car to where the work was going on. Well enough to roar at us, too, if the work was not to his liking. He was still on his pills, but the doctor no longer came to him. He went to see the doctor once a month. But he had to be driven. He did not trust the pony on the road any more. All his great pride in the strength of his wrists and his ability to stop a horse on a plate seemed to have gone.

It was Tom now who drove with fury, sweeping dangerously out on the road, tearing at a gallop down the hills, grinding to a halt with a clatter of sparks on the village street, throwing the reins carelessly across the horse's flank and sauntering off to stand in a shop doorway and glance about to see if anyone had been observing his dashing arrival.

On a fine afternoon, between the hay and the corn, my father took the notion to go for a drive. He insisted on yoking the Croydon, in spite of my mother's objections, and giving me the reins.

"It's time you got the feel of driving it," he kept saying.

All morning he had sat in the yard in the sun, watching me wash the bodywork and polish the mountings. I was pleased—and flattered—because he had never trusted me with it before. I was only let out in the pedestrian old pony and trap and there was no excitement in that any longer.

I drove, as he directed me, down dusty by-roads between green hedges, the horse trotting at a brisk pace, the car gently swaying, my father sitting straight, for all his years, with his two elbows projecting over the backrest.

It was pleasant driving along like a man with my father sitting relaxed and trusting beside me, looking into fields of tanned haycocks and late potatoes still in bloom—purple and white and purple again in striped patterns—fast ripening corn, cattle grazing, tails a-swish, young horses dashing in circles, manes, tails, heads, feet aloft, the sky, high, wide and a washed-out blue, the clouds massed cumuli out over the drifting islands.

My father was in a reminiscent mood, talking about his boyhood, pointing out the changes that had come over the years—here a new farmhouse, there, where nettles grew rank on a mound and tall saplings thrust upwards, the ruins of a house where a family of ten had been reared. We crossed the tarred road, known as the New Line, though, since it had been laid before I was born, there was nothing very new about it to me, and came to a public house.

"We'll go in here and see Mick Rennick's woman," my father said.

Mick's marital affairs had long been a puzzle to me. I knew he had a wife somewhere, whom he visited now and then, but I had no idea she lived so close. I pulled in the pony and tied him to a gate.

"You were never down this way before, were you?" my father asked.

"No," I said.

"I'll have one little glass of whiskey, that's all," my father said.

"Are you sure it won't do you any harm?"

"Devil a harm!" he said.

We went down a step into a long room which was dark and cool after the sunshine. It was all brown varnish and dark shadows. It took my eyes quite a while to adjust to the gloom. We were served by a thin girl of about twenty with untidy rat-tails of black hair.

"Is the missus around?" my father asked.

"Gone to town," the girl said and continued with her task of washing glasses behind the bar. I was disappointed at not seeing the mysterious Mrs. Rennick.

"Did they ever live together?" I asked my father.

"A month or two maybe."

"That was strange, wasn't it?" I continued, determined to get to the root of the mystery if I could.

"It was—and it wasn't," my father said, savouring his whiskey and holding it out for me to siphon a little soda-water into it.

"What happened then?" I asked.

"They weren't long married when her father died and she came back to run the place."

"Couldn't she have sold it?"

"Her mother was alive then."

"Couldn't Mr. Rennick have sold the farm?"

"And they all live together here, is it?" my father said.

It seemed a reasonable solution to me and I said so. My father shrugged, gave a kind of laugh, made as if to say something and changed his mind.

"Well, they didn't," he said at length in a tone of dismissal and I knew he intended to say nothing further. I sipped my Orange Crush and wondered what had really happened. My father seemed to be in a thoughtful mood, too. It was quite a while before he stirred himself and said:

"I'll tell you one thing, boy. Never get married in a hurry."

I thought of the years that must pass before I could possibly marry Helen and there seemed to me no need for his advice.

"D'you hear me now?"

"Yes," I said obediently.

I wondered if he had married in a hurry, if he—as well as my mother—had been repenting it ever since.

"Never buy a beast from the son of a widow—she'll be sure to think you done him—and never marry in a hurry," he said. "You'll be sorry if you do."

I tried to think of my father in love, as I was, but the very idea was ridiculous. Then I began to wonder what Helen would think of my father, what he would think of her.

We were out on the road again when my father, who seemed to have been following some consistent train of thought all the time, said:

"Your mother and me were never—close. You know that?"

"N—No!" I lied.

The truth was too distressing to be put into words so casually. My father looked at me shrewdly. I knew he didn't believe my denial. Perhaps he understood it, for he let it pass.

"She didn't want to get married," he said.

"Oh!" I said, embarrassed, not knowing what else to say.

"Her father was anxious for it."

"Oh!" I said again, without looking at him.

"But that's all in the past," he said after a silence and shrugged his shoulders. "There's no use talking about things like that now."

"No," I said.

I thought of how I loved Helen and she loved me. We would always love each other and go through life hand in hand together. I was sorry for my father and mother, because they had missed the greatest thing in life.

We came by a quiet road, which was new to me, to the old graveyard of Templemunn. It was a place we visited once a year on Pattern Day, when crowds gathered to dress the graves, and candy cars with canvas awnings sold liquorice and Peggy's Leg and bottles of hot lemonade that fizzed up in our noses and made us sneeze and brought water to our eyes.

We tied the pony to the gate, which was locked, and I helped my father in over the stile. We picked our way through the unkempt grass that bent before us, through the little ruined church with its simple, Romanesque doorway, out through a gap in the broken wall, until we reached the grave in the shelter of the southern gable.

"It's a scandal with all that grass and weeds," my father said.

I went on my knees and cleared the grave, until it was bare except for a thick stubble that bled green juice. My father had his pen-knife out and was clearing lichen from the tombstone.

IN LOVING MEMORY OF THOMAS FOLEY,
DRUMGOWAN,
WHO DEPARTED THIS LIFE MARCH 30TH, 1890,
IN THE 69TH YEAR OF HIS AGE,
AND
OF MARY FOLEY, WIFE OF THE ABOVE, WHO
DIED
SEPTEMBER 16TH, 1896, AGED 71 YEARS
AND
OF NICHOLAS FOLEY, SON OF THE ABOVE, WHO
DIED
APRIL 10TH, 1922, AGED 52 YEARS.
ETERNAL REST GRANT UNTO THEM, O LORD!

"Poor Nick," my father said. "They found him dead in bed. God rest his soul!"

He always said the same thing at the grave. It was always Nick he mentioned first.

"The wife sold out and went back to her own people," he continued. "They had one girl, Mary. She's married now, up the country with childer of her own."

"There's only myself to go in here now," he added.

"Isn't the graveyard nearly full up?" I asked.

"It's closed, except for the odd one like myself with graves here already. It's thirty years since a new grave was opened here."

We knelt at the graveside and I thought of those three who had been buried here, long before I was born. There must be traces of them in me somewhere, looks, gestures, qualities of mind. I wondered how life had looked to them and what they thought about, when they were my age and knelt on the graves of their dead.

"I should have bought the home place when poor Nick died, only I hadn't the money then." My father stood up and blessed himself.

"It's very quiet here," I said.

There was no sound beyond the hum of insects and no movement, except for tiny eddies of air that stirred the grass. There was a drowsy other-worldliness about the place. The lichened tombstones leaned haphazardly, an unlikely regiment resting on their long march to doomsday.

"Look," my father pointed away to the north-east, "you can see the mountain."

It was about eight miles away, a faint blue, except where the quarry, gouged into its face, gleamed white, like the slash of a scalpel that lays bare to the bone. Way down in the valley I caught a flash of fire.

"There's the sun on our sheds." I said.

"You can see the house on a clear day," my father said.

On the way back he was quiet, withdrawn into himself. But in an amiable way. He seemed satisfied about something. We stopped in the village at Mr. Wadding's. We went into the bottling store and, when I knocked on the door with the tiny diamond pane,

Mr. Wadding himself, fresh from his accounts, with his glasses high on his hairline, came to take our order. He shook my father's hand and insisted on him having one on the house. He sat with us, while we drank and talked of long ago. My father and he laughed over all the old stories and sighed over times gone and friends dead. When my father got up to go out to the stable, Mr. Wadding remarked how well he was looking, though, when he was gone, he said he had become very feeble. I told him that the doctor had said he was on no account to drink much and hinted that he had had enough already.

My father surprised me, when he came back, by suggesting that we should be on our way. Mr. Wadding did not press him to stay. He came out to the yard with us and helped my father into the Croydon and shook hands. My father asked to be remembered to all the old crowd and they shook hands again, and Mr. Wadding remarked that I was a man now, and well fit to drive the Croydon. My father smiled and said that I was more of a townie now than a countryman like himself, and maybe it was as well for me, after all, because everybody couldn't be suited to the land—which was a long way to have come for him.

Then we were off, with Mr. Wadding waving from the street corner and my father lifting his hand, until we were at the bottom of the street, when he said—as much to himself as to me:

"There's no dacenter man in Ireland than Wat."

Nearing home, he ordered me to draw in to a gateway and stood up in the Croydon to inspect a field of wheat that belonged to Mick Rennick. The head was a rich brown and already getting top-heavy.

He ran his expert eye over it and praised the crop.

"Another week or so," he said, and the binders will be out. "We'll have an early harvest this year."

CHAPTER EIGHTEEN

My last year in college. I lean over the railings and drop pebbles into the fetid gardens. Kieran Maher beside me, sweeping wheaten hair out of his eyes.

"What do you want to do with your life?"

"I don't know."

"Neither do I."

"But we'll have to decide soon."

Slogging away in the study-hall. Homer, Calculus, The Medieval Papacy, Irish Poets of the Eighteenth Century, Hamlet—who loved his father. Our eyes fixed on June. And after that? Who knows! THE READINESS IS ALL . . .

Father Creame snooping around outside the windows, his face a white balloon. Sweeping in to exact retribution. Long on justice; short on mercy. Now, men, I'll say it once and I'll say it no more . . .

Kneeling there in the shadows, sick and apprehensive. Rasp of slide, click of door. Footsteps on the bare tiles. Smell of sweat—smell of sin. Moment of panic. Bless me, Father. You'll ruin yourself, soul and body . . .

Leaning out of a window in the darkness. Sound of revelry from below. Entertainment for some visiting team.

"The Training College, I suppose."

"Junior Ex., perhaps."

"What about the E.S.B.?"

"We could try the Cadets."

"They're not recruiting this year."

"Customs and Excise?"

"Of course, if we could get a University Schol."

"We could try everything."

"And, maybe, one . . ."

"It's early days yet anyway."

"Let's go down and see what's happening . . ."

Before Christmas my mother wrote to tell me that my father had had a slight seizure. He was out of bed by the time Moll and I arrived home for the holidays. He seemed to have got smaller, to have shrunk into himself. His great appetite for life had deserted him. On Christmas Day he allowed us to prop him in the armchair in the parlour without protest. He drank one small glass of punch just to please us—and didn't even finish that. His pipe remained unsmoked in the tin box on the dresser.

He had changed in other ways, too. Once, shortly after Christmas, when his strength had improved, I returned from the village to find him sitting at the fire, talking to Dr. Reilly. The purple veins in his face were like worms under the skin. He was holding up his left hand, on which the skin was stretched and shiny, showing it to the doctor. I knew before he opened his mouth what he was going to say and felt embarrassed, because Dr. Reilly would consider him silly and childish. We had all noticed that he was getting childish of late—pleased with little things, like a baby laughing over the discovery of its limbs.

"Doctor, did you ever meet anybody who could do that?" he asked.

He held his hand very stiffly to quiet the tremor and separated his fingers so that the first and second fingers were close together, then a gap, making a broad V, with the third and fourth fingers close together on the other side.

Dr. Reilly held up his own hand and shook it. The four fingers flew apart, as if springs were forcing them. We all laughed and felt easier. I might have known that the doctor would understand.

Dr. Reilly tried again. As soon as he brought two fingers together, the others slid apart. He caught two fingers with his other hand and held them there.

"You're not allowed do that," my father said.

"I give up," Dr. Reilly said. "Your hands are more flexible than mine. You're a remarkable man for your age."

My father did his trick again.

"I could always do that from the time I was a boy," he said, proudly.

"You wouldn't be double-jointed as well?" the doctor asked.

"No!" my father's tone was regretful. "But I knew a man with a double-jointed thumb. He could bend it right back and touch his wrist."

His face was flushed with his little triumph. It was easy to please him when he was in that mood.

I cycled to the convent in Wexford to do the Easter Orals for entry to the Training College. In a long, bare room, all brown furniture and hard chairs, smelling of polish and piety, an inspector was waiting for me. A patient man in a tweed suit, his hair standing straight up like the head of a brush, giving him the appearance of being permanently taken by surprise.

Irish, English and Music.

"We'll start with the Music," he said.

A bad beginning. He sat at the piano.

"What are you going to sing?"

"SHE MOVED THROUGH THE FAIR," I said.

He played a few notes and I started off.

> "MY YOUNG LOVE SAID TO ME
> MY MOTHER WON'T MIND
> AND MY FATHER WON'T SLIGHT YOU
> FOR YOUR LACK OF KINE."

"God bless us!" the inspector exclaimed.

I stopped and blushed.

"I can't sing," I said lamely.

"Well, you got an odd note." He was more charitable than I deserved.

He sat round to the piano again.

"Would you like to try another bit?"

"No!" I said.

"I tell you what I'll do," he said, "I'll play two notes on the piano and I want you to tell me which is the higher."

"I'll try," I said.

He played two notes.

I hesitated and he played them again.

"The second one," I said, though I could see no difference between them.

"Actually, it was the first," he said, turning around to me with a smile. It wasn't a superior or offensive smile, just a friendly one. It made me smile too.

"I think I'll leave the music at that," I said. "I don't have to go on, do I?"

"Of course not," he said. "Music is optional for boys as you know."

"I'm tone deaf," I said. "I can't sing at all."

"Never mind!" he said. "You aren't the only one."

The failure, though I had been expecting it, undermined my confidence. I had always assumed—for no particular reason—that the music would come last. While I did well enough in the rest, I felt I was not doing myself justice. The Irish was straightforward enough, a passage in prose to read and explain, conversation designed to test my knowledge of such things as the Conditional Mood. The English was rather similar. A passage from Dickens about a door-knocker that was like a man's face or a man's face that was like a door-knocker—I forget which. Something from Scrooge, I imagine. General conversation, loosely about literature.

Afterwards I collected a prescription for my father, who had had another of his attacks and was confined to bed. Tom had found him slumped on the steps leading to the loft and carried him in, as if he had been a baby. Dr. Reilly arrived and came downstairs after his examination with his lips pursed. My father's condition was serious, he said. He had suffered a severe attack and the condition of his kidneys was such that they placed a massive strain on his heart.

He was very low for a week, unable to do anything for himself. Then began a slow recovery, the doctor giving us little hope that he would be able to get up again for a long time. I spent part of each day sitting with him. He seemed to like having me there. I think he preferred to have Tom or me do the menial intimate things for him, though my mother was very patient with him and never complained. Tom and I lifted him out of bed into a chair, when the bed was to be made. I think it gave him pleasure and recalled his own youth to feel our arms strong about him. Tom was over six feet now, and could heave a twenty-stone sack about without any trouble.

Once or twice, when he had eaten his supper of brown bread and buttermilk and was ready to go, Ned Rafter asked to see him and clumped awkwardly upstairs, his cap in his hand, to stand at the end of the bed, twisting it about this way and that, talking in an over-hearty voice, assuring him that he looked well and would be up and about again in no time. But, when he came downstairs again, he would scratch his head and remark that the Boss had never taken care of himself.

"Look at them broken blood vessels under the skin for a start," he said. "I read some place that every time a blood-vessel breaks, a little bit of the man dies and, when they start to burst in the brain, it's all up with him. It comes from all this mad rushing about, driving at top speed.

"The human frame, Mrs. Foley," looking earnestly at my mother, "wasn't made for that kind of treatment. The mechanicals of a man are a deal more delicate than the workings of a watch. They're more easily shook. It stands to reason now, don't it? If the Lord had meant us to travel fast, he'd have fitted us out with wheels. Speed only brought a man one place fast—to an early grave."

Then, in case he had outstepped the bounds of good taste with his pessimism,

"Still, it's amazing what a bit of rest can do to build up the blood vessels again. It's all a question of the cells, you understand, and how they stand up to the shock. The Boss was ever a strong man and we'll have him on his feet again in no time."

I met Helen just once during the holidays, a sweet, brief meeting at the gate-lodge. She was taller, more beautiful than ever, her breasts plumped out in the white sweater she wore under her open coat. I had dreamed of her so long, had carried her image in my mind so long that, always, on meeting her, it was a surprise to find that it was a flawed, imperfect thing beside the real Helen. It was the feminine difference of her that thrilled me, the scent of her hair, her slim fingers and slender wrists, so unlike my own, the delicate curve of cheek and nostril, the soft fairness of her skin.

We talked of the coming summer, when the exams would be over and we could be together—really together this year, because she would be at home. We would go on our first real date together to the pictures in Wexford. The thought of it would nourish the imagination in the trying days ahead.

Back to school then for our last term. A gathering together of all the powers of intellect and reasoning and memory. A concentration of them on that final goal. Extra classes. Extra study periods. Boys lounging around the yard in the May sunlight, books clasped to their chests, their lips working. Boys in pairs, catechising each other. Boys strolling around in earnest argument.

Smell of lush grass in the playing fields, of cut grass on the summer lawns. The annual sports, stretched out in the long shadow of a fragrant evening. Cheers, cries, the loud, commanding whistle. Smell of embrocation in the pavilions, smell of sweat, smell of victory. Laughter and ironic cheers for the silly races—Three-legged, Egg-and-Spoon. White daisies in the grass, delicately edged with pink. Thud of feet into the pit over at the long jump. A spread field in the distance races. Father Creame yelling encouragement from the sideline.

The time is almost upon us.

Lord, desert not Thy servant in the hour of his tribulation!

The junior classes had all packed and gone. We were alone in the college. The corridors rang hollow with our diminished footsteps. There were gaps in the dormitories, as in billets after a battle. The refectory was strangely empty. Like condemned men, we were fed to our own whim—square slabs of butter on dishes in the middle of the table, jugs of milk, fresh loaves.

Teachers came, herding us together in corners for last minute advice, talking to us, man to man, at last, the old mask of authority and reserve off. Except for Cuffe, who belted and barged away to the end, a teaching automaton with all his bearings oiled and greased, clicking away blindly like a tin robot, impervious to the natural demands of flesh and blood.

Then the long hours in the examination hall, while the clock strode on inexorably. I must be cool, rational. I must not allow myself to panic. In a sense, a feeling of freedom, of release, as I cast off the received opinions of the years and became myself at last, attacking savagely, where comment was called for, manipulating the facts of history to argue a thesis, questioning the orthodox judgements of literature. I was surprised to find that my mind functioned well under stress. Ideas, convictions I never knew I had, came to me out of the air. Comparisons, analogies floated by. I grabbed them and made use of them. The felicitous phrase flowed from my pen. A feeling of exhilaration, of exaltation seized me. I felt I was engaged in a creative act. I was giving birth to my adult self.

When it was over, I was soaked in sweat and limp as a rag. But

I felt happy, partly because I believed I had done well, but even more because I had got something out of my system.

It was impossible to relax. I tired of everything almost as soon as I began it. I walked about in a nervous way. I gave it up for a few cracks in the alley. I sprawled on the steps, yawning and rubbing my eyes. I sprang up to kick a ball. I turned a few pages of a book and flung it aside to start pacing again. Neither sitting nor standing nor walking nor running nor lying nor lounging gave me any ease. And so it continued for ten days.

Once, because I woke and it was light and I could not content myself to lie still, I got up at five in the morning to read Greek history and watch the sun come up over the river in long streaks of lemon light. The railings were wet with dew, the classrooms like empty coffins, ghostly with chalk-dust. I tiptoed around in a hollow emptiness, mouthing to myself about the Delian League and the constitutional reforms of Cleisthenes. It was a supremely lonely experience, and it was a relief when the others began stirring and I could join them.

It was a time for reminiscence and nostalgia. Most of us realised that we would never meet again. An era was passing. We recalled the glory of past days, the terror and the grandeur, elevating the squalid and the sensational to the level of legend. We had lived to see great things happen, to control events. Some day we would be heroic figures in an epic frieze to our juniors, a glamorous link in the long chain of myth that bound all who had passed that way.

Kieran Maher and I would meet again—we were definite about that—when I came to Dublin, perhaps to work, perhaps to study, but certainly for a holiday. Sometime! When the final day came, we drifted off in ones and twos, like an ice-floe breaking up, shaking hands, talking half-seriously of a re-union in a year, five years, ten. Sometime!

Then it was all over and I was on my way home, feeling, oddly, the same as I had felt on that first day, leaving home. Apprehensive, aware that something familiar and known was coming to an end in my life, that I was again on the edge of change, my future in flux. But I was older now, had experienced change and come to terms with it. I was not without hope that I would be able to do so again. It was the uncertainty I feared more than the change.

CHAPTER NINETEEN

MY father had grown worse. He lay in bed, propped up by pillows, bloated and fidgeting, his distended fingers clasping and unclasping the coverlet. I was unprepared for my first meeting with him and the deterioration shocked me.

"John, boy, you're here!" It was a statement rather than a question or a greeting.

"Yes," I said. "How are you feeling?"

"There are men in the garden," he said, looking at me in a manner I did not understand then, though I was to know it well enough later. "Tell them to go away."

I looked at him in surprise, but he seemed to be serious. I went over to the window and looked down. I saw the apple tree, Beauty of Bath, with its red fruit; I saw the border of Sweet-Pea; I saw the flower beds. But I saw nothing else and told him so.

"They're there all right!" he said. "They're watching me."

"There's nobody there," I said.

I had never experienced anyone with hallucinations before, but it came to me suddenly, with a chill of horror, that my father was raving.

Then he looked at me in that strange way of his again, half cross—like his old self—half appealing.

"You don't believe me either," he said.

There was no point in annoying or distressing him further, so I asked him what the men were like.

"There's one with a beard, a brown beard, like Parnell, and there's a young, clean-shaven man. Have a look again and you'll see them."

To please him I went to the window again and looked out.

"I can't see anyone."

"They're hiding," he said. "They do that. Then, as soon as you come away, they're back again. Try it now and see!"

Feeling foolish and, at the same time, upset to see my father in such a pitiable state, I did what he told me.

"Well?"

"Nobody!"

"They're too cute," he said. "But they're there all right. They're there all the time."

"Even at night?"

"All the time. They come and look in the windows at me at night."

"How do you know?"

"I see them, dammit," he said with some of his old spirit.

"I hear them talking, too. They had a woman with them one time, but I couldn't hear what they were saying. Tell them to go away, do you hear!"

"Yes," I said.

It was distressing to see him like that. As soon as he had settled and closed his eyes and seemed at peace, I tiptoed out and down the stairs.

"He's like that for a while, now" my mother said.

"Sometimes, they're in the room with him. Once, he said they were on top of the wardrobe."

I laughed in a hysterical way and checked myself, appalled at my own reaction. Whatever it was, it was not funny.

"He's—not going—to do—any good, is he?" I asked.

"I—don't know."

"What did the doctor say?"

"He's old, you know," she said evasively. "We must be prepared for anything."

"Is that what the doctor said?" I insisted.

"The doctor doesn't give opinions. He does what he can, as long as he can."

"What do *you* think?" I pressed.

"I think we must be prepared," she said, without any sign of emotion.

"Is it as bad as that?"

"There's men younger than him died with less."

"Does the doctor know about—the way he's raving?"

"Yes."

"What did he say about it?"

"He said it was to be expected."

"You're not to be thinking about it or worrying yourself about it," she said after some thought.

"He's in the hands of God. He's had the priest and doctor. Everything that can be done is being done for him. He's contented enough in himself—except for imagining things, and nothing can be done about that."

"Can't I do anything for him?"

"You can sit with him and talk to him, if he wants to talk. He was asking about you coming home all the week. Maybe, if we have to stay up with him at night, you'd take your turn."

"Of course I will."

"You must get out now while you can and get some fresh air. If he gets worse, he'll need someone with him all the time. So take the chance while you can."

"Would it be all right if I went to Wexford one evening—soon?"

"Of course it would—if he gets no worse."

"People might be talking."

"People like the Breens!" she said scornfully. "Why should anyone care what people like that think? You won't be doing your father any harm by going out now and again."

"If—something happened—while I was away?"

"If he was that bad, you wouldn't go, would you?"

"No."

But I was worried about going all the same. I had promised Helen that I would. I wanted to go, because I felt the need of her company and the assurance of her love now more than ever.

"Isn't this picture night in the village?" my mother asked.

"Couldn't Tom and yourself go?"

"Maybe!"

Helen might be there. I could explain how things were and we could plan our evening out. Better soon than later, if what my mother said was true.

"Moll and myself will look after the place until you get back," my mother said.

Moll, who had finished her Intermediate a few days before my exam ended, was worried about my father too. The raving had upset her as much as it had disturbed me.

"He really believes it," she said, "and he gets very cross if you don't take him seriously."

"Did you see the way his hands are swollen?" I asked.

"His knees, too," Moll said. "I saw them when I was making the bed. Does he know he's bad?"

"I think he does. Do you know what he said to me? He said Tom and I were to look after you and my mother."

"Did he really say that?"

Tom had been busy thinning turnips all day and was glad enough of a few hours off in the evening. We cycled in to the pictures together.

"My father is dying," he said in his abrupt way.

"I know," I said.

"She never says a word about it!"

"She's worried all the same. I was talking to her."

"She doesn't show anything."

"It's not her way."

"He told me to look after her."

"He told me the same."

"You know about his men?"

"I know," I said.

"I used to argue with him about them, but now I don't."

"It wouldn't be any use, would it?"

"No use at all!" Tom said.

I met Helen after the pictures. We hadn't long together, as I was anxious to get home. She knew of my father's sickness. Her voice coming out of the darkness, as we stood and talked, was sweet and reassuring. To be with her was like coming home after a long and dreary time away. She was to spend the weekend at the house of a school-friend in Wexford, and would meet me there at eight on Saturday night and we would go to the pictures to see Larry Parks and Evelyn Keyes in THE JOLSON STORY. She loved the singing of Al Jolson and was looking forward so much to seeing it. She gave me her friend's address and telephone number, in case I needed to contact her before Saturday. She was sorry about my father and would pray for him. I felt better about life—about everything—after seeing her.

My father was lucid again, when I went in to see him, before going to bed. He was talking about the hay and when it should be cut. He was questioning Tom about the work for the following day and advising him to keep Ned Rafter on the go.

"You know Ned," he said, "always ready to stop and argue the toss. Day and date, chapter and verse for everything. Your hay might go mouldy and your corn rot, while he explained the exact spot he was standing on—and what way the wind was blowing—the day he first heard of the Easter Rising in Nineteen Sixteen!"

Saturday was a day of thunder and sunshine, with sweeping showers of hail tearing the leaves of the sycamores ragged and beating on the roof like shot into a basin. The morning was fine and calm, not a breath stirring, with an oppressive heat that made me feel limp and in need of air. Then the thunder rumbled in from the Saltees, pushing before it a creeping, menacing mass of black clouds with a metallic blue sheen to their undersides. A brilliant flash, as it broke overhead, an explosive crack, booming and reverberating across the sky and then, in the inspissated gloom, the heavens opening.

It retreated and came back again and retreated, growling gutturally like an animal foiled of its prey. Then it was off inland, rolling back over the mountain with a receding murmur. Next, the rain in a solid sheet, slicing down. Then easing, thinning, lightening to a fine spray, stopping as the sun broke through, radiant, glittering on the wet leaves, from which the water dropped, splashing to the lower branches, squishing into the grass, dripping on the ground, dribbling into pools. And, louder than all, the roar of water through the chutes, gushing into the rain-barrels.

Last of all, high and wide across a gleaming blue sky, the rainbow, one foot on the islands and the other down in the bogs by the leafy pool, where Moll and I had bathed in the old days.

It was a beautiful evening when I left for Wexford about half-six. I found the house of Helen's friend easily enough. It was along a tree-lined road near the hospital at the northern end of the town. The houses were big, hidden discreetly behind high walls or set well back among deep lawns with white picket-fencing along the curving tarmacadam drives. The houses of professional folk, business people. Trellised roses, copper beeches on the lawns. Brass plates on the walls.

Ivy Lodge had no ivy, but a red creeper on the walls. It was three-story Georgian, with a graceful fanlight in coloured glass over the door. I was hesitant about ringing, but eventually did, pulling on an old-fashioned bell-chain that set up a quivering peal somewhere deep in the house. There were steps in the hall. I hoped it was Helen. The thought of meeting strange people disturbed me. It was Helen, all right, looking very sophisticated with her hair up, her slender neck rising like the stem of a flower out of a red, cotton dress with no sleeves. She looked cool and sweet and desirable.

Luckily for me, there was no one in but herself. Her friends had gone sailing on the estuary and the house was hers. I stood in the hall, examining a brass gong and straightening my tie with the help of a looking-glass in the hallstand, while she got her bag and gloves and joined me.

We walked along in the evening sunlight, past the West Gate and Selskar and out on to North Main Street, where the houses leaned towards each other across the narrow way like gossips whispering. Through the Bullring with its heroic statue of the Ninety-Eight Man, along South Main Street to the Capitol Cinema.

The streets were full of country people in for the evening, shopping and gossiping, full of couples, too, like ourselves, sauntering along, looking into shop windows, laughing, happy. I felt very adult and mature to be one of them. It amused—and pleased—me when some men neglected their own girls to stare at Helen. Boys at the street corners whistled as we passed, idle boys, feinting blows at each other, giggling, staring. Their jealousy was encouraging to my vanity. I felt like a king in triumphal procession. The pride and glory of my achievement had me choking with emotion. If Helen was aware of the interest she aroused, she gave no sign.

In the intimate gloom of the cinema we ate sweets and talked until the film began. The hum of conversation was loud about us. To make herself heard, Helen sometimes leaned over to whisper in my ear. The brush of her hair against my face and her warm breath on my ear was exciting, dangerous. It set beating deep within me the tidal rhythms of the flesh. It awoke in me again with passionate intensity a desire to kiss her. I had been struggling with this feeling for some time, but the moment had always been unpropitious, or my own timidity had led me to postpone it. But it could be postponed no longer. As the lights went down and the curtain lifted, I made a resolution that it would have to be accomplished before the evening ended.

Larry Parks in blackface, miming to the singing of Al Jolson, was agreeable enough, but my mind came fully alive only in the romantic scenes. Of the songs April Showers appealed to me most, perhaps because of its optimism, perhaps because of its reference to violets, which had special significance for me since childhood days, when we collected them from the grass under the trees and presented them to my mother, who sniffed them and smiled and looked young and happy, as she put them in water.

But I was to remember April Showers for none of those reasons. I was to remember it as the moment when I reached out boldly in the darkness, captured Helen's hand and held it prisoner. It was a willing prisoner, resting softly in my own, our fingers twined. When I squeezed, she returned the pressure. It was beautiful there in the conniving darkness, sealed in the intimacy of song, taking emotional soundings through our fingertips.

When the lights came up again—much too soon—our hands slid reluctantly apart, mine, at least, feeling like a plant wrenched from its roots, no longer an agent of love, but a mere physical appendage. By the light of the street lamps we strolled back, Helen with her hand laid lightly on my arm. I was thrilled by its presence there, the first time she had ever done it. I was preoccupied by the impending necessity of proving myself further, and our conversation was in trivialities—the film and our reactions to it. Up over the roofs the sky was still bright with summer. But it would be dark enough along that tree-lined road to kiss unobserved.

We passed from tree to tree, my heart thumping, calling coward to every footstep I took. I'll do it at the very next one. But it's too small and there's a street lamp right beside it! The next then. Is that a man watching us? Why doesn't he go away and mind his own business! Has he forgotten what it is to be young, the diffidence, the uncertainty! She might say no! Slap my face! Scream! Don't be silly. She wants it as much as you do. Remember those messages from her fingers in the dark. I can't go home without kissing her now. A kiss is my passport to manhood. The final seal of acceptance. Here, in the shade of this friendly tree.

It was the last tree before Ivy Lodge. There would be no other chance. I stopped abruptly and her fingers slid off my arm, as she continued to walk on.

"Helen!" I cried awkwardly as she stopped and turned back.

There was surprise—perhaps alarm—in the stiff way she held herself.

"What's wrong?" she asked.

It had to be said now, and there was no going back on it. Feeling like a man throwing himself blindly over a precipice in the faint hope that, by some miracle, he might learn to fly, I stammered.

"W—W—Would—Would you—Would you kiss me—before you go in?"

It was out at last. But only in my graceless, hangdog fashion. There was none of the dashing, chivalrous gesture about it that I had planned.

"Y—Yes—if you like," Helen said in a tiny voice that barely carried to where I stood.

She said YES!

Rainbows of light Catherine-wheeled in my head. Trees, houses, swivelled, swayed and danced a jig. The whole universe expanded before me.

She said YES!

We stood there, looking at each other Helen out in the mellow evening, looking in at me, looking out at her from under the kissing leaves. I was waiting for her to come in and she seemed to be waiting for me to come out.

"It's more . . ." (I couldn't think of the right word, the right *inoffensive* word). "It's more . . . sheltered in here."

I tried again.

"We—we might—be seen—out there."

"Oh!" Helen said.

She moved in and stood beside me, waiting. I was unsure about what should be done next. She definitely had said yes. Or had she? Did something else need to be said? We stood awkwardly, looking at each other, she looking up, I looking down. ALL I HAD TO DO WAS LOWER MY HEAD AND KISS HER.

I put my arms clumsily about her, feeling her shoulder-blades through the thin dress, pressing her to me. I brought down my mouth on hers. It was exquisiiely soft, warm, intimate. The scent of her hair, her body, the softness of her breasts against me, her sweet breath on my face completely seduced my impressionable senses. They fed back a flood of passionate sexual information to my brain, which promptly sent out urgent demands for more. It seemed to me in that one minute that I absorbed her completely, through every pore and avenue of knowledge in my body, that when we parted—if we could ever be said to be parted again after that—I would take her away with me as an integral part of me and would be able to re-create her down to the last seductive detail, to my dying day. Her smell and feel and taste are with me now, as I write, as much a part of me as the food I eat, the air I breathe, the thoughts I think.

We parted reluctantly, Helen a little breathless, smoothing down her hair. It was as painful as tearing off my arm to let her go. I stood there under the tree, possessed of her, exalted. The whole world was concentrated for me in her slight person. All that I ever wanted, could ever want, could ever dream of wanting, was in her. To love her, to be loved by her, was power, fame, riches, glory to me. Heaven would be hell without her. Hell a paradise, if she were by my side.

"I'll have to be going," I said.

Banal words, trite words that gave no clue to the intensity of my feelings, shouting away beneath the skin of love and eternal union.

"Yes," Helen said, "it's time I went in."

No clue there either.

What was wrong with us at a moment like this, using words as a mask?

"I hope you enjoyed the evening," I said.

"Very much!"

"So did I!"

Then the mask was off and I added, "It was the nicest evening of my life."

There were lights in the lower windows of Ivy Lodge. My bicycle was by the wall. I stood beside it, reluctant to leave.

"Would you like to come in and meet Eileen and the family?" Helen asked.

"I'd rather not, if you don't mind," I said. "I'll have to be getting home. My father isn't so good these days."

If I couldn't be alone with her, I wanted to be alone by myself. I wanted to give my full attention to the new relationship that, I felt, had begun between us. Kissing had changed and deepened everything. I was not sure how much it meant to Helen, but to me it was the consecration of our lives to each other.

We arranged to meet again when she came home. She stood watching as I put on my bicycle clips and adjusted my lamp. We said goodnight. I can still hear her voice, low and sweet, saying, "Goodnight, John!"

I watched, as she closed the gate and went up the broad steps to the front door. I expected her to turn and wave when she got to the top, but she must have imagined that I had already gone, because she turned the key in the lock and went straight in. My last image of her is her slender figure and dark head in a frame of light. Then the door closed and I was alone.

But I wasn't really alone. Her presence was about me like an incense, as I cycled home. I drifted along in languorous euphoria, light as a feather in the saddle, swooping and soaring, leaping off to dance up the steep hills, gliding down in a pleasant rush of air.

When I came up over Half-Ways-The-Lane, I knew there was something wrong. There were too many lights in the house. There was one in the kitchen and one in the dining-room. There was a candle on the ledge where the chiming clock stood at the turn of the stairway. There was a bright light in my father's room and on the drawn blinds I saw the shadows of my mother and someone else moving about.

CHAPTER TWENTY

DOCTOR Reilly's car was in the yard. Inside, Tom and Moll were pacing the floor. Tom looked at me and shook his head. Moll's eyes were red.

"How is he?" I asked.

"As bad as he can be," Tom said.

"He had another attack," Moll said.

"He's unconscious," Tom said.

Moll began to cry. She dabbed her eyes with her apron and sat down with her head in her hands. I felt guilty about being away when it had happened.

"I knew when I saw the lights," I said.

"Moll found him at nine o'clock," Tom said. "He was all blue in the face and gasping for breath."

At nine I had been sitting in the cinema, holding Helen's hand.

"Did you go to the pictures?" Tom asked, with his uncanny instinct for probing me on the raw. He may have meant nothing critical at all, but, to my guilty mind, it sounded like an accusation.

"He was all right when I left," I said. "I wouldn't have gone if I'd known."

"Of course, you wouldn't," Moll said. "There's nothing you could have done by being here anyway."

Father Donnelly had come and anointed him. Moll and my mother had sat by him until the doctor came.

When Dr. Reilly and my mother came down the stairs, I searched their faces for the truth. I felt that they might try to keep the worst from us, and I wanted to know. Both of them looked worried. My mother was twisting her wedding ring in a way I had sometimes observed her doing before when she was upset. Dr. Reilly was pulling his left ear between finger and thumb in an abstracted manner.

He spoke in his hoarse, soft voice, as if his throat was troubled by phlegm which he could not clear.

"Your father's condition is very serious," he said to me.

I looked across at my mother. She nodded her head in agreement with Dr. Reilly, but said nothing.

"Will he regain consciousness?" I asked, intent on finding out the worst.

"Impossible to say," Dr. Reilly said. "I've told your mother— to prepare for the worst. She thinks—and I think—it's better for all of you to know."

He put his stethoscope and sphygmomanometer into his bag which was open on the kitchen table. We stood there, looking at him, as if we were absorbed in his actions, as if the closing of his bag was the most important thing in the world. He seemed to take longer than was necessary over it. When it was closed, he took it in his left hand and swung it to his side. He shook hands sympathetically with my mother and said.

"I'll give a call in the morning after Mass—unless I hear from you before then."

Tom and I followed him out.

"Look after your mother," he said. "See that she gets her rest tonight."

He got into his car and started up the engine. The lights came on, and he was off into the blue, velvet night that smelt fresh and sweet, and not at all like death.

"I should have stayed at home," I said, as I followed my mother upstairs.

"You weren't to know," she said wearily.

"I'm sorry all the same," I said.

"Don't be blaming yourself. You couldn't have done anything. No one could do anything."

"I wish I had been here!"

My father was lying on his back, his breath coming in a snore. His head was thrown back and the openings of his nostrils looked like dark pits. There was a film of sweat on his forehead. My mother wiped it off with a small towel which was on the chair beside the bed. It was a gentle gesture and it brought tears to my eyes. I had never seen any tenderness between them before and it affected me to see it now, and under circumstances like these.

"He's dying, isn't he?" I said.

It was strange to be standing there, talking in such a detached way about it, wondering why I could feel nothing except horror at his physical deterioration and pity for his distress. The skin of his face was taut and tense, as if there was tremendous pressure from underneath and the bone was about to burst through.

"He's dying, isn't he?" I said again.

"Yes," she said.

I could detect no emotion in her voice. But she must have been feeling something, now that this strange union that had bound them for so long was coming to an end. Perhaps, like me, she felt dazed, unable to take it in.

"He's well prepared anyway," I said.

It was the sort of consolatory thing one said, but I remember wondering, even as I said it, what I really knew of my father's spiritual state, what I knew about him at all, what he had thought of the world and of life and of death and of us. I didn't know. Would never know. If I felt any grief, it was sorrow that my father and I had been strangers for too long, sorrow that my final grief could only be a shallow thing, because he and I had only recently come to know or love each other at any depth.

"Call up Tom and Moll," my mother said. "We'll say the Rosary around the bed."

Tom was looking very white and shaken. A little thing would make him crack. I envied him his distress. He had been closer to my father than any of us. Tears would come easily. He would have no feelings of guilt afterwards.

I began the Rosary and they answered it, starting every time my father's breathing changed. I could not concentrate on the prayers. All I saw was my father's face and my mother's gesture, as she wiped off the sweat. If only he had been conscious to see her do it. But it was too late to think of that now. He would never regain consciousness again. He would stop breathing and then it wouldn't be my father there in the bed any more. He would be gone and any chance of them getting a better understanding of each other would be gone, too.

Tom insisted on staying up all night. I stayed with him until two and then went to bed. There was no change in my father. I told Tom to wake me first, if anything happened.

When, eventually, I slept, sometime after the sky lightening for day, I dreamed of standing under a tree from which a thunderstorm was stripping all the leaves. Then the branches came tumbling down and the whole tree seemed to split and fall on top of me. I remember no more, until I woke, anxious and disturbed, with the feeling that some unbearable call would shortly be made on my emotions and that hitherto untouched depths in me would painfully begin to bleed.

My father's condition had not changed. He still lay there, laboured in his breathing, his head lolling, his fingers jerking in spasms. There was nothing easy or restful about him. His forehead was damp and cold. The grey stubble was pushing through his face and his moustache hung limp, like seaweed after the ebb tide.

Moll and I looked after him, while Tom and my mother went to Mass. We wet his lips with water, once or twice, and smoothed the pillows. When they came home, Tom went to bed and Moll and I went to last Mass in the village. It was a beautiful morning with dust rising. I thought of the day we had gone driving in the Croydon and of how my father had sat upright in his Sunday best, saying "tch, tch, tch" through closed teeth to encourage the horse, and flicked carelessly at low-hanging leaves as we passed under trees.

We went tiptoeing about the house all day with an air of expectancy. Every time anyone went upstairs and came down again the rest of us jumped up, as if we were determined not to let death take us by surprise.

Tom got up about five and we did the evening's work. When it was done, we sat around, not knowing what to do, leafing through magazines, getting up to stand at the foot of the stairs and listen. I went for a walk through the fields, but turned around and ran back when I was in the middle of the second field, because I thought I heard someone calling me. Tom and I banged a ball about against the cowhouse, but Tom deliberately drove it high over the roof and neither of us would go and look for it. We went inside again, where my mother was washing sheets. We hung them out for her and returned to stand in the doorway, looking out at the beech trees, brushing their leaves against the roof of the shed. And so the long June evening stretched out the shadows tediously and moths flickered and bats swerved and crows came home in a noisy line and the mountain darkened and bulked larger and stars pinpricked the velvet twilight.

No change in my father. No change at all.

We said the Rosary about his bed, had our supper, and Tom and my mother retired for the night, my mother reluctantly. Moll stayed up to keep me company till two o'clock. We sat by the bed, talking in whispers. My father lay, gasping and twitching. There was something titanic about his struggle for life. All that great animal energy of his that had helped him claw his way into the possession of land and security was now channelled into this last battle of a war he had been fighting all his life—the struggle for survival. I lifted his hand and laid it inside the coverlet. It fluttered in mine as feebly as an infant's.

It was lonely when Moll went to bed at half-two. I sat there, thinking of the past and how much I had been afraid of him. I thought of the day I had let the pony escape. I thought of all the times he had come home from fairs, roaring drunk, and terrorised us all. I thought of the clink of glasses in the kitchen at night, as I lay in my wet bed upstairs, the tipsied singing and shouting about the yard. I thought of the long, agonised childhood I had spent, sitting on upturned barrels, listening to maudlin philosophising. I thought of my mother tiptoeing up the stairs and the closing of this same bedroom door and how I had waited in apprehension for the sound of my father coming up. I thought of them sleeping apart in our cold Catholic form of divorce. I thought of how I had hated him for blighting our lives, of how I had come to the reluctant realisation that I couldn't hate him as I hated people like Father Creame, because he was part of myself. I thought of how shocked and disturbed I had been to realise that in some way, deep in my blood, I loved him. I thought of how that love had begun to develop between us over the past year.

Now that there was no one to see, I cried, because I had never loved him as I had wanted to love my father. I cried, because my love for him was not the boundless, totally committed feeling I had for my mother and Moll. I cried, because I felt it had been an ungenerous, unfilial withholding of myself. Crying was no comfort to me. I felt that I was crying as much for myself as for my father.

I was crying, because I was being denied the luxury of a perfect and impassioned mourning.

Day was well advanced and there were wedges of sunlight on the bedroom floor, when I noticed that his breathing had changed. The deep gasping had given way to a quiet whisper. I thought, at first, that he had stopped breathing altogether, but, when I leaned over him, I could hear it, faint as a sigh. He looked peaceful and, for a while, I had almost persuaded myself that he had passed some sort of crisis and would pull out of it after all. But by the time my mother was up and came in to relieve me, the gasping had started again.

"Your breakfast is ready," she said. "Hurry up now, and then off to bed."

There were motes floating in a shaft of sunlight from the landing window as I went down. Moll had a weak fire going on the hearth. The kitchen had its empty, early-morning smell. Tom was rattling buckets in the yard. I walked out in the light and stretched myself. The day was sweet and wholesome, a scent from the fields heavy with summer. The calves in the shed behind the barn were bawling for their milk.

I sat at the kitchen table and ate porridge. The spoon was one I had taken to College in my first year. It had my name engraved on the handle. I drank tea and ate brown bread. Moll went off glumly to start the milking. A squeal of the lane gate as Ned Rafter arrived. I waited till he came in, boiled his egg and served up his breakfast. No. There was no change in my father. Yes. He was putting up a great fight. No. There was not much hope.

I went upstairs to bed, looking into my father's room on the way. My mother was sitting by the bed, watching him.

"His breathing is strange, isn't it?" she said.

It had grown very quiet again.

"I think he rests easier when there's someone with him," I said.

"Go to bed, like a good boy! You look very pale."

"I'll never sleep on a nice morning like this."

But I did sleep. I left my mother there, smoothing out the sheets and quieting my father's restless hands. I made the sign of the Cross with Holy Water on his forehead and went to my room.

I closed the curtains and got into bed. In a short time I slept.

As soon as I woke, I knew my father was dead. I was aware of voices first and running feet and then of Moll shaking my shoulder. I leaped out and ran to his room.

My father was lying there, quiet at last, all the agony of living drained out of him. His face was white and had the texture of wax. There was a dignity and peace in his expression that gave me strength when I looked at him. I took the Blessed Candle from my mother and put it, still lighting, back in its candlestick. I held back the bedclothes while she joined his hands and put the beads between them.

"We'll say the Rosary," my mother said.

We knelt down and I began. Tom was choking and could not answer. My mother, who was kneeling beside him, laid her hand in a gentle gesture on his head and stroked it as if he were a child. He buried his face in the blankets, sobbing. Moll, who was beside me, was crying, too. I held her hand in mine and she looked at me in a pitiful, pleading way, her eyes big with tears. I stopped, uncertain whether I should—or could—continue.

"Go on," my mother said. "I'll answer it."

Her face was pale, strained. She held her head high, kneeling upright but, I knew by the way her hands were clenched white that she was deeply affected, as I was, by their distress.

I went on again, a quaver in my voice, my eyes on the bulk of my father's body under the bedclothes. I was not affected by the fact that it was a body and no longer my father. Thinking of him dead was, in a strange way, comforting to me. I thought of him at peace in some remote place, free of the flesh that tied him down with its raw appetites craving satisfaction. Never again would he lacerate us or we him. Never more would there be anger or mis-understanding between us. It was as I knelt there, looking at his untenanted face, that the conviction came to me that in those past months I had come to love my father as he should be loved, that I would continue to love him—not as the idealised father of pious memory, but as the wild, roaring man of flesh and blood who towered over my childhood. I had come to love him for his weakness as much as for his strength—just as I loved Tom now in the infirmity of his grief.

For my father's sake I would have to be strong now. I who was a coward, who dreaded pain, who lacked all the qualities of leadership, would have to support the others in their sorrow. I lifted my head and knelt upright like my mother. Tom and Moll were answering intermittently, breaking off quite suddenly in the middle of a word to sob again. Every time they did it, I was in danger of being swept away, too, on the tide of their emotion. Then I looked at my father's face, peaceful in death, and kept going.

When it was over, I went downstairs for a drink of water, because my mouth was dry with strain. As I drank from the enamel bucket on the dresser, a strange thing happened. My eye lit on the box where my father kept his pipes and tobacco, his shaving gear and his Woolworth glasses. The sight of it did what his body could not do. It sent me heaving to the closet, where I stood behind the closed door and cried, until I could cry no more and the whole agony of his death wrenched its way out of my system.

When I came out, I felt stronger. I went back and took on myself the arrangement of his funeral. For the rest of the day I was busy. I went through it all in a daze. I arranged with Mrs. Morgan to come and lay him out. I went to the village to send telegrams, to have a death notice inserted in the newspapers, to make arrangements for his Office and funeral with Father Donnelly, and—the thing I dreaded most—to order his coffin. I left a long list of provisions for the wake at Mr. Wadding's, and collected them when I had finished my other business. Mr. Wadding was very kind to me. There were tears in his eyes as he spoke of my father.

"They're nearly all gone now, the old breed," he said, wiping his glasses—and wiping his eyes furtively, too. "Your father was the straightest and decentest man I ever knew."

In the course of the next few days, I was to hear a great deal in praise of my father, but none of it meant anything to me, except what Mr. Wadding said then, and what Mick Rennick was to say on the following day, when he came across me in the shed, running my hand over the smooth wood of the Croydon that had been my father's pride.

"We had many good games of cards," he said simply, "you and your father and myself and nothing pleased him better than to see you win."

By the time I got home the news had spread and neighbours were coming to the wake. He was to spend the night in the house and would be taken to the Chapel on the following day for burial on Wednesday. It was awkward meeting them and having them shake my hand and offer their embarrassed condolences.

Sure, that's life!

It had to be!

He was well prepared to go!

It's the same way we'll all go, God help us!

Above in the wakeroom my father was laid out in his brown habit, his eyes shuttered against the glare of eternity, his beads clasped between joined hands, a silver crucifix on his breast. His face was freshly shaven, the straggly ends of his moustache trimmed. His skin, pale as freshly churned butter, shone with a bright translucence. His features were soft in death, peaceful, almost gentle.

Very like himself, people said, as they came and knelt and sprinkled Holy Water and retired to the chairs around the walls to sit and whisper, until others arrived and convention decreed that it was time to go downstairs for refreshments.

My mother and Moll were serving tea in the parlour and Tom and I drew corks in the dining-room. It was just like old times. Bottles and glasses everywhere, the smell of whiskey and Guinness. Cigarettes, trailing a long ash from the corners of lips or sending up thin lines of smoke from the mantelpiece. Talk about the great times long gone, when they had made rollicking trips to the Curragh and my father had outspent and outdrank and outlasted the best of the party.

Sometimes, I met my mother or Moll, as we rushed about, seeing to everything, and we exchanged a weary look, a tired sigh. Tom moved like a waxen robot, speaking hardly at all, withdrawn into himself, remote.

Later in the evening my uncle Ned and my aunt Nelly arrived. Their coming was a great comfort to us all. They took the burden of coping from our shoulders. Uncle Ned hustled the drinkers from the dining-room to the kitchen, clearing the way for aunt Nelly, who shooed us before her into the dining-room and made us sit down, while she prepared a meal for us. As soon as she had us safely seated at table and eating, she excused herself and went off to look after the mourners in the parlour.

My mother ate nothing except half a slice of bread. But she drank some tea and a little colour came back into her face. I could not determine from her eyes whether she had been crying or not, but she had the same blank, withdrawn look as Tom.

She kept talking of the necessity of getting mourning clothes for herself and black mourning diamonds for our sleeves. Moll would have to have black stockings and a black beret—if not a complete outfit in black. Tom and myself would need black ties. Had I arranged with Father Donnelly about the number of priests at the Office? Would Tom Hayes, the undertaker, be able to provide a wreath?

CHAPTER TWENTY ONE

My father and I in the graveyard of Templemunn again. He in his coffin, secure, boarded up in the beauty of death, his senses closed forever to the hurt of humanity. My father going like a bridegroom into the earth he loved. There was a breeze soughing through the trees, setting the grass whispering. From the hedges blackbirds were singing for my father, a clear, happy call, piping him to rest. The priest prayed. People shuffled and coughed.

I stared at the mound of yellow clay piled by the open grave. There were stones in it, dried out by the sun. Inside the grave the earth was dark at the top and got lighter as it went down. Ned Rafter had dug it. He had asked to be let do it, because, he said, the Boss was an exact man, and liked things done right, and young pups like Dan Morgan couldn't be trusted to dig the kind of grave a man wouldn't be ashamed to be buried in. Ned was standing by in his overalls, leaning on a shovel, waiting for the priest to finish, so that he could begin his own part of the ceremony.

Moll on my left hand, Tom on my right. Looking down like me, worn out by the long ritual of death. My mother, following the custom of our parts, was at home. Doing what? Feeling what? In the middle of the night, I had heard her coughing and blowing her nose as if she were crying. The middle of the night was her time for crying. She would be troubling no one with her tears. She would be making demands on no one.

Moll had heard her, too. She had come, wrapped in a blanket, to sit on my bed. We had comforted each other and sworn that, whatever happened, we would always stick together. Moll and I piecing together life's jigsaw. But could we ever again piece it together to both our satisfactions?

Ned Rafter was lowering the first shovelfuls, gently, decently, lovingly over my father. They fell with a soft murmur like the greeting of a lover. My father stooping at seed-time to pick up a handful of loam and caress it with his fingers, letting it fall through again and brushing his palms together in a praying gesture. My father on his knees in the turnip drills. My father's clay-encrusted boots, as I saw him from under the kitchen table, where I had sought refuge from his anger. My father impatient at Ned Rafter's slow, precise way of doing things. Was he impatient still, looking on from wherever he was at Ned's deliberate laying of the earth over him?

Out over the heads of the crowd the quarry on the mountain gleamed like a bleached bone. Somewhere down under was our house. My mother. Doing what? Thinking what? Of my father being lowered into his grave, his real love, his only love, the earth, beneath him, around him, above him at last? My mother in her cold room, crying in the middle of the night, her sorrow, like an inward bleeding, leaving no mark on the surface.

We had followed his coffin out of the Chapel, Tom and Moll and I, walking behind the hearse to the outskirts of the village before getting into the mourning car. The blinds were down in all the shops and people stood at the corners to watch us pass. As I walked along with my eyes on the coffin, I was conscious of a blur of faces. It would have been a comfort to search and find Helen's among them, but I owed it to my father to let this day be his only.

People were getting impatient, shuffling about, whispering. Burial was a thing nobody wanted to linger over. Someone had seized a shovel to help Ned, but he waved him off. He would bury the Boss in his own way at his own pace.

The fall of the clay had affected Tom and Moll very deeply. They were rubbing their eyes in soggy handkerchiefs and coughing to contain their emotion. Moll had a tight grip on my arm. I pressed it to my side to encourage her. What was to become of Moll who loved me more than a sister should, and needed my love as much as I needed Helen's? Moll with her laughing, tomboy ways and passionate nature. I wanted to tell her that my father didn't need tears, that he was happier now than he had ever been. But tears for her and Tom and my mother were filling my own eyes and no words came.

Twenty-eight priests at the Office, I heard a man say. My father would have liked that. He enjoyed travelling in style—if only to his grave. In any other situation he would have been embarrassed to be surrounded by priests. They were a race apart, infinitely superior, in close rapport with God, whose instruments of anger they often were. They had strange powers, were not men to tangle with or cross, because they might use those powers. Peasant mythology was full of stories where they had. Like most peasants, my father respected priests, obeyed them, feared them—and, occasionally, loved one. But (in his sober senses) he would no more argue with a priest or express a contrary opinion, or quarrel with him, than he would with the devil. And for the same reason. One behaved with caution in the presence of the supernatural.

The grave was now at ground level. Ned Rafter crossed two shovels on it and everyone knelt down for a decade of the Rosary. My father was six feet underground. His nails and hair were still growing. I had read that somewhere and never forgotten it. Would his face need a shave on Resurrection morning? Or what body did one rise with? Pious folk said we would all be thirty-three in Heaven, because Our Lord died at that age. What about those who didn't, or wouldn't live so long? If my father is thirty-three in Heaven, how will I ever know him when—shouldn't I say, if—I get there? How will he know me?

Thistle and coltsfoot in the long grass, trampled by the careless mourners, hurrying away from my father's grave. Hum of insects in the ivy on the ruined church. Thick, garish flowers under a glass dome on the raw earth. My father should have a wreath of wild flowers, not this lumpish abomination. My father picking clover from the pasture and smelling it. My father pointing to the white flower on spring nettles, with simple astonishment that God should take such trouble with weeds. My father showing us how to suck honey from purple fuchsia bells. My father placing his boot on a dozen daisies and announcing the arrival of spring. Soon the grass will grow, healing the raw wound of his burial and Nature will supply his wreath.

Only Ned and ourselves left. Ned smoothing off the mound, shaping the corners with conscious artistry, resting on his shovel to admire his work.

"God rest the Boss," he said. "He always liked a job well done."

He took off his cap and bent his head in prayer. Then he gathered up his things, shouldered his shovel and walked away. There was nothing more he could do here for my father.

I admired the confident way he left the graveyard. He had come to terms with the world outside, knew his place, was content in it. The future might hurt, might even harrow, but could never destroy him. I was not sure if the same could yet be said about myself. But I was determined that it would be. I felt myself drawing strength from the grave of my father. For the old me, the simple thing would have been to stay here, bent over the dead past. But life was not lived like that. I, too, must go out like Ned, like my father before me, to build my own world in hope and gratitude—my endeavour, a memorial, more lasting than granite pillar or funeral hatchment, to this strong, wayward, lonely man who had given me life.

The blackbirds were piping again from the hedge. A robin picked in the earth on my father's grave. A breeze of summer shook the trampled grass. It was time to go. With Moll holding my arm and Tom beside me, I walked out of the graveyard.

OTHER TITLES
from
BLACKSTAFF PRESS

THE ARAN ISLANDS

JOHN M. SYNGE

WITH DRAWINGS BY JACK B. YEATS

In 1898, acting on the advice of W.B. Yeats, J.M. Synge visited the remote Aran Islands in the west of Ireland. The primitive lifestyle and complex ancient culture of the island people had a profound effect on the young writer and his work. The memory of his Aran experiences, brilliantly distilled in this account, was to provide a rich quarry for his great masterpieces *Riders to the Sea* and *The Playboy of the Western World*.

This beautiful new gift presentation, in buckram hardcovers, is a facsimile reproduction of the 1911 Dublin edition, including twelve magnificent line drawings by Jack B. Yeats.

198 x 129 mm; 272 pp; illus; 0 85640 412 8; hb
£9.95

NIGHTFALL

AND OTHER STORIES
DANIEL CORKERY
EDITED BY FRANCIS DOHERTY

'That terrible promiscuity of rock, the little stony fields that only centuries of labour had salvaged from them, the unremitting toil they demanded, the poor return, the niggard scheme of living; and then the ancient face on the pillow, the gathering of greedy descendants – he had known it all before; for years the knowledge of how much of a piece it all was had kept his mind uneasy.'

from 'The Priest'

Passionately committed to the idea of a unique but vulnerable Irish identity, Daniel Corkery was nevertheless clear-eyed and unsentimental in his observation of peasants and poor town-dwellers. Widely recognised as among the finest Irish writing of this century, his masterly short stories, of which twenty are presented here, spring from this tension and from his sense of an unknowable mystery at the heart of common experience.

'The simplicity of the writing at times reminds you of Hemingway, but it has a warmth and passion that Papa rarely showed. Powerful, elemental themes – exile, death, blindness, loss – are dealt with in flexible words that add to the pathos of what is being written about.'

Irish News

198 x 129 mm; 224 pp; 0 85640 414 4; pb
£5.95

DECEMBER BRIDE
SAM HANNA BELL

'And what was it ye said? To marry one of the men. To bend and contrive things so that all would be smooth from the outside, like the way a lazy workman finishes a creel.'

Sarah Gomartin, the servant girl on Andrew Echlin's farm, bears a child to one of Andrew's sons. But which one? Her steadfast refusal to 'bend and contrive things' by choosing one of the brothers reverberates through the puritan Ulster community, alienating clergy and neighbours, hastening her mother's death and casting a cold shadow on the life of her son.

'a story of the eternal triangle, held, like the land, by stubborn force'
Fortnight

'a quiet, compassionate story'
New York Times

'stands out as a remarkable novel'
Benedict Kiely, *Irish Times*

'invested with a disquieting and sullen beauty'
Saturday Review of Literature

198 x 129 mm; 304 pp; 0 85640 061 0; pb
£4.95

SOON TO BE AN IMPORTANT FEATURE FILM

ORDERING
BLACKSTAFF BOOKS

All Blackstaff Press books are available through bookshops. In the case of difficulty, however, orders can be made directly to the publisher. Indicate clearly the title and number of copies required and send order with your name and address to:

Cash Sales
Blackstaff Press Limited
3 Galway Park
Dundonald
Belfast BT16 0AN
Northern Ireland

Please enclose a remittance to the value of the cover price plus: 60p for the first book plus 30p per copy for each additional book ordered to cover postage and packing. Payment should be made in sterling by UK personal cheque, postal order, sterling draft or international money order, made payable to Blackstaff Press Limited.

Applicable only in the UK and Republic of Ireland